Workplace
Superstars

Workplace Superstars
in Resistant Organizations

SETH ALLCORN

QUORUM BOOKS

New York • Westport, Connecticut • London

Library of Congress Cataloging-in-Publication Data

Allcorn, Seth.
    Workplace superstars in resistant organizations / Seth Allcorn.
      p. cm.
    Includes bibliographical references and index.
    ISBN 0–89930–657–8 (alk. paper)
    1. Performance. 2. Achievement motivation. 3. Organizational
behavior. I. Title.
HF5386.A528   1991
658.3'14—dc20   91–186

British Library Cataloguing in Publication Data is available.

Library of Congress Catalog Card Number: 91–186
ISBN: 0–89930–657–8

First published in 1991

Quorum Books, 88 Post Road West, Westport, CT 06881
An imprint of Greenwood Publishing Group, Inc.

Printed in the United States of America

The paper used in this book complies with the
Permanent Paper Standard issued by the National
Information Standards Organization (Z39.48—1984).

10 9 8 7 6 5 4 3 2 1

Contents

Preface

This book has one message—people, not organizations, achieve excellence. The advocates of excellence talk about many things management should do, but they do not really talk about people. This book does. The advocates of organizational excellence have seemed to point the way; however, scholars have been baffled to find out what is new about what is being said. It has even been asserted that our organizations may be in some instances so poorly run that if excellence were pursued as advocated they would merely rise to mediocrity. This book takes a different approach by starting with the people who make organizations run. It searches for the basis of individual excellence and, just as important, the psychological aspects of people and the workplace that keep outstanding employees from achieving excellence.

This book is written by a manager who works in middle management. It is not written by a chief executive officer of a giant company. This book is also not written by a consultant although I have occasionally worked as one. Neither is it written by an ivory tower educator, although I have helped teach group dynamics in the classroom. It is not written by a management researcher, although I have performed research. It is also not written by a dreamer, a hero, or a snake oil salesman. If I don't get my job done as a manager, I don't have one—and no golden parachute. This book arose from a personal quest to understand individual excellence; it began with technical knowledge and skills and concluded in an attempt to understand people. I learned somewhere along the way that people can make an organization outstanding or keep it from achieving anything.

This book is about working with people who are sometimes happy and sometimes sad; people who work for other people who are sometimes kind, caring, and nurturing and who are sometimes not. It is about working in organizations that are many times led by people who are interested only in advancing their own careers and people who sometimes do poor work, no work, or the wrong work.

The book is written to make the psychology of people accessible to executives, managers, supervisors, foremen, and human resource managers—anyone who wants to learn more about what makes people tick and what it means to strive for excellence. The book talks about things we all have in common and that we all run into at work. If one is going to talk about people, one must talk about feelings and thinking, about personalities, about personal idiosyncrasies, and, most of all, about the psychology of people.

The book is not about the quick fix or the ten easy steps to a better organization. People cannot be sensitively nurtured and cared for in one minute. Leaders, managers, and administrators cannot practice transformational leadership without first having to acknowledge the egocentric nature of the idea—after all, doesn't management have to tell employees what to do? People, real people, are just too complex to be treated all in the same way, a situation which occurs when a simple set of behavior modification strategies is used.

This book is also about you. You can learn more about yourself by reading it. You can learn more about what it means to work. This book is about your friends, your fellow workers, your superiors, your subordinates, and your organization. This book is about your life at work. I hope you find it helpful.

Acknowledgments

I wish to acknowledge a debt of gratitude to my friends and colleagues who were willing to devote their valuable time and energies to reading and commenting on my work. Their many insights and not always so easy to respond to criticisms have made it a challenge to write an ever better book.

I wish to acknowledge my first reader, my wife Jean, whose patience and management experience permitted her to make many insightful suggestions. I wish to acknowledge my friend, colleague, and collaborator Michael Diamond for his support, advice, criticisms, and for his pointing the way. I also wish to acknowledge Howell Baum who provided me with many challenging opportunities to improve my work, the input of Glen Swogger, Richard Yepez, and Jim Hagen who provided me with many valuable insights and suggestions, and Ray Mayewski who provided me sheltered time to write.

Last, I wish to acknowledge the companionship of Lt. Savik, M.C.C., throughout the endless weeks and months of labor involved in bringing this project to fruition. THANKS.

Introduction

The pursuit of excellence in the workplace has taken on the significance of a cultural imperative in the United States. Competitive survival in the world's marketplace is at stake. The United States has lost much of its dominance in research and development, innovation, and cost-effective production of superior products and services. Other societies that are dedicated to becoming leaders in commerce through efficient production of superior products have had their dreadful effect. One need not read a newspaper or magazine long to find Japan or some other nation reported as taking the lead in an important research enterprise, or beginning to market a new product that is a substantial improvement over the previous one. America's response to this threat during the 1980s was a rededication to the pursuit of excellence in the workplace.

The pursuit of excellence provided the incentive to redesign organizations to free up creativity, action, and entrepreneurship. These efforts made a difference. It is also important to appreciate that many of the nostrums advocated by the evangelists of excellence do not address the paradoxes of human nature which often militate against achieving excellence.[1]

People all too often say one thing and do something else.[2] What they say they want is contradicted by their actions. They may unwittingly sabotage work in pursuit of fulfilling a personal agenda. One need not look far to find this type of contradictory action. A manager, for example, may advocate decentralization, delegation, and individual initiative but develop a reporting structure that funnels everything to the manager for final review and approval. Similarly, managers may espouse the pursuit of excellence but not support the pursuit with their actions.

Much has been said about the pursuit of excellence in organizations. Less understood and appreciated is the pursuit of excellence by individuals. Who in his or her right mind would not want an outstanding employee to achieve the maximum possible? Doesn't everyone benefit? The answer is Yes and No. Yes, superior individual creativity, innovation, leadership, and productivity are desirable; and No, others often find superior individual performance hard to handle. No one wants to feel outshined by another person. No one wants to see someone else receive promotions, pay increases, recognition, and prestige. No one wants to be reminded that he or she is not as good as someone else. As a result few people may really want a superstar to achieve excellence.[3]

We are thus confronted with a paradox of human nature in the workplace. Those most able to lead the way to achieving excellence may find themselves inhibited by others. They may be rejected, ostracized, and set apart from rewarding friendships and peer interactions. Outstanding performers whose self-esteem is injured by others may react in ways that further alienate them from the organization, management, and their friends and colleagues. Set in motion may be a self-defeating cycle of envy, fear, and rejection, on the part of others; and anger and contempt toward others on the part of superstars. The cycle leads to the self-fulfilling prophecy that superstar performers will not achieve their potential for the organization.

Freeing up outstanding individual performance must be a goal of the 1990s. To achieve this an appreciation must be gained of the aspects of human nature at work that serve to at times tragically limit what can be achieved by outstanding individuals. It is to this end this book is dedicated.

The chapters of this book are organized into three parts. The first five chapters describe the attributes outstanding performers, hereafter superstars, must have and some of the reasons for the problems they encounter in the workplace. Chapters 6 through 12 introduce a cosmology of burned-out superstars who have been turned off by their own feelings and actions, the feelings and actions of others, and the leadership of their organizations. Solutions to the problem of burnout are provided. Chapters 13 and 14 look at what is involved in developing an organizational culture that supports the pursuit of individual excellence. Chapter 15 concludes the book with additional reflections on achieving individual excellence.

Chapter 1 begins with a case that introduces the superstar problem. The literature on the search for excellence is then reviewed and contrasted to the individual psychological perspective, the focus of this book, and what it means for individuals to pursue excellence at work.

Chapter 2 provides a description of the attributes of superstars. Problematic aspects of defining or describing human behavior at work are discussed. The question of where superstars come from is then asked. Superstars may be hired in or rise to shine from within. Their origins and their gender are found to impact upon their likelihood of success.

Chapter 3 reviews many of the factors that surface to limit and alienate superstars. Superiors, colleagues, and subordinates will often unconsciously act to limit superstars. The chapter explores the possibility that, while organization members may espouse the pursuit of excellence, they, in fact, act to maintain mediocrity. The unconscious motivations for these actions stem from unacknowledged feelings of fear, envy, and lowered self-esteem which arise from working with outstanding performers.

Chapter 4 further elaborates the interpersonal and organizational dynamics created by the presence of superstars in organizations. Many of the possible interpersonal interactions others may have with superstars are listed. Of equal importance is an assessment of the implications of the interactions of superstars with groups of people with whom they work. Those who appear to be stars but are not superstars, like those who are good talkers or who are overly ambitious and power seeking, are also discussed. The chapter concludes with a discussion of others who fall short of stardom but are nonetheless outstanding in some way.

Chapter 5 provides an overview of the typology of burned-out superstars. The intellectual limitations of using a typology are discussed along with the threat that misinformed applications of typologies will create unfair outcomes for others. The chapter introduces a number of different ways of understanding human behavior that will be used in the book to illuminate the superstar typology in Part II. The levels of analysis are intrapersonal, interpersonal, group, and organizational. Each level of analysis introduces new factors to consider.

Starting with Chapter 6 the typology of the cosmology of burned-out superstars is introduced. The cosmology includes the pulsar in Chapter 7, the supernova in Chapter 8, the black hole in Chapter 9, the red giant in Chapter 10, and the white dwarf in Chapter 11. Each type of burned-out superstar is described both in behavioral and psychological terms. Fictional case examples are provided and discussed using each of the four analytical perspectives of the book: intrapersonal, interpersonal, group, and organizational. Prevention of superstar burnout is discussed. Organizational interventions to avoid extinguishing superstars and the problem of recovering poorly functioning superstars are explored. Chapter 12 further examines the cosmology and problems associated with outstanding individual performance by introducing the psychological perspectives of self-esteem and the development of a sense of self. The use and abuses of the typology will be revisited before encouraging readers to think critically about their work environment and the development of additional superstar types. The chapter concludes with an introduction to the importance of organizational culture for nurturing outstanding performers.

Chapter 13 begins the last part of the book by introducing the concept of organizational culture.[4] Organizational culture is found to include many essentially unconscious basic assumptions people hold about the world, themselves, others, and work. Organizational culture is also found to include organizational elements that allay anxiety about working within an organization and about the outside world the organization exists within. Many taken for granted aspects of work life such as language, groups, power and authority, and goals and objectives are found to contribute to making work less stressful. Chapter 14 further develops the concept of organizational culture by showing how it can be used as a means of creating a superstar-friendly interpersonal, group, and organizational operating environment.

Chapter 15 looks back over the book's major arguments and offers suggestions for superior performers who want to avoid burnout.

PART I

THE SEARCH FOR EXCELLENCE

Understanding what has been said about achieving organizational excellence lays a foundation for understanding what is involved in advocating for the achievement of individual excellence. The way to understand individual excellence is by understanding some of the unconscious workplace dynamics that limit the pursuit of excellence by outstanding individuals—superstars. Part I reviews the literature on the search for organizational excellence and then looks at workplace superstars who may have their best efforts blocked by organizational trends and unconscious interpersonal processes that may alienate and burn out the best of performers.

1

In Search of Excellence: The Superstar Factor

The search for excellence begins with people who think and feel. It is thought by many that if people learn thinking and management skills, they will use them to pursue excellence.[1] It is obvious that we all can learn and use new skills to improve our performance. It is equally clear that we do not always feel like it. We may even feel angry and intentionally not use our skills to our organization's best advantage. Similarly we all learn interpersonal skills which permit us to function effectively relative to others.[2] We learn how to work together and how to motivate others to perform better. However, we do not always act intentionally relative to others. Sometimes we are frustrated with what someone else has done or we are envious of their performance. It is the irrational side of organizational life that so often defies effective management, and it is this side of organizational life that creates hard to resolve interpersonal problems and conflicts.[3] The irrational side of organizational life can also have a devastating impact upon individuals who distinguish themselves by their performance and, by extension, negatively impact organizational performance. The Jenferni Corporation is a good example of this problem.

THE CASE OF THE JENFERNI CORPORATION

It seemed that the Jenferni Corporation had been around forever. Founded in the late 1800s by Joseph Jenferni, the company's 500 employees produced some of the finest wood products in the Southeast. Lately, however, losses of market share had all but eliminated the long list of back orders. Management and employees believed that their problem was their failure to adopt the design and production innovations already made by three of their biggest competitors. Production managers had to use new equipment, improved manufacturing methods, and more aggressive raw materials acquisition. What was also needed, they believed, was a top-notch "big city" marketing executive to shake up the demand for their products. These changes, everyone agreed, were critical to avoid layoffs that would have to be made to, in many cases, lifelong employees.

Janet Evening, an MBA and a rising star in marketing in a similar company in Chicago, was hired within a few months. Upon arrival she found that the management and employees of Jenferni were wonderful to work with. Within months Janet developed an enthusiastic staff and the needed research to identify the company's marketing problems and opportunities. Her skillfully prepared and presented strategies were well received by everyone. Her many ideas, which often impacted design, production, packaging, and distribution, were warmly received and, in most instances, acted upon. Janet's strategies began to bear immediate fruit. By the end of the third quarter sales had increased 27 percent and exceeded the highest levels of past sales. Continued fine-tuning of her strategies over the next year combined with good management of production methods made Jenferni a profitable organization which was able to provide its employees bonuses. Things had never been better for the employees of Jenferni.

Janet's continued successes gradually made her a household name among employees and within the local community. Her marketing exploits had been highlighted in local and regional newspapers and publications. She received a number of community recognitions for her work.

Janet's stellar performance and success had not gone unnoticed by her colleagues. Thomas Jenferni, president of the company and a highly visible member of the community, found, however, that he had lost some of his limelight to Janet. James Stuton, assistant vice president for production, had had several obvious but heretofore unnoticed production problems embarrassingly pointed out to him by Janet. Several other assistant vice presidents, who had hoped for promotion to vice president, watched in awe as Janet did, within two years, achieve the sought after status of vice president.

Initially it was thought by some of Janet's upper management colleagues that she might leave or that her successes would become fewer and further between. Gradually, criticism of her began to surface in the grapevine. Critical statements were occasionally made at social functions and in meetings when she was not present. Some of her ideas began to encounter energetic resistance. She began to find that Thomas Jenferni was rescheduling some of her time toward less productive and less visible work. Those in upper management began to require more of Thomas' time to discuss their thoughts and feelings about Janet and her ideas, her plans, her actions, and her rewards. "Yes, she had accomplished some remarkable things but so had others. We all made some solid contributions.''

Janet found the going got a lot tougher after the first two years. Even though the company's market share and profits had never been better, her ability to keep the ball rolling was diminishing. Problems and missed opportunities were beginning to reoccur. Janet felt frustrated by her loss of progress and the reduced flexibility on the part of others. At times, she felt bitter about the personal attacks made on her and what was becoming an endless process of sniping at her behind her back. She was being maligned and limited for no good reason she thought. And, despite her best efforts, her ability to get things done continued to gradually evaporate.

By the end of three years, the market share was beginning to falter. Profitability and back orders were down. Worse yet, some of her key marketing ploys were beginning to deteriorate without adequate nurturing by the company and a willingness to continue to change and innovate.

Janet gradually realized that those she worked with were, in fact, opposed to her rather than her ideas. Many of her colleagues, she found, were actively blocking her from accomplishing her work. This self-defeating process continued even after Janet began to draw attention to what was going on. She pointed out that it was not in the company's best interest to keep her from making her marketing programs work.

By the end of four years things had deteriorated to the point that the viability of the company was again in question. Janet felt that no one wanted to listen to her. No matter what she suggested or how she presented it, her efforts yielded no results. She found, after a long vacation, that she did not want to go back to work. She did go back, but she went into her office and closed the door. She just did not want to face the constant bickering and rejection. She attended meetings but rarely spoke up to avoid being attacked. She did work that was requested but without her old vigor and willingness to constantly try to improve the company. She felt bad about herself, her work, and the company as she helplessly watched the company fail.

It was not long before Janet was recruited by a nearby competitor to head their marketing department. Janet's departure was approved of by most of her colleagues who inwardly felt relieved she was leaving. ''She should have left years ago.'' Even though Jenferni was about to go under, there was an excitement in the air. There was a sense of hard-earned pleasure. A victory had been won and, naturally, the source of all the problems would magically depart with her.

THE DYNAMICS OF THE CASE

What happened to Janet has happened to many superstars. Her outstanding skills, which led her to correctly analyze the situation, develop good solutions to problems, and participate effectively in implementing change, helped the organization but eventually threatened her superior and her colleagues. She had inadvertently demonstrated by her work that they had not been effective leaders of their company. Her quick analysis of the situation made this readily apparent. Her many rapidly developed and sound ideas made them feel that they were not, by comparison, informed, creative, or resourceful. Her talented use of interpersonal and group process skills also made her a highly visible leader within the organization; someone whom others thought made important decisions and pointed the way to profit. Everyone knew about her, and employees began to wonder why top management had for years been so ineffective.

Even though they liked her and enjoyed working with her, her fellow workers and subordinates also occasionally felt overwhelmed by her rapid thinking, fast-paced work, well-developed information base, analytical skills, network of connections, and expectations that they achieve excellence in their work. Some felt incompetent and overwhelmed by comparison. Those who had been leaders and decision makers were, in some instances, displaced, and they resented the loss of their status. Many including those in upper management resented feeling that they had been part of the problem and that they had had to rush to catch Janet's bandwagon. The best solution, they began to think, was for her to leave. As a result, strong negative feelings toward Janet developed along with an undiscussed collusion on the part of those most threatened by her to try to cut her down to size by blocking her from more success, promotions, and raises. However, overlooked by almost everyone who knew what was going on was the all too obvious loss of the benefits everyone received from her skillful development of outstanding marketing strategies.

So one must ask, were the leadership, management, and employees of the company really seeking excellence? Why were the management and members of Jenferni willing to forgo Janet's quest for excellence and, by extension, organizational excellence? To learn more we may turn to the advocates of organizational excellence to see what they have to say about Janet's situation. In particular we can consult two important books by Tom Peters and his colleagues.

IN SEARCH OF ORGANIZATIONAL EXCELLENCE

The most influential contemporary work on the subject of organizational excellence is Tom Peters and Robert Waterman's book *In Search of Excellence.*[4] Peters and Waterman found successful American companies to have eight properties. Although it is not possible to review this book in depth here, it is important to appreciate the subject matter and its treatment. To this end the properties are listed below along with many of the key words and concepts used to describe and discuss them. To the uninformed reader of management literature many of these words and concepts may not be readily recognized or placed into the context of the workplace. Should this be the case an apology is extended, and I encourage you to locate and read the book.

The following encapsulated overview of the book reveals that much of what is said are, by now, familiar slogans. It is equally important to understand that the approach to and the discussion of organizational life have detached scholarly, theoretical, and "organizational" perspectives. Although the authors claim the book is grounded in how to help get people to do better, it deals only superficially with how people might feel at work and how these feelings might influence behavior. There is no explicit discussion of the limitations, contradictions, and irrational side of organizational life although this is, in part, the stated purpose of the book.[5] This is not to say that what is said is not important and that these important organizational properties are not associated with high-quality operations; however, they provide little insight into what it means to be someone striving for excellence at work.

The eight properties of successful companies are listed below.

1. A Bias for Action. Key words and concepts: less complexity, fluidity, adhocracy, informality, communication, breaking work down into doable tasks, small groups, project teams, willingness to try things and experiment, and simplifying systems.

2. Close to the Customer. Key words and concepts: customer orientation, caring, customer satisfaction, people orientation, top-management involvement, feedback, quality and service orientation, tailoring via market segmentation, listening to users, and cost consciousness.

3. Autonomy and Entrepreneurship. Key words and concepts: encourage entrepreneurship by allowing autonomy, messiness, overlap, lack of coordination, chaotic conditions, internal competition, champions of causes and zealots, parallel projects, sponsors, and risk taking, and by permitting failures, support systems, heroes, and mythology.

4. Productivity through People. Key words and concepts: rules assume that people are incompetent; people respond to being treated as adults; dignity; respect; set reasonable and clear expectations; training; autonomy; lip service is a disaster; hold people accountable for their performance; people programs; monetary and nonmonetary incentives; language used to represent how people should treat each other—crew members; informality; free flow of information; role models; management training; smallness.

5. Hands-on, Value Driven. Key words and concepts: values are not policies and procedures; beliefs should inform policies and procedures; it should be clear what the organization stands for; focus; articulation of values; values are diffused through stories and myths; values should inspire the people at the bottom; leaders should have vision and promote excitement.

6. Stick to the Knitting. Key words and concepts: Stay with what the organization does best; rampant diversification is not encouraged.

7. Simple Form, Lean Staff. Key words and concepts: Simple and stable organization form; unifying organizational themes focus work; flexibility; fluidity; pressing authority down in the organization; decentralization; flatten; and three pillars—stability, entrepreneurship, and breaking old habits/reorganizing.

8. Simultaneous Loose-Tight Properties. Key words and concepts: control versus autonomy; control associated with values; culture; information systems; autonomy associated with champions; flexibility; risk taking; simultaneous external and internal focuses.

There is, regrettably, little to learn from the book about the unconscious and subjective nature of individual and group dynamics that act to limit the pursuit of individual excellence. It may be observed that many of the managerial devices identified as associated with achieving excellence use impersonal organizational variables such as task breakdown, creation of small groups, market segmentation, internal competition, accountability, incentives, training, stable organizational form, flattening the hierarchy, control versus autonomy, and information systems. These traditional organizational concepts all, of course, involve people, but they are abstract concepts and strategies which guide management behavior. They are a list of ingredients for an organizational stew. They are topics for discussion, and they are subjects to be learned about. Decisions may be made to flatten the hierarchy and promote communication to save money, and to promote participation, personal investment, and ownership of work. They are, however, one step removed from the people who make up the organization.

Another batch of terms imply people but are not discussed in terms of what they really mean to people. Examples of these impersonal people terms are communication, willingness to try, customer orientation, listening, allowing autonomy, heroes, people responding to being treated like adults, informality, articulation of values, flexibility, and risk taking. These are concepts that people would be expected to do or experience. Keeping everyone informed is important. People should be willing to try new things. Others should be listened to. Informality is usually appreciated. All of these are important people-oriented organizational attributes; however, they are not discussed in terms of exactly how it might feel to receive adequate communication—to be confided in and treated as an equal. How does it feel to be expected to be flexible and accommodating? How might it feel to be expected to be a team player? How does it feel to be encouraged to take risks at work? Are people really all that accepting of failure? What impact may one failure have upon being encouraged to take another risk? And even if failure or less than complete success is welcomed by others and management, isn't it likely that those who take the risks and fail may still feel defeated and diminished relative to their own expectations?

In Search of Excellence does briefly touch upon some aspects of emotional life at work. Pointed out in the book is the paradox that an organization member may wish to be both part of an organization and a team player and, at the same time, autonomous—a star in his or her own right, a seeker of freedom and self-determination. The discussion includes neither the social and psychological origins of this duality nor the meaning of the internal conflict and anxiety that it may create. Furthermore, the implication of this important organization psychodynamic is never explored relative to managing the members of an organization toward achieving excellence.

We also learn that there are contradictions to human nature, such as wishing to see ourselves as better than we really are, but why these might be so and what they might mean are not mentioned. We learn that we have two sides to our brains, a creative side and a logical side, and that both sides should be considered to be of value to organizations. We learn that our minds have a limited ability to process information. We also learn we may have our behavior modified by a system of rewards and punishments, that we may be intrinsically motivated, and that we seek meaning in life from others, from organizations, and from social institutions. We do not learn much about people and what makes them tick. We do not learn why these all too human attributes and tendencies may affect achieving organizational excellence.

The overall orientation of the book leads the reader to the conclusion that people and their work life are to be managed, organized, and motivated. It is top management, in all of its beneficence, who must create the correct mix or organizational variables and provide the transformational leadership that provides organization members with meaning and purpose. It is top management who must provide the incentives we need to change our behavior, thoughts, and feelings.

Missing in the book is any real sense of humanity and what it means to rise in the morning, leave for work, perform work, and leave work only to return. Missing is any real appreciation for the true complexity and paradoxical nature of human beings and their nonrational feelings. Lost in the reification of the organization is the need to deal with the people who create the organization when they come to work, who make it run, and who use it to meet their own needs for interpersonal safety and security. *In Search of Excellence* does not tell us about the feelings Janet and her colleagues experienced which motivated their behavior. Her colleagues did not act as Janet recommended, nor did they logically. Espoused theory and theory in practice diverged.[6] And it may not have been because the management and staff of Jenferni did not know better; very likely they did. More important, they, for very personal, undiscussable, and perhaps unacknowledged or unknown reasons, did not feel like it.

A second leading book on excellence is *A Passion for Excellence* by Tom Peters and Nancy Austin.[7] This companion book to *In Search of Excellence* is described as a Whitman's Sampler of the passion for excellence. The book, based on additional years of experience gained from 500 training seminars, does not profess to have scientific validity nor to extend management theory. The book is rather more inspirational and motivational.

The reader expects this book's content to be more concrete and sensitive to how people really are. After all the authors point out in the introduction, "We got so tied up on techniques, devices and programs that we forgot about people— the people who produce the product or service and the people who consume it."[8] Regrettably the key words of the five parts of a passion for excellence demonstrate there is, once again, a shortfall in understanding the psychological side of organizational life.

1. Common Sense. Key words and concepts: management by walking around; care of customers; constant innovation; turned-on people; external focus; adaptation; staying

in touch with consumers, suppliers, and employees; listening to your customers; use the devices advocated in the book with integrity.

2. Customers. Key words and concepts: courtesy; listening; respect for the customer; customer orientation; support people as heroes—the receptionist who does a great job; make your product special through differentiation; price/cost are not necessarily a common denominator for successful competition; perceptual skills—look for variations; do not be impersonal; listen to complaints; measure consumer satisfaction; quality not so much a technique as a philosophy of caring; the customer is all important.

3. Innovation. Key words and concepts: messy world—innovation is not renderable to orderly and controlled processes; constant experimentation; must be able to accept uncertainty and ambiguity; move quickly; small teams are more effective than big ones; interproduct line compatibility is important; optimization is not critical—no one design is best; leading users of your product or service point the way to improvement; understand personal attributes of champions; assess performance of decentralization; trust; volunteerism; locate the best people for skunk works; reward entrepreneurship; innovative groups feel different; sloppy process; failure is OK; networking; nurturing champions; creating heroes; working around or violating routine administrative systems.

4. People, People, People. Key words and concepts: people philosophy; lead by inspiration; believe in people; personal integrity; encourage ownership of work; involvement; pride; empower others to act; provide information; commitment; decentralization; trust; demeaning regulations are unproductive; celebrate success with meaningful awards and recognition.

5. Leadership. Key words and concepts: Leadership is show biz; cheerleaders; enthusiast; nurture others; dramatize; coach; managers are powerful—they influence values and what others believe; promotion is an important signal of what behavior is valued; attention is symbolic behavior—what is attended to indicates what the leader values; use drama to communicate values; language and stories teach values; preaching vision; care and love; doable tasks make stars; limit bureaucracy; limit formal central control processes in favor of individuals paying close attention to their work; flatten the organization; coaching is face-to-face ongoing leadership; coaches encourage, excite, teach, listen, facilitate; management by walking about; sponsoring; counseling; confronting; commitment; courage.

The book is exceptional for its down-home, good neighbor style. Filled with interesting anecdotes on how great people achieved great things, the book is motivational for the legions of zealots of excellence. However, a review of the key words and concepts does not show much progression toward understanding people. Some is common sense—such as getting to know your employees and customers—certainly sage advice for at least two millennia. There are, of course, important things to know about relating to customers such as being courteous, respectful, and attentive to their needs, dreams, and aspirations. It goes without saying, in a time of "permanent white water," that innovativeness and organizational flexibility and adaptability are musts.[9] To improve, it is pointed out, it is important to support people who mess up tidy organizational life with change that tries to make the organization better and its employees more effective. We learn that the backbone of an organization is its employees and that these important people should be treated respectfully and encouraged to take risks and to treat each other as adults. And naturally all of these aspects of organizational life must be led by an insightful, enlightened, and visionary management which coaches and counsels its inspired teams of employees to victory in the marketplace. Few would disagree that these ideas are important contributors to making organizations work better, but they overlook the extraordinary complexity of human nature with its many limitations, paradoxes, and irrationalities. Overlooked is providing the reader with insight into what it really means to use this big bag of management devices effectively and sensitively in an organization filled with real people who have many personal needs, aspirations, and feelings.

REFLECTIONS

Perhaps my assessment of these two books is too harsh. Perhaps they have been set up to fail because they were assessed relative to a perspective that they were not intended to cover. Perhaps a hopelessly overstuffed strawman has been created and then mowed down as part of a traditional intellectual ritual. To the extent that a strawman has been created, it serves the purpose of focusing on what these books do not cover. To the extent that the books were not intended to deal with the psychological aspects of life, the limiting, paradoxical, and nonrational aspects of people, then it is clear that it is time to consider them. In either case the point is made. To understand why people do what they do, one must consult them. One must understand what they think and feel and what about their life serves to, in part, unconsciously determine their behavior at work. Psychoanalytic psychology permits us to do this. The subject of this hermeneutic science is people.[10]

A NOTE ON PSYCHOLOGICAL LIFE IN ORGANIZATIONS

Understanding people at work means understanding and appreciating the underlying psychodynamics of their motivations. A son who was dominated by his mother may feel he has to, in turn, dominate women at work or otherwise be dominated by them. A daughter who received little attention may have developed a low self-esteem and, as an adult, be excessively concerned with receiving the approval of others. The compulsive pursuit of this approval may, in turn, lead to self-sacrificing behavior that is organizationally adaptive but self-defeating.

Understanding the psychological aspects of life at work implies prying into the unconscious motivations for our behavior—our prior life experiences. There are many ways to apply psychoanalytically informed psychology of individuals, groups, and organizations, and there are many legitimate views of the irrational side of organizational life. The extent of this theory and literature precludes even the most expansive efforts to summarize it. It is diverse, complex, and abstract;

nonetheless, it is highly informative. The works of Karen Horney and Wilfred Bion, object relations theory, and the work of many contemporary authors form the basis for the examination of individual excellence undertaken in this book.

The case of the Jenferni Corporation highlights the importance of being able to understand the not so rational aspects of organizational life. What happened in the case has been played out countless times in almost all organizations. In this case, Janet was simply very good at her work. She possessed many of the attributes of a superstar, which are discussed in Chapter 2. Her intelligence and skills permitted her to excel. Despite her thoughtful attentiveness to interpersonal and group dynamics, her many successes and rewards and the occasions when she embarrassed others eventually caused some of her coworkers to feel bad about themselves, which unconsciously motivated them to act to limit her and to get rid of her. Janet eventually got the message. She was just not wanted and she left.

Understanding the psychological side of work life will aid in understanding why people like Janet are high achievers and why, when the going got tough, they might decide to leave rather than stick it out. Psychology also permits a much better understanding of how superiors, colleagues, and employees come to feel about superstars and why they, without discussing it, might collude to limit and to get rid of them.

The balance of the book makes it clear that superstars are people too. They may be motivated to achieve for not entirely rational reasons. And, if these star performers are rejected, maligned, and limited they, like everyone else, have emotional feet of clay and may well respond with strong feelings which lead them to predictable, emotionally motivated behavioral outcomes. In sum, they can be hurt and become angry like everyone else.

The book also examines how others feel about superstars which, in Janet's case, resulted in self-defeating hostility and aggression. Those who work with superstars are also found to have emotional feet of clay which lead them to feel threatened and envious; feelings that, in turn, unconsciously motivate actions to limit or defeat the superstar who may, in wild West terms, be seen to be "the fastest gun in town."

A WORD ON LESSER STARS

Chapter 2 provides a list of superstar attributes. Many employees have some of these attributes but have thus far fallen short of achieving stardom although outstanding work is often accomplished. There may also be instances where someone performs brilliantly in one area but is weak in others or inconsistently produces stellar results. These individuals may be effective leaders who, for example, lack vision. There are many possible combinations of the superstar attributes which can create lesser stars who, when they shine brightly, may experience the positive and negative feelings others hold for superstars.

Although this book uses superstars as a point of discussion, it applies equally to everyone who achieves outstanding performance and who becomes the subject of fear, envy, and rivalry. In sum, this book is dedicated to everyone who shines at work.

CONCLUSION

The search for excellence should begin with people, and understanding people means venturing into psychology and what it can teach us. It is time to make this trip before it is too late. Achieving organizational excellence in the 1990s is going to mean finding ways of enabling individuals to achieve excellence— it is people, not the organization, who strive for excellence.

2

Who Are the Superstars?

We have all heard the word superstar. We all associate it with someone who is outstanding, such as a Joe Montana in football, a Magic Johnson in basketball, and in the business world a Ted Turner, Lee Iacocca, or Donald Trump. These men are superheroes to the young and provide important role models to emulate. In the workplace superstars are found throughout organizations but possibly more often where performance is easily quantified such as in sales.[1] Superstars of the workplace, like their counterparts the super athletes, salesmen, and CEOs, possess many skills and personal attributes which permit them to function highly effectively as workers and managers. Understanding superstars at work begins with understanding the skills and attributes they possess which permit them, and may even compel them, to achieve individual excellence. Before proceeding, however, a word of caution needs to be invoked. Any list of skills and personal attributes has limitations that offer its users problems in wisely and fairly using it to understand one's self and others.

LIMITATIONS OF THE LIST OF SUPERSTAR ATTRIBUTES

The list of attributes given in this chapter is no exception; it has some limitations that are worth noting.

The first limitation is that no matter how thorough a list is, it is not comprehensive. There will always be attributes that are not discovered or, if discovered, were not listed for reasons known only to the author. The second limitation is that a list of attributes can be seen to be much like a horoscope. The reader may think, ''Most of them fit me at least to some extent.'' We all have good attributes that we are proud of and rightly so. A third limitation is the problem of deciding whether an individual needs to possess all the attributes in the list or just some. Are there some that are mandatory and others that are not? A closely related issue is the degree to which they should be possessed and how they can be documented. A fourth limitation is that some if not many of the skills and attitudes may be difficult to define in operational terms. For example, leaping ability is important in basketball. Leaping ability can be measured and a standard set for outstanding ability. However, to say a person must be quick witted creates a dilemma in developing an operational description of the attribute. How do you measure the ability when the process goes for the most part unobserved? How do you control for variations in the situation requiring quick thinking? Is the person expected to be equally quick witted in all, most, or some of the situations? And what product is expected? There may be a vast array of possible responses. And, last, how will the response be evaluated and compared to the responses of others?

These limitations lead to considering how useful it is to use attributes to describe someone. A worker may get good results without having the qualities of a superstar. A person may have superstar qualities and not get stellar results. Similarly, some individuals may look like superstars but only because they are good at attracting attention to themselves and their work. These people, who work with great flair, prefer to focus on aspects of work or the workplace where their efforts will be quickly spotted and acknowledged. These eventualities do not invalidate the approach of making a list, but they do make it clear that one must accept the limitations of the approach, be patient in applying it, and be prepared to observe enough behavior to discern a clear trend before deciding whether someone is superstar material.

In sum, it is important to appreciate that what seems like a simple and straight-forward concept, such as a list of attributes, can conceal important problems in understanding and using it. This chapter does not presume to solve the problems or to overcome the limitations of making a list, but it is informed by them and hopefully minimizes them where possible.

SUPERSTAR ATTRIBUTES

The list of superstar attributes was assembled from experience and informed by the attributes of gifted children and, to a lesser extent, those attributes associated with entrepreneurship and creativity.[2] The list includes many admirable traits that everyone possesses to some degree. The difference is that the superstar possesses most of them at a fairly high level of functionality. As a result, it is usually easy to spot people who have the attributes and are encouraged to use them. When given the chance, people who have the skills and attitudes in the following list will usually distinguish themselves. The superstar will exhibit many of the following personal and behavioral attributes:

- Time efficient
- Organized
- Persistent and able to concentrate on a project for long periods of time
- Energetic and self-initiating
- Diligent
- Capable of risk taking
- Open to feedback and criticism
- Visionary and willing to offer guidance and direction to others
- Tolerant of stress and ambiguity
- Not preoccupied with
  Pursuit of power and authority
  Pursuit of title
  Receiving the approval of others
  Competition
- Highly informed about many subjects and eager to contribute to discussions
- Well prepared to work and participate in meetings
- Equipped with good administrative skills
- Sensitive, self-reflective, and considerate of others
- Willing to make tough, controversial decisions
- Imaginative—flexible, adaptive, resilient
- Innovative
- Creative
- Good at communicating
- Curious about what is going on around them
- Interested in pursuing excellence for its own sake
- Equipped with good interpersonal skills
- Equipped with good leadership and group process skills: assertive, and able to resolve conflicts, accept criticism, and deflect or absorb aggression
- Charismatic

The Provisos

Before proceeding, several important provisos need to be made about the nature of this particular list: The list of attributes are personal attributes that are usually associated with achieving high levels of personal competence and performance; the attributes are skills and attitudes that can be learned by everyone;

learning to be time efficient and organized are the subjects of time-management seminars; everyone can improve administrative, communication, interpersonal, and group process skills; and everyone can learn to be more risk taking, persistent, and innovative. However, all of these attributes do not add up to a fully functioning person. The first proviso is then that the list of superstar attributes is just that. They are skills and attitudes that are prerequisites to being successful at work. They leave out that part of us that makes us human: our feelings and our personalities.

This chapter does not explain how the attributes are acquired. In the case of the gifted child, they seem to naturally emerge from the child's genetic heritage. For others, they are hard earned for not always the most rational of reasons from formal education and trial and error. The cosmology of burned-out superstars described in Part II emphasizes the sad fact that many who achieve high levels of performance are driven to compensate for personality deficits in the form of compulsive solutions to cope with neurotic anxiety. The second proviso is then that people at work may be motivated to acquire superstar attributes and achieve great feats for less than rational reasons. This proviso also applies to the gifted who may also use their talents to fend off the distressing experience of neurotic anxiety. This is not to say many people who have or acquire the attributes and achieve great feats are not acting for rational reasons; they are. However, it must be appreciated that even the best of people can become disorganized if put under enough stress and will respond by trying to minimize anxiety by using their skills and talents.

Last, the list of attributes may seem to imply that anyone who has them is not merely on the right track to achieving personal excellence and superstar status but also on the track to becoming superhuman. This is not the intention of this chapter or the list. The most fundamental presupposition of this book is that superstars are people too. Not only do they have many fine and highly developed skills, they also have feelings that make them just as vulnerable as everyone else to having their feelings hurt by the actions of others and then reacting in an emotional way to that hurt. Superstars feel fear, anger, envy, and rejection just like everyone else and perhaps more often because their skills tend to make them the focus of a lot of attention. The third proviso is then that superstars, like everyone else, have emotional feet of clay and do not always rise above their feelings to do the right thing or to achieve excellence.

The list of superstar attributes must then be appreciated for what it is, an effort to list the skills and attitudes that are associated with being able to excel at work. It is also noteworthy that many of the attributes are not explicit parts of the curriculums of business schools which traditionally provide their students with highly technical and analytical skills which contribute to fulfilling but a few of the items in the list.

Now that the provisos have been made we may return to the discussion of the attributes of superstars.

Time Efficient

Superstars get a lot done. They are very productive. There are a number of elements involved in their time efficiency. First, they just simply work fast. They move and think quickly. They can be intense and high task at times. They focus themselves on the work at hand. Second, they are effective at handling multiple tasks. They may work on dozens or even many dozens of projects simultaneously. This strategy is necessary when their work on projects is invariably delayed by slow responses from others, groups, and the organization. Working on multiple tasks permits them to keep going by permitting them to shift back and forth between projects to keep productive. Working on multiple projects also creates synergistic outcomes in that the products of some of the projects may positively interact with work on other projects. Third, they are effective at identifying what is important from what is not. They do not waste a lot of time working on or worrying about an aspect of the work that has little effect on the final outcome. Fourth, other abilities, such as being well organized, informed, creative and self-critical, contribute to the superstar's finding ways of being efficient. Many people are time efficient and rigorous at scheduling what, how, and when they work. Superstars are just simply better at it. They are better able to handle a great many projects and to tolerate the ambiguity and self-imposed stresses they create. For the superstar, it is a challenge to be met.

Organized

Superstars are effective at organizing their work and their resources and at sequencing tasks. They are effective at organizing meetings, work schedules, and priorities. They have had to learn to be organized to handle the, at times, large and diverse volume of projects mentioned above. Part of their effectiveness is their willingness to remain flexible about their priorities and scheduling to take advantage of opportunities that develop. By having many projects under way simultaneously, superstars create the opportunity to be flexible and increase the likelihood of serendipitous outcomes. To the extent that they are permitted to be flexible by management, they usually take good advantage of it.

Persistent and Intense

We have all known people who are tenacious in their pursuit of their work and goals. We have all known people who block out everything else and focus on whatever they are working on. These same individuals might think nothing of spending whatever amount of time it takes to achieve a goal or complete a project. These individuals might be described as compulsive achievers, mono-maniacs, single-minded persons, overachievers, and industrious workers. Superstars are willing to persist on projects and to work long after their friends and colleagues have given up. This intensity is, however, balanced with a self-awareness that helps mediate it thereby permitting superstars to avoid becoming overly obsessive and compulsive about their work. They are not compelled to work this hard to achieve; rather, they enjoy their work for its own sake.

Energetic and Self-Initiating

Superstars have a lot of energy to bring to bear on their work. They usually have something to contribute. Their high energy levels permit them to work harder and longer and to be more active than many of their colleagues. Superstars are also self-starters but not to attract attention to themselves to gain status and power. Since they enjoy thinking, manipulating ideas, and doing, they originate new ideas and act on them. They are hard to hold back, which is the good news for their supervisors.

Diligent

Superstars are responsible people and, although they have a lot of ideas, they are good at following through with proper execution of what can become painstaking details. They can be depended upon to get the job done. As a result, they are able to take many projects from start to finish.

Capable of Risk Taking

Superstars are willing risk takers. They take risks all the time in their thinking. They are willing to risk rejection and being chided for constantly exploring the limits of new ideas. Superstars enjoy developing and presenting their ideas, defending them, and expanding them, and they are willing to drop them if they do not have merit. They are also willing to implement change and accept the risks of failure. When problems and failures do occur, their persistence often pays off and so does their personal resilience. They are not overly affected by problems which they view as a challenge rather than as a personal threat to their self-esteem or their reputation.

Open to Feedback and Criticism

Superstars seek feedback from others. They understand that feedback is important to improve their ideas and methods. Superstars are receptive to receiving constructive criticism even though it is not always pleasant. They can be expected to respond with change once the nature of the criticism is understood in terms of their behavior. In sum, superstars are always learning to improve themselves and their work from others.

Visionary and Directive

Superstars frequently envision what should be or what will happen before others do. Superstars who serve as leaders can be inspiring as a result of their ability to develop insightful long-term goals that are then communicated to others in an inspirational and motivational manner. Superstars provide direction and coaching and counseling to others, groups, and organizations as needed. They can be depended upon when needed for good insights and instructions.

Tolerant of Stress and Ambiguity

The self-imposed pressures of being efficient, organized, and risk taking make it important for superstars to be able to tolerate ambiguity and work-related stress. A strong sense of self-esteem and self-other boundaries contributes to regulating the degree to which stress comes to be experienced and the amount of anxiety experienced. Superstars will appear calm during stressful times, not because calm is an important attribute for image management, but because they are calm, thoughtful, observant, and self-reflective.

Not Preoccupied with Pursuit of Power and Authority

Superstars enjoy thinking, creating, working, and achieving much for their own sakes. They climb the mountain because it is there. Although superstars often obtain power and authority as a result of their achievements, they are not overly motivated to acquire them to feel good about themselves.

Not Preoccupied with Title

Superstars may have their work acknowledged by promotions and other accoutrements of organizational success but, once again, they do not seek them for their own value. Superstars are not particularly motivated by extrinsic organizational rewards. Their motivations are, for the most part, intrinsic.

Not Preoccupied with Seeking Approval

Superstars are not seekers of approval for its own sake. They are also not usually motivated by the need to prove themselves to others nor do they particularly feel the need to attract positive attention to themselves. Superstars have achieved fairly high levels of personal autonomy and self-esteem and are not dependent upon the approval of others to feel good about themselves.

Not Preoccupied with Competition

Superstars may feel competitive toward others but it is seldom a strong motivator. They may understand much competition is self-defeating and counterproductive for the organization as it usually serves to create winners and losers and to advance one person's interests. They more often compete against absolute standards they set for their performance. They work hard to perfect their skills to achieve their goals. They do not, however, lose the joy of the pursuit of excellence and do not become driven by impossible to meet standards.

Highly Informed

Superstars are voracious consumers of information on all sorts of topics. They take advantage of opportunities to learn, and they are effective at generalizing their information to other subjects. They can often see many sides to a subject but may pick one to explore and argue in favor of in a group. They will have a great deal of expert information on topics of primary interest to them and their work. They are diligent researchers and will gather information from many sources before arriving at a conclusion. Their opinions are highly informed and, as a result, difficult to refute. This difficulty is further accentuated by their being informed about the weaknesses of their position.

Prepared to Work

Superstars come to meetings ready to work. Their level of preparedness can be disarming to others who may not have prepared as well (or at all) for the discussion of a topic at a meeting.

Equipped with Good Administrative Skills

Superstars are good at their jobs and good at management and administration. They have gained mastery over such customary skills as planning, organizing, coordinating, delegating, and directing. They are insightful consumers of management information and resourceful users of computers and other information resources; they are informed about the literature and attentive to what other organizations are doing; and they are pursuers of continuing educational opportunities.

Sensitive, Self-Reflective, Considerate

Superstars are aware of others. They have learned to appreciate what others think and feel for few people are indifferent to superstars. They are attentive to what others say and do not say, to their body language, and they are aware of the symbolic meaning of their actions. Superstars are sensitive and aware of what goes on around them. As a result, they are more apt to perceive being manipulated, controlled, and rejected. Because their feelings can be readily hurt, they have learned to be self-reflective and able to understand what they are feeling and why.

Willing Decision Makers

Superstars, because they are risk takers and tolerate stress and ambiguity well, are usually willing to make decisions. Their behavior may be seen as paradoxical. In a crisis they are usually calm and thoughtful. They succeed in controlling their emotions which they know will impair their thinking. As a result others may believe they have no feelings, which is not true. They are simply able to override them when necessary to be able to bring their abilities to bear on the distressing problem. The paradox is that, during periods of calm, they are more active, trying to encourage more work and change.

Imaginative, Innovative, and Creative

Superstars have good imaginations and possess an active fantasy life. Superstars see opportunities everywhere. They may surface many ideas quickly and build quickly on the ideas of others. Superstars will usually be field independent and divergent and critical thinkers. They invariably come up with new and interesting ideas. Their thinking is seldom limited by the norm. Superstars are resourceful thinkers who consider many sides of a problem before selecting one or more avenues for pursuit. They are able to envision the likely outcomes of the current course of events, to assess the impact on the organization, and to respond by taking effective action to head off the problem or further developments. Superstars are especially effective at continuous innovation where the first, the second, or even the third effort is not entirely successful. As they are critical, nondefensive consumers of their own ideas and efforts, they quickly identify problems with their decisions and actions and are ready to make adjustments as needed. Creativity involves many things and shares similarities with imagination and innovation. Creativity is a highly sought after personal attribute that we all possess but do not always have opportunities to develop because we are not encouraged to use it.

Good at Communicating

Superstars have good verbal skills. They think clearly and as a result they can usually express themselves fluently. They are attentive to their audience and adjust their pace and content to improve understanding. Their ability to think quickly further accentuates this skill. Superstars are also good listeners. They encourage others to speak to them by hearing what they are saying, asking questions, giving feedback, and permitting the other person to be the focus of attention. There is little competition for air time. People enjoy talking to superstars who usually will make the encounter interesting, personally rewarding, and even entertaining.

Curious

Superstars are unusually observant about what goes on around them. They often discern details others miss. They may pursue a course of investigation merely to see what is there or a course of action to see what will happen. In some ways they are a living industrial lab that Thomas Edison would have been proud of. It is also worth noting that their curiosity may lead to blind alleys and "wasted" time and resources. However, the waste they create is more than made up for by the opportunities they spot along the way.

Interested in Pursuit of Excellence

Superstars enjoy trying to do things better, not better than others per se, just better. All of the above attributes almost involuntarily lead the superstar in this direction. They enjoy the challenge of trying to perform better or to improve things beyond current levels.

Equipped with Good Interpersonal Skills

Superstars have people skills. They are interesting people to be around and to talk to. Their many ideas and life experiences and their substantial data base make them enthusiastic and warmly received contributors to discussions. Superstars are attentive to others and good listeners who provide constructive feedback. Superstars are attentive to interpersonal and group dynamics. They pick up meaningful actions that may go unobserved by others. They are good observers of human nature, and they enjoy meeting and being around people. They are also comfortable with being alone or remaining on the periphery of a social event. Superstars do not have compelling needs to be around others and are not overly preoccupied with social approval. They are people who like to be with others who stimulate their minds with new thoughts and information.

Equipped with Good Leadership Skills

Superstars are natural leaders. Their self-esteem permits them to seek the responsibility and power of leadership roles without becoming immersed in the pursuit or wielding of power and the politics of influence. Superstars are effective at using group process skills and building consensus. They, when necessary, will make tough, even unpopular, decisions. They are effective at leading others in taking action and are attentive to the need to attend to resistance to change.

Charismatic

Superstars will often develop a charisma about themselves. Others will come to like and admire them because they merit it. They have earned the positive attention they receive. Superstars enjoy their enhanced status (as any one would), but they make others comfortable in their presence. People are willing to follow the superstar because they trust the superstar to take care of them with the direction selected.

ORGANIZATIONAL ORIGINS OF SUPERSTARS

Superstars can have a major impact on an organization and others in it. One irreducible variable that may impact responses to superstars are their origins, either from within or from without.

Superstars may be hired to work for an organization. Those doing the hiring will usually know they are hiring a superstar, however, they may not if the superstar has not been encouraged to shine in the past. A known superstar who is recruited into an organization will encounter several predictable problems. The superstar may be dumped on and expected to accomplish great feats which may not be readily achievable.[3] The superstar may be hired into an organizational setting where others were opposed to the recruitment and will resent the superstar's presence. These individuals may be the first to point out the superstar is not living up to expectations (perhaps set too high to ensure failure) implying it was not a good hiring decision. The superstar may also be viewed as a "hired gun" who has been brought in to shake things up. Others may fear the superstar or set themselves up to take the superstar on in a showdown. Of course, there is always the possibility that the superstar will be warmly received and set up to succeed.

Superstars who enter organizations where their abilities are not known by the recruiters may pleasantly surprise everyone when they begin to shine. In this event, and as will be seen in subsequent chapters, there are things that can be done to nurture the superstar in the pursuit of excellence.

Superstars may also rise from within organizations where others have provided them with a receptive and nurturing setting. Should this occur the superstar should be more readily accepted, however, how management responds is critical. The superstar may, at this point, be set up to fail by being singled out for excessive praise and rewards which attract a lot of attention and envy, a contributing factor to Janet Evening's problems.[4] However, the fact that the superstar emerged at all is a positive statement about the organization and its members who may feel they have watched and contributed. The work and products of the superstar's talents may have already benefited them, and they may understand the connection between enabling the superstar to achieve and the overall success of their organization. To the extent that a superstar had a difficult and tortuous rise, the person will no doubt possess some superstar burnout characteristics that may tend to make the superstar less productive.[5] Subsequent chapters will deal with this phenomenon. It suffices to note that nurturing a superstar into full production requires a commitment by management and others.

GENDER OF SUPERSTARS

When one thinks of superstars it is rather natural in our culture to think of men who have achieved superstar status; however, superstar traits and abilities are not peculiar to men. Women possess them too. The response of others, management, and, by extension, the organization to a superstar's gender will very likely differ. Gender discrimination is alive and well in most organizations.

Males who are superstars are more likely to be encouraged to shine because the stereotypes tell us that high levels of achievement are expected of men. This is not to say male colleagues and supervisors may not come to feel envious and threatened; they will. However, it will not be because the superstar is the wrong gender. The superstar may also respond to others who attack him by fighting back which is more consistent with men and often attributed to be part of achieving success in organizations. Female colleagues can be expected to permit the male superstar to strive for success possibly by admiring him and nurturing him. He may offer little or no threat to women who have learned men are expected to move ahead. In contrast, women who achieve superstar status have distinguished themselves from other women and most certainly from their male colleagues.[6] It may seem strange that other women may be adamantly opposed to one of their own distinguishing herself, but it must be appreciated that women are competitive among themselves. A female superstar may be welcomed at one level as vindicating the gender and possibly leading the way to other successes for other women in the organization. At another level these outstanding women will be the focus of envy and jealousy and may represent a threat to other women who may feel it is they who should have been recognized or who may feel that they are deficient by comparison.

A female superstar presents men with a more difficult situation regardless of whether she rises from within an organization or is hired in from without. In either case she threatens the masculine world of achievement and dominance. She may provoke their worst fears and encourage them to surface feelings relative to past encounters with female authority figures such as their mothers. And regrettably, the female superstar who has adopted some of the more aggressive attributes of her male colleagues will further increase the threat she represents. In sum the female superstar can be expected to have more problems with her fellow workers than a male superstar.

CONCLUSION

This chapter has provided the reader with a lot of material to consider. The list of superstar attributes is thought provoking. One may ask, is the list complete and representative and, more important, is it clear that executives, managers, and supervisors who consistently deliver outstanding performances must share many of these attributes? Do professionals who are expected to excel within their narrow range of expertise and workers who usually have more narrowly focused jobs share the attributes when they achieve excellence in their work? The assertion made here is Yes, they possess many of the attributes of the list, and even more important many can shine if provided with the opportunity to do so.

The chapter also pointed out that gender issues will influence how much an outstanding person is permitted to achieve by others. Regrettably it is likely that a large part of our work force, the women, are held back from achieving excellence by old but socially ingrained values and stereotypes.

The chapter also points the way toward creating a concrete and challenging agenda for developing important attitudes, knowledge, and skills for talented and intelligent members of our society and work force. What should people know to achieve excellence? This chapter provides some direction.

3

Organizational Trends Opposed to Achieving Individual Excellence

It somehow feels better to think of an organization achieving excellence rather than an individual. The organization is an abstraction. It is something we do not compare ourselves directly to. In contrast, when someone we know achieves excellence—makes the A or the 4.0 in college—we have a reaction. Our feelings may inform us we are less than completely sincere when we offer our congratulations. We, of course, wish it could have been us and rightly so. Most of us aspire to higher levels of achievement. The problem is, that while we *think* others should be encouraged to achieve excellence, when they do, it does not always *feel* good to us. They have achieved something we wish we had. We wish we had received their recognition no matter how much we try to think otherwise. We feel envious, left out, and outshined.

These are feelings all of us including superstars have experienced, and it is only natural to want to avoid them. The all too human response of avoiding pain can, however, have an accumulative effect in organizations. Trying to avoid feeling outshined can become institutionalized in many ways that inhibit the individual pursuit of excellence. This chapter looks at several aspects of organization life that block the pursuit of excellence. The focus is on the often unacknowledged and undiscussed aspects of work that include such things as fear of elite groups and fear of change.

Not fully appreciated at work is the fact that some organizational values and

dynamics arise from unacknowledged, undiscussable, and unconscious motivations aimed at assuring us that we feel good about ourselves by limiting the
need for change and doing away with the possibility that some people are more
equal than others. We also do not appreciate the significance of how these hidden
agendas are acted out in what is said and done at work. For example, many
things that sound fair and reasonable and influence decisions often subtly communicate that we are all equal and will be treated as such. After all, ''Aren't we
all in this together?'' Egalitarianism has, as its underlying appeal, the provision
of equality and the likely suppression of too much individual achievement.

This chapter looks at concrete examples of how managers and coworkers may
unconsciously conspire to oppose the individual pursuit of excellence and inadvertently perpetuate mediocrity. The chapter also provides some examples of
how unquestioned ''business as usual'' organizational dynamics also perpetuate
mediocrity and alienate those who could do better. We begin by looking at the
impact of unacknowledged fears of elite groups that limit the pursuit of individual excellence.

THE ELITIST REACTION

Organizations face tough problems every day. For a university it may be a
problem of how to achieve meaningful integration of administrative and research
computing. For a service organization it may be how to develop a service
orientation in its staff. For a manufacturing organization it may be a problem
of how to achieve quality and efficiency in making a product. For a public
institution, such as a city, it may be a problem of how to ensure that its administration is achieving the best results with our tax dollars.

One strategy for pursuing excellence is to locate within the organization or
community the very best talent to bring to bear on problem solving. And why
not? Wouldn't you prefer to have the best possible surgeon at your side during
an operation? It is equally logical that, if you want to try to achieve excellence
in solving a problem, you want the best people singled out to contribute to its
solution. The reality, however, is that, while this strategy seems logical, those
who must implement it often do not and, in fact, may unintentionally prevent
it from occurring. Identifying the very best and calling them together to form a
group, it may be thought, will be felt by others to smack of elitism. And, without
a doubt, most people in organizations do not like anything that smacks of elitism.

Elite groups, at least in Western civilization, are often felt to be bad. One
need think back no further than Nazi Germany and the Aryan race to find a
horrible example. The creation of an elite group is usually felt to be threatening
and bad. However, the courageous fliers of the Royal Air Force who served
during the air invasion of England were no doubt members of an elite group
which possibly single-handedly stemmed the tide of the invasion. These fliers
were not regarded as members of an evil elite; they achieved a great success.
Even so, it should go without saying that, were these fliers to have been singled

out for abundant special recognition and rewards, many others would have been offended. They were part, after all, of a much larger effort.

Elite groups present a problem. Those who could call them together are usually hesitant. They fear that they may open a Pandora's box or create an organizational Frankenstein. Even if the group produced a great feat, others might feel threatened or offended or might wish it had not happened. Avoiding elite groups is an organizational dynamic that gets played out in many ways. Before looking at some of these ways, it is important to restate that when fear exists of elite groups it often goes unacknowledged, and it is seldom open to discussion. As a result, fear is suppressed from awareness and becomes part of an unconscious individual and group dynamic where the underlying motivations for avoiding elite groups are unknown and, if pointed out, may be disposed of by denial or rationalization. We may now turn to some examples of this process.

Already mentioned above are some common problems typical organizations face. Let us begin with an example of a proposal made during a brainstorming meeting to convene a task group of the best talent available, regardless of organizational status, to figure out a strategy to integrate complex computer systems. The only criteria to be used will be that the individuals chosen must be the best available. Those present in the meeting agree it is a good idea. Following the meeting the group's leader makes telephone inquiries to single out employees who might make outstanding contributions to solving the problem. A list of names is developed. However, as the list takes shape, the leader gradually comes to fear calling the group together for the reasons mentioned above. These fears are operationalized by thinking, "There may be some individuals who are not liked by others." Other thoughts rapidly follow. Creating the elite group may be seen by others as exclusive and threatening. It could get out of hand. It could develop into something undesirable. It might create a platform for some individuals to press forward with some of their "pet" projects or points of view. It might be dominated by a few individuals. The group might be hard to control.

The list of cons can grow long rather quickly. In the end no action is taken and the next meeting of the group occurs. During the meeting the same individual who had suggested the creation of the elite task group questions why it has not been called together. "Hadn't it been agreed to?" The group leader responds with the all too familiar refrain, "It is still being worked on." Problems have been encountered in identifying the people. Problems are anticipated in negotiating the needed release time from the employees' respective departments. Finally, the idea has been temporarily held up to receive upper management's endorsement. The number of reasons for not taking action are limited only by imagination. Subsequent meetings yield similar outcomes. Getting the group together has become too complex and time consuming; ultimately, it is not assembled. Group members tacitly approve the no action outcome as they silently learn that continued questioning and advocacy makes the group leader uncomfortably defensive and angry.

A second example of avoidance is the administrative maneuver of assembling a group with some of the best people but watering it down with a few key individuals who are judged to be able to keep the group from getting out of hand. For example, the group leader may be appointed for being effective at controlling groups and getting an organizationally suitable outcome. Those who could have made an outstanding contribution find themselves labelled as zealous, dysfunctional, overly eager outliers who are singled out for special attention by the group's leader and shunned by some group members who are better "team" players.

For example, an engineer recently has been hired in from a competitor who has many new ideas. The ideas are listened to quietly; the engineer is gently questioned, and then, just as though the ideas had never been offered, the group moves on to consider the ideas of others. It is not as though the group will reconsider the ideas later; it is as though the ideas were never presented. They are soon forgotten. Days and weeks later the ideas may not be recalled by most of the members of the group.

In a second possible scenario, the engineer's ideas are aggressively challenged by some members who are prepared to argue about their veracity until "the cows come home." As a result other group members become uncomfortable with the tension and delays and may begin to feel that the engineer is too defensive—a reasonable feeling based on the behavior at hand. They may also feel that this newcomer does not understand their customary group processes and has begun to counterattack those who are merely offering him critical feedback. The hostile feelings of those doing the questioning are, in an unconscious process, attributed to the engineer who, it is understood, must have done something to make them feel angry. The final outcome may be that both the ideas and the engineer become too hot to handle. Continued discussion is unacceptable, and discussion at a later time, it is felt, will only recreate the bad feelings associated with the first meeting.

A third method of avoidance is, for example, a mayor's reaction to a city council that decides to assemble a blue ribbon panel of citizens from the community to review the city's operations for improvement. Despite the fact that the idea is made very clear, the mayor begins to handpick the names of cronies to serve on the prestigious committee without considering their qualifications. Selection of the best is not a factor; avoided is the likelihood that the group will have the expertise or the interest to point out the problems with the city's operations. As time passes, the list of names grows as everyone on the city council offers more names. The list becomes the unconscious focus of the process and displaces the original intent of assembling the group. The names of friends and relatives of friends are surfaced for participation. When the name of a qualified individual in finance is placed into nomination, the person is passed over, not because of a lack of qualifications but because no one knows the person. A politicized process such as this raises the question of how often leaders resort to selecting group members because they are friends or politically wise appointments to the exclusion of choosing those best able to perform.

A fourth elitist avoidance mechanism is to, rather than worry about finding the best talent, worry about fair representation. Fair representation may involve consideration of minorities, departmental or divisional representation, balances between different professions, and organizational status. In a large organization the size of the group that has to be assembled will usually become cumbersome. The inevitable conclusion may be that a group of the size needed will not get anything done and that it may be better to have the manager of the area where the problem exists try to work the problem out alone. Being fair, in this case, precludes assembling the best talent in favor of what seems like a more balanced approach.

In a fifth approach, upper management has already decided what the answer is but wishes to develop a group that can be steered into endorsing their point of view: "the rubber stamp." A group of outstanding employees is not likely to comprise the easiest individuals to herd into adopting the already decided upon solution. Without a doubt, unless they are carefully handled, they will question what is occurring. In the end the group may be assembled with a rigid and narrowly defined set of guidelines. Group members are then pressed to learn quickly that their real role is to reach for the rubber stamp and lend credibility to the proposal and perhaps to support it later.

In a final avoidance strategy, upper management feels threatened by the possibility of being outshined by the elite group. Top management may be concerned that they will be made to look bad. They may also fear that some of their pet projects, their strategies, and their worldview may be negatively impacted by the elite group's work. In order to protect themselves from these possible outcomes but let the group continue, they, at the minimum, make sure that any outstanding product of the group will be attributed to them. This is accomplished by making public pronouncements of their calling the group together. Naturally, if the group produces a major improvement, management is responsible for this achievement; they had the foresight to establish the group. However, if the group produces little, nothing more is heard. If the group produces something negative, the group leader and its members can be expected to be scapegoated. A process such as this is transparent; the hidden agenda is apparent.

In sum, an elite group can be felt to be threatening for a number of reasons, and these unacknowledged fears can be seen to motivate unconsciously those responsible for assembling the elite group to avoid doing so or to do so only after expending a lot of energy making sure it will be under control. Regardless of exactly how this dynamic is acted out, those with superior talents, skills, and insights do not get a chance to shine.

THE UNCONSCIOUS QUEST FOR MEDIOCRITY— MANAGEMENT MAGIC

We have all observed magic at work. What the magician conjures is real for those who observe it. There are instances where things disappear in organizations which have, for all practical purposes, ceased to exist. Examples are abundant but often go unnoticed. The magic works because unconsciously we wish it to undo, correct, or remove a distressing problem. In each of the examples below, the outcome is magically changed, and improvement is not necessary. Excellence is not needed, and those interested in achieving excellence are left holding a ticket stub to the magic show.

The Disappearing Critique

Take, for example, a group of organization members who are confronted with a distressingly long list of criticisms developed at considerable expense by a consultant. Many in the group including the leader may wish that the criticisms had not been made. Everyone may wish that things were different. It may suddenly come to the leader's mind that, despite this depressing news, the organization has some strong points overlooked by the consultant. "We can't be that bad." The group is then led in the development of a list of strong points to be juxtaposed with the list of criticisms. Helpful hint: A list of strong points of equal proportions to the criticisms aids in this feat. Once the list of strong points is developed, it is compared to the list of weak points. Suddenly, things are not as bad as they appeared when only the list of criticisms existed. The two lists become fused in the minds of the group's members. Similar to mixing colors of paint, the two lists disappear. Reality is altered. The list of criticisms is disposed of and it disappears from future agendas. As a result, payment of the consultant may be handled in wonderment. No one is quite sure what the consultant did, and certainly no effort is made to relocate the report.

Rabbit Tracks

Members of organizations have to solve problems. However, some problems are more difficult to deal with than others because of complexity, lack of information, people, or organization politics. Take, for example, the problem employee who is transferred to another department or is even promoted out. The employee makes tracks. The magical solution fulfills the wish for the problem employee to vanish into thin air. The manager does not have to deal with facing the guilt and fear of confronting the employee's poor performance.

Another example is a group of employees who, after seeming to have tracked down every conceivable solution to a problem, perpetuate the problem by intentionally making the wrong decision. They may have, for example, systematically avoided dealing with the problem's true origins, which may be located in a powerful other such as the CEO. Dealing with the real problem and its associated fears and anxieties is avoided by following the wrong but safe rabbit tracks and then believing it will work.

The Rabbit's Foot

Some managers and employees seem to lead a charmed life. Virtually no bad news or problems ever reach their desks. If something does go wrong, it disappears when the employee responsible for the gross oversight is sacrificed or when someone else is blamed. The rabbit (scapegoat) is slaughtered to restore good luck (the rabbit's foot) to the manager. The problem, it is understood, did not really exist for the manager or the group; it was always the fault of the targeted employee. The same can be said for making the problem disappear by ignoring figures, redefining the problem, presenting fabricated information, or reinterpreting the information or the situation. Everyone may wish to believe that there is a silver lining if only it can be found.

Pulling a Rabbit from a Hat

Sometimes others are encountered who are neither part of the solution nor part of the problem. These individuals do not wish to be discussed along with their possible contribution to the problem. Their responsibility seems magically to disappear. Careful scrutiny of these individuals may reveal that they hold a black top hat from which may be drawn all manner of undesirable outcomes. Who wants to be faced with a yelling or sobbing employee or a manager who is bullying or intimidating or who threatens punitive action? Who wants to deal with vigorous assertions that the problem lies elsewhere when it does not? In this case, contemplation of a rabbit being yanked from the hat may make others act as though the person is not part of the problem in order to avoid having to deal with him or her.

Envision, for the moment, a room filled with tense employees who must deal with a problem. The situation is distressing to everyone. The need for a solution to cut the tension is nearly absolute. Like a rabbit out of a hat, the group's leader, who perceives these needs, suddenly announces a major new program that, although it would normally have taken months to develop, is to be implemented upon leaving the room. The solution is greeted with both enthusiasm and skepticism; however, everyone leaves the room with a rabbit in hand. Everyone silently wished for a solution and they got one. Work is then expected to proceed despite the fact there is no basis for accomplishing the program.

Little more needs to be said. Everyone—every group and every organization—may develop magical outcomes. The power we have to alter reality in our minds is without limit. In psychological terms we defend ourselves from the anxiety a situation holds for us. We may deny, rationalize, pay attention only to what relieves the feelings of anxiety, attribute the cause of the situation to others, or simply not feel or think anything to avoid the distressing experience of anxiety. The message of the magic is that excellence need not be pursued. There are also less magical processes that occur at work that send the same message, which must also be appreciated.

ORGANIZATION TRENDS THAT CREATE AND PERPETUATE MEDIOCRITY

Other kinds of organizational influences limit the quest for excellence. There are any number of organizational attributes that can serve to limit individual achievement and perpetuate mediocrity.[1] Some of the more common organizational attributes are discussed below.

Little Steps

The little steps approach to management is an unconsciously conservative, risk-aversive style which is rationalized as meaningfully analytical. It is believed that little steps do not get you into too much trouble at any one time. People who could achieve more find that they are limited to moving at an unchallenging pace that misses opportunities. A by-product of taking little steps is having plenty of time to analyze everything, which leads to "analysis paralysis." The unconscious wish is that, with perfect knowledge, no one has to make decisions or take any risks; the choice will be obvious. The little steps approach also contains a hidden agenda in that it is a high control administrative strategy. Problems and opportunities are broken down into many parts for separate consideration. The many steps lead to the need for coordination by management. In the end, opportunities to be innovative are often precluded because of the complexity that has been created and because everyone is obliged to follow the work plan handed down by top management.

Words and Thinking

Words and thinking go together. Talking helps us to think through our ideas. Words are also a reflection of our feelings. When we feel anxious and defensive at work we may use words to minimize the accompanying feelings of anxiety. The following statements are examples of language used to allay anxiety and to perpetuate mediocrity.

1. You are the only one who has complained.
2. You can't have what you requested because no other department can afford it. It just wouldn't be fair to them to let you have it.
3. You can't have the resources requested because you are too good at defending your requests in relation to your colleagues.
4. Everyone is in the same boat (for example, underpaid). We can't let anyone get out of line.
5. I can't approve your request because my office should be doing what you recommend.
6. Rather than confront the employee over poor performance, just make the job so bad that the person will leave.

7. We are a great organization.

8. What are the minimum requirements for the work involved?

9. We plan to enhance the program in the future.

10. We have always done it this way. Why fix it if it isn't broken?

When you hear comments like these, watch out; allaying anxiety and perpetuating mediocrity are the hidden agendas. Hearing these kinds of statements may also make those wishing to do better feel angry, ''Who the hell cares anyway?''

Quick and Dirty

Quick and dirty are also code words for the unconscious imposition of mediocrity. What is meant is that we do not have (choose one or more of the following) the information, systems, expertise, money, time, or resources to do it right. Either the information and systems do not exist, or, if they do, they are too difficult to work with to get the needed information. There may also be an appalling lack of insight by some in top management as to what is really going on at operating levels. Some in top management may wish to believe anything will work when, often, it is the operating managers who make these quick and dirty solutions work, sometimes at considerable personal and organizational cost. Accepting this strategy means there is no need to improve the systems, processes, and plans that led to the problem in the first place. Also, the wish that no one is to be held accountable is also fulfilled.

Poor Leadership and Strategic Direction

Poor leadership and strategic direction can deskill even the best performers. What good does it do to have developed a major breakthrough in the manufacture of buggy whips? Dedicated, productive, innovative, and resourceful organization members may occasionally discover their best efforts have been for naught. Outstanding achievements may become inconsequential and even counterproductive. The employees may have, with eager anticipation of approval, presented management with a new development only to discover that a recent, heretofore uncommunicated management decision makes their achievement of no use. Employees are left holding an empty bag of expectations, which, an instant before, was filled with an outstanding achievement.

Leadership plays an important role in identifying and defining mission, goals, and problems for others to work on. If an organization's leaders are ineffective at this, its members may not know what to work on or may possibly even work on counterproductive projects. Leadership and vision are important ingredients for organizational success.

Organizational Politics

Organizational politics have a crippling impact on almost any endeavor. Many individuals, groups, factions, and coalitions may want a "piece of the action." Key organizational members may expend valuable energy and time advocating their point of view or their department's to the exclusion of considering the well-being of the organization as a whole. No one may be willing to give up power or prestige to improve organizational performance.

An organization is more than the sum of its parts. Chronic and occasionally explosive political infighting can bring even the largest and most powerful organization to its knees. One need look no further than the military for a good example. Infighting among the branches of the military service over participation, it was reported, contributed to the catastrophic failure of the Iran hostage rescue attempt. A second example of the pursuit of branch interests to the exclusion of the whole effort is seen in the fact that an officer who had to coordinate fighting during the invasion of Grenada had to make a long distance telephone call. The communication equipment the various services used was not compatible. Each branch pursued its own interests. Outstanding men were less than completely successful as a result of organizational politics.

Bureaucracy Without Rational Advantages

We have all encountered bureaucracies, and many of us are working for one. Bureaucracies are usually filled up with people who are expected to comply with policies and procedures developed to govern most if not all aspects of their work. Bureaucracy is noted for its slow responsiveness to change and the creation of "red tape" which slows down even the best of performers.

However, bureaucracy is not all bad. Bureaucratic policies and procedures make work and decision making more predictable and less subject to personal preferences of managers and employees.

Regrettably there are many organizations that have all the negative attributes of bureaucracy without managing to garner many of the advantages. Clients and employees often find bureaucracies unpredictable, and the members often are unable to make decisions, unable to make exceptions, and unable to come up with the same answer twice. A good example is a personnel department which, when called for advice about a progressive discipline problem or a complicated raise or promotion, generates as many responses as the number of people consulted. In effect all the policies and procedures are not "perfectly clear." Achieving excellence in a climate like this is unlikely.

Chronic Fire Fighting

Some organizations or divisions of organizations always seem to be responding to crises. Poor planning and leadership combined with inappropriate staffing and information systems can lead to a chronic process of discovering new problems which require immediate response. Opportunities for improvement are everywhere, but no one has a chance to respond to them because everyone is working first on one thing and then another. Brilliant solutions may be developed to fight the fires, but the overall battle for excellence is lost. However, top management will usually feel that their staff is doing well; after all, "They just managed to put the fire out last week."

Limited Access to Key People and Resources

Organizations are filled with people who can make insightful and even outstanding contributions if only they had access to a key person or could secure enough resources to invest in a risk-taking innovation. Superstars go unheard if their immediate superior is intimidated by them or does not like them. It is, of course, natural for superstars to find problems with the status quo which others, however, often experience as personal criticism. Superiors may, for example, feel defensive when an outstanding employee offers an insight that directly or indirectly implies criticism of an earlier decision. Inevitably, the superior acts to limit the damage inflicted by the superstar by blocking access to others who might also be critical of the superior.

Another way of limiting the superstar is sidetracking. A superstar may be assigned to a new department or project that precludes making a contribution on a current project. If outstanding employees are moved around enough, their overall impact on people's egos and the status quo will be limited and so will the pursuit of excellence.

Do It by the Numbers

Do it by the numbers relies on using budgeting and financial information as the principal and perhaps only basis for running an organization. After all, it is easy to add up numbers with computers. They look concrete. They can be readily graphed. They can be analyzed ad infinitum. They can be used to show others what you want to show them. They also consume valuable time of operating managers who must prepare them, defend them, make out requests to increase them, and explain variances in them. In many organizations budgets and financial reports are the unacknowledged purpose of the organization. The machines and "green shaders" must be fed their numbers. There may develop a tyranny of financial management which, in the end, is hopelessly disconnected from making things run.

For example, a typical response to hard times is to, of course, cut the budget. The word is passed down through many layers to operating managers who must make the 12.5 percent reduction. And if they are really unlucky, the reduction is retroactive to some prior period. Of course, there may be some effort to assess the impact of the across-the-board cuts and not all may be made. The organization is then assumed to be able to produce as much with less; it is leaner and meaner. The fat has been cut. But is this necessarily so? Has the fat been cut? More important, why did the fat exist in the first place? Why wasn't this known to the number crunchers?

The financial approach to managing operations overlooks one key thing— reality. Budgets are an abstraction. You can't look at a budget or a bottom line and tell how well a division or a department is run. You can't tell what it is really like to make a widget. The financial approach essentially eliminates the need to know how to be more effective. Those who might know are not asked. They are simply expected to turn in the numbers.

CONCLUSION

There are many commonly accepted and hard to change trends in organizations which have as their implicit outcomes limiting anxiety and perpetuating mediocrity. This chapter discussed trends against achieving individual and organizational excellence that are encountered in organizations. It is also important to appreciate that, if changing these trends were easy, everybody would do it. Change creates anxiety when the previously well-understood ways to limit anxiety are removed. Resistance to change can range from ignorance and no perceived need to change to "Don't fix it if it is not broken" and lack of better performance (past or future) having no apparent negative effect on the organization's competitive position. Other resistances to change block considering it: There is too little time, resources, or people; it is too difficult, complex, or interdependent; and everyone agrees to make changes, but no one takes any action. These common responses are disheartening to anyone who is striving for excellence.

Leading and implementing change are the topics of many books and are not to be dealt with here. It will suffice to say that changing these kinds of trends can be dangerous, difficult, and unrewarding to anyone striving for excellence.

4

Feelings in the Workplace: The Superstar Versus Others

An organization with one or more superstars should count itself fortunate. Management should be pleased to provide superstars with challenges, opportunities to succeed, and rewards consistent with their performance. Peers and colleagues should feel that they benefit by learning from the superstars and from their productivity. Superstars, like Janet Evening, can turn events around. They can make things happen. They can lead the way to organizational excellence.

The happy and productive incorporation of superstars into organizations is, however, all too often not accomplished. Their energies and abilities are often wasted. Managers and peers who feel threatened by and envious of the attention superstars receive may advocate greater fairness and equality. Others who feel superstars look down on them and feel less than capable by comparison may wish the superstars were not around. In sum, superstars should be excited about producing outstanding work but may not be permitted to as a result of the negative feelings of others.

The fact that others have negative feelings for those who achieve excellence prompts the asking of two questions. What kinds of feelings do superstars provoke in others? How do superstars feel about themselves and the envious, fearful, and punitive reactions of others when they occur? These are questions that must be dealt with to maximize the advantages of having superstars in the ranks.

Organizations are full of conflicting experiences. People who attract attention to themselves will be confronted with more conflict than others. Superstars are likely to become the subject of intense scrutiny by those who fear and envy them, those who admire them, those who depend on them, and those who find them challenging to compete with and to emulate.

This chapter explores the feelings others develop when confronted with the superior performance of a superstar and how their reactions affect relationships with these outstanding performers. The chapter also begins to explore the feelings superstars experience toward others especially when others reject them and limit their efforts to achieve excellence. Understanding these negative feelings is essential for understanding the resulting psychological, defensive organizational dynamics that are created.

NEGATIVE FEELINGS IN THE WORKPLACE

Everyone who works is confronted with organizational events, interpersonal relationships, and superior-subordinate authority relations which can result in good and bad feelings. Organizations and work life are by no means all bad. Membership in an organization, work, and relationships at work can be exciting and personally rewarding. This book, however, examines the darker side of emotional life at work and does so, hopefully, in a compelling manner that deserves to be considered an important aspect of understanding the workplace.

Work life is not always fulfilling, exciting, rewarding, and self-actualizing. Organization life can provoke negative feelings about oneself, one's work, others, superiors, subordinates, departments, and the organization as a whole. Ten feelings or emotions encountered at work can create a gloomy and pessimistic worldview of organizational life: feeling attacked, fear, anger, hate, rivalry, love, envy, shame, guilt, and admiration.

However, before continuing, it is important for balance to point out that feelings of being attacked, fear, hate, and anger can be adaptive to organizational life and may even be promoted.[1] All of these feelings are found, for example, in the military during wartime or in organizations that are under external attack where the attackers (corporate raiders, the media, the government, or competitors) are feared and hated. Anger may fuel self-defensive actions and counterattacks. However, it is equally important to appreciate that, when these same adaptive responses are turned inward against others in the organization and between elements of the organization, the results are destructive and limiting.

We may now return to the examination of how these ten feelings arise, how they are experienced, how they are handled psychologically, and how they fuel behavior that will have predictable social reactions which, if anticipated, may inhibit acting on the feelings and perhaps change them to actions that are more interpersonally and organizationally acceptable.

Feelings may develop for many reasons. One not explicitly stated here is the circumstance in which one or more superstars are encountered. Superstars, by responding to situations, events, and others can both unintentionally and unconsciously provoke the feelings considered in this chapter. The cosmology that begins in Chapter 6 explores how and why superstars may unconsciously act to develop interpersonally self-destructive and personally self-defeating behavior. Accordingly these tendencies will be briefly mentioned in favor of focusing on the aspects of superstar behavior that may also inadvertently and unintentionally provoke the feelings.

In sum, the perspective of this chapter examines how others respond to those who excel at work. It starts from the position that star performers can become the innocent victims of others who come to malign and limit them as a means of coping with their own anxieties. And, despite the best efforts of the star performers to head off the problems, they can occur as they did to Janet Evening.

Feeling Attacked

Superstars can be informed, critical, and eager participants in any discussion, group, or meeting. We have all had the unexpected and unpleasant experience of having what we thought was a pretty good idea quickly and insightfully belabored by someone we knew to be a superstar. The superstar may have plunged ahead asking questions, offering insights, making criticisms, exploring implications and possibilities, rapidly manipulating and moving through the idea leaving the originator of the idea and others feeling surprised, anxious, and defensive. The superstar's actions may, even when most tactful, leave the originator of the idea feeling set upon, attacked, exposed, and anxious to defend the idea. What is important to appreciate in this interaction is that the superstar bears no ill will and is responding to a cue—an opportunity to explore a new idea. However, some participants may feel that the superstar is using the opportunity to show off and to boost his or her ego.

The feelings and reactions others may experience by the threatening provocation provided by a superstar are explored to a greater extent below. This detailed analysis of feelings in the workplace begins with a list of synonyms for the word ''Attacked'' to semantically anchor the sense of being attacked. An example of a typical workplace provocation is then provided that includes not only the above actions of a superstar but also the actions of others who, like the superstar, might innocently ask questions or, unlike the superstar, might not so innocently ask questions and make criticisms. Others might, in fact, be trying to personally attack and humiliate the originator of the idea to make themselves feel powerful, superior, and better about themselves—motivations that might be attributed to the superstar.

Within the example of the provocation there is one additional implicit but important element that must be noted. To the extent that the originator of the idea needs approval to feel good and finds that it is not forthcoming, the individual may feel crushed, defeated, and rejected. To the extent that compulsive needs for approval exist, the actions of others become powerful and forbidding. The slightest criticism may signal loss of approval and momentary feelings of anxiety, panic, falling apart, and annihilation. Even if this is not the case, others may well react by unconsciously attributing these feelings to the person and then act to defend or heal the person even though it is inappropriate. For example, the most aggressive and self-seeking personal attack may fail to affect an individual whose self-esteem is such that it permits him or her to maintain his or her feelings of assurance and security, which further frustrates the attacker.

The analysis continues by providing a list of feelings that may arise from the experience of being attacked. Feeling hurt, confused, and defensive and wanting to fight back are natural. It would be unexpected if they did not exist. Typical psychological responses to these feelings are then provided. Psychology permits us to understand ourselves as products of our pasts. How we act under stress is, in large part, determined by how we learned to respond in the past—how we learned to act, think, and feel so that we could restore our feelings of safety and reduce our anxiety.

Throughout life we have all learned to use psychological coping strategies to help us deal with stressful experiences. These strategies, which are defined in the appendix, play an important part in our daily lives and may go unnoticed by ourselves and unobserved by others; we may not acknowledge them even if they are pointed out. In fact, should someone point out a coping strategy, the anxiety created would probably provoke additional psychologically defensive strategies. For example, an individual, when confronted by another who points out an obvious rationalization, may first deny it. That failing, the rationalization may be undone by apologizing for it while perhaps projecting angry feelings about being questioned onto the questioner who is then felt to be perpetrating an angry attack. If the situation continues, the subject may regress to feeling rage but acting on this rage is simultaneously felt to be dangerous, and it may be displaced by throwing or kicking something or knocking a hole in a wall.

The analysis concludes with descriptions of likely reactions to feeling attacked, which, if acted out, will result in predictable social perceptions, reactions, and associated repercussions which, if anticipated, may inhibit action. The threat of social disapproval constitutes a sanction which serves to maintain socialization.

Synonyms for *attacked* include: set upon, aggressed, invaded, assailed, assaulted, and violated.

Provocation. One's decision, idea, or statement is rigorously questioned by a superstar. However, it does not seem that the superstar is being objective, fair, or sensitive. The superstar's questioning, it becomes clear, is leading to an eventual humiliation. However, there is no stopping the process.

Feelings Generated. One may feel defensive, fearful, angry, hateful, helpless, confused, and hurt.

Psychological Responses. Anger and fear fuelled by past defeats and narcissistic injuries must be suppressed. It is unacceptable and unprofessional to become overtly aggressive and counterattack the superstar. At a less conscious level it is understood that a response might result in the uncontrollable annihilation of the superstar, a response best left to the fantasy of instant replays.

Reactions and Public Perceptions. There are a number of familiar reactions to this situation that may not always be positively received by others. For example, fighting back for purposes of self-vindication may be thought to be juvenile, emotional, and unproductive even though some may gain vicarious pleasure from seeing the superstar cut down to size. Similarly, withdrawal and retreat from the situation may be perceived as being the reaction of a sore loser who may carry a grudge and has to be watched. Another reaction might be no response at all which may be seen to be a fearful response that includes tacit admission of failure and weakness. Last, the evasion of, disowning of, and distancing from the issue or problem combined with scapegoating someone else may be seen to be an astute diplomatic avoidance and flight from ownership of the problem.

In each of these cases, common workplace responses result in foreseeable double binds where social perceptions are unacceptable and, therefore, inhibit taking action. These double binds underscore the importance of being able to deal with superstars in intentional nondefensive ways to avoid social disapproval.

Fear

The presence of others who are felt to be more powerful and more knowledgeable and who are predictably critical consumers of ideas can lead to pervasive apprehensions. Fear of being attacked and publicly humiliated are very real; these fears are, after all, the basis for stage fright and writer's block. We fear that our product or performance will be found to be deficient, and we will be cast in a negative light. Comparing ourselves to superstars often lowers our self-esteem and makes speaking up anxiety provoking. These fears can become immobilizing, and new ideas may be lost in an intrapsychic process that is unobserved by others. The effects of fear on people at work are further illuminated by the following analysis.

Synonyms for *fear* include: apprehension, alarm, fright, dread, dismay, and awe.

Provocation. One feels, by comparison to a superstar, that one's ideas and thinking are naive and deficient. Apprehension arises about speaking up to offer one's ideas. Not acting, it is felt, is safer as the threat of being embarrassed by questioning and criticism is avoided.

Feelings Generated. One may feel deficient, self-hateful, defeated, insecure, panicky, intimidated, and relieved by not having acted.

Psychological Responses. Low self-esteem and fear of abandonment, rejection, and punishing criticism lead to self-minimization to avoid feeling powerful, effective, and, by extension, willing to speak up. Denial and rationalization of this self-defeating behavior are necessary to avoid painful knowledge of the self-victimization. Projection onto others of anger held toward and fear of the superstar defends against feelings of vulnerability, while making others seem more helpless than this individual.

Reactions and Public Perceptions. Flight, avoidance, and not speaking up may make this individual appear to be fearful, panicky, nervous, and unthinking. Behind-the-scenes discussion to get ideas heard may appear to be politicking and behind-the-back maneuvering that offers this frightened person safety from public scrutiny. Presenting one's idea, just to get it over, will be understood to be an action filled with fear that results in a hurried and nervous presentation accompanied by disclaimers and a rapid retreat from discussion. Getting someone else to present your ideas, if known, may appear to be a presumptuous manipulative maneuver that is risk aversive. Once again, being able to deal directly with the threat is critical to avoiding these defensive self-defeating outcomes.

Anger

When an idea is subjected to insightful questioning by a superstar, it is natural to become anxious. After all, we may feel any problems should have been foreseen. One result of a critical examination of an idea is for the originator to become angry with others, the process, and himself or herself.[2] All three of these outcomes are likely to be experienced together. Anger may develop against the superstar who develops an uncomfortable line of questioning. Anger may be directed toward the group leader for permitting it to happen. Anger may be felt for others for not speaking up or acting to limit the criticism. Anger may be felt for oneself for having so stupidly presented the imperfect idea in the first place. The tripartite aspect of anger in this example illustrates that more feelings of anger may exist than can be readily understood or appreciated by the individual or others. Not locating a constructive way to act on the anger may result in the one safe avenue of pursuit being taken, turning the anger against oneself.

Synonyms for *anger* include: rage, infuriated, incensed, embittered, inflamed, furious, and hostile.

Provocation. One's decisions, ideas, and statements are regularly and systematically questioned (attacked) by one or more superstars for what is felt to be less than objective reasons. This insidious and unrelenting process is feared and detested. Deeply felt animosity fuels defensive and embittered responses which may lead to further discrediting that is infuriating.

Feelings Generated. One may feel defensive, hateful, vindictive, hurt, depressed, and feel like fighting back or fleeing.

Psychological Responses. Children learn that being angry is not good. Not acting on one's anger, it is understood, avoids self-defeating behavior in the form of loss of approval and affection and avoidance of counterattacks and punishment. However, the object of the angry feelings may, as a result, become the subject of obsessive thinking and fantasizing about getting even. Added to this may be splitting and projection that create an all-bad threatening object that merits destruction. (See also "Attack.")

Reactions and Public Perceptions. Acting out and attacking back may appear to be juvenile, brutal, and dangerous behavior that is vindictive and excessively defensive. Turning the anger inward may result in moodiness, irritability, depression, and apathy. Displacement of the anger onto a safe object will give others the appearance of being unpredictable, as someone or something not associated with the problem is attacked.

Accepting or ignoring the objectionable behavior may give the appearance of being resigned to the situation and lacking the courage to resist. Selection of a safe, acceptable, and politically correct response may give the appearance of being disciplined but also contribute to dysfunctional organizational gamesmanship.

Hate

Hate and anger in life are often parallel emotions. We can feel both hatred for and anger toward others and ourselves. We can hate what is happening. We can hate those who contribute to a humiliation. We can easily come to hate those who frequently best us and receive the rewards. Hating others is particularly counterproductive at work, and, if not worked through, it must be vigorously suppressed. Hate, like anger, is multidimensional and can be felt toward others, the group dynamic, and ourselves for having exposed ourselves to personal attack and humiliation. It is also important to appreciate that hatred is often fuelled by injustices encountered throughout life.

Synonyms for *hate* include: loathing, detest, dislike.

Provocation. As the subject of what seems like personal attacks by a superstar and colleagues, one feels disliked and held in contempt. Others in the work group also report that, at times, they see their actions as excessive, which further encourages the feeling of being victimized. However, they do not do anything to stop what is going on and, if confronted, may assert that the criticisms—for the most part—are correct. Public criticism and behind-the-scenes back-stabbing become the norm as efforts to resist these actions fail.

Feelings Generated. One may feel angry, enraged, fearful, attacked, victimized, rejected, humiliated, helpless, and hurt.

Psychological Responses. The hatred held for others may be generalized to include all those in the group who tacitly support what is happening. Paranoid feelings of persecutory anxiety tap into similar punishing and detested experiences from childhood. The hate, however, must not be acted on directly and suppression or its acting out through passive aggression may help to cope with it. Distressing feelings of hate may also be projected onto others who are, in turn, experienced at being hateful. The hate turned inward creates self-loathing, adds to low self-esteem and depression, and it may be unconsciously felt that the attacks and humiliations are deserved.

Reactions and Public Perceptions. Asserting that others are being unfair and vindictive may give the appearance of being overly suspicious and organizationally naive. Defensiveness relative to others who have hurt one's feelings may appear to be an overreaction and includes personalization which shows a lack of insight into interpersonal and organizational dynamics. Avoiding hated other(s) may give the impression that one's feelings are too easily hurt and that there is no willingness to defend one's self. Angry counter-attacks that include harsh, personal, and condemning statements may be treated as ineffective and inappropriate self defense. Acceptance of the provocation, combined with withdrawal, may appear to be a weak response that includes contempt for others and one's self.

Rivalry

Feelings of being competitive and beating or defeating others is commonly associated with success. The best competitor wins the gold. However, competing against others on your own team can be counterproductive. Superstars are inviting targets for the rivalrous intentions of others. Depending upon how these competitive urges are acted out, they can be good or bad. Superstars set a high standard. To the extent that their performance represents a challenge, their presence promotes achievement. However, to the extent that others are angry and embittered by the superstar, the competition, although still producing a benefit, is undermining and potentially explosive. Working in a group that includes members who are out to get someone can be unrewarding, filled with tension, and threatening.

Synonyms for *rivalry* include: competing, antagonism, opponent, and match.

Provocation. Members of a group are constantly looking for ways to improve upon ideas. The focus becomes one of trying to generate the best ideas as evidenced by their drawing the least criticism. For some the need to generate the most grandiose idea is apparent and their efforts gradually shift toward ideas that are more risky. Others who are more reflective and analytical use their skills to receive attention by introducing so many factors for assessment that it makes it difficult for others to readily handle the instant complexity.

Feelings Generated. One may feel alert, attentive, excited, overwhelmed, and threatened by criticism and others getting ahead.

Psychological Responses. Competitive feelings arise as many seize the moment to elaborate the best idea. Similar experiences as a child who had to compete for parental attention may well up to influence thoughts, feelings, and actions that further fuel the wish to receive group and top management attention. Participation in this stressful group dynamic stimulates interpersonal rivalry that may lead the group from the task. Feelings of being threatened, angry, disgusted, and left out may lead some to withdraw and remain silent.

Reactions and Public Perceptions. Working ever harder to keep up may appear to be a juvenile male response to competition. Taking personal offense at the competitive and rivalrous actions of others may create the appearance of being a sore loser who has had his or her pride hurt. Trying to outshine others for the attention of the group, its leader, or top management will appear to be self-serving careerism that contributes to dissention. Withdrawal combined with thinly veiled contempt for competitive colleagues may be felt to be judgmental and inconsistent with being a good team player.

Love

Love is an emotion filled with many meanings.[3] Love is an important part of life which has both positive and negative meanings. Negative or neurotic love may be sought from others to fill up the perception of oneself as being empty, worthless, and undesirable. Love becomes a need and a demand which lead to selfless devotion in which the object of the love is felt to be faultless and able to provide perfect care for the dependent, devoted lover. Love, in this case, arises from the compulsive pursuit of affiliation, approval, and affection, and leads to impoverishment of all concerned.

Because of their skills and personal attributes, superstars are good subjects for the unselfish and unquestioning devotion of some individuals. Bonding of this nature is seductive to the recipient who is made to feel to be the center of the other person's universe. This outcome, however, occurs at a cost of having to take care of the bonded other(s). The partners in this dance become interlocked in a system of mutually reinforcing and limiting thinking, feeling, and action. The superstar learns the behaviors required to keep the devoted and dependent others happy. After all, it becomes the superstar's responsibility to take care of them. The loving and devoted others have their expectations of being taken care of by an omniscient other reinforced and their wish for dependency fulfilled. In return they maintain what can become a morbid dependency on the subject of their affections. Breaking or frustrating the development of this self-sealing dance is fraught with difficulty and pain. The superstar will be seen to be an uncaring and rejecting person. The dependent other(s) will be seen to be hurt and rejected. Everyone can become a loser if this process is not dealt with firmly and sensitively.

Synonyms for *love* include: affection, attachment, devotion, kindness, support, fondness, and infatuation.

Provocation. Outstanding others who are superstars, leaders, thinkers, and doers are frequently the focal points for attention. Colleagues may be enamored with them, act nervously and humbled in their presence, and become attached, devoted, and dependent upon them. These individuals become special people in the minds and hearts of organization members and are looked to for direction, care taking, and kindness. As a result, many may feel left out of receiving these feelings while being expected to give them to the special people.

Feelings Generated. One may feel relieved, attached, attentive, idolizing or adoring, proud, safe, secure, taken care of, awed as well as unloved, envious, and jealous.

Psychological Responses. These individuals become idolized as organization members project good parts onto them making them bigger than life. Idolization may lead to blind followership where personal responsibilities are shed in favor of these now specially endowed others taking care of everyone and everything. These special individuals may also be a threat to one's self-esteem in that their approval may not always be forthcoming, may be manipulated, and may have to be competed for. An unacknowledged wish to share in their fame and become the focus of attention may also exist.

Reactions and Public Perceptions. A high degree of support accompanied by a lack of criticism may appear to be slavish devotion and reckless abandonment of personal responsibility that contributes to the development of an exciting personality cult. Protection of these special individuals from bearing responsibility for problems may give the appearance of unhealthy group solidarity that insulates the idolized leader or superstar from reality. The constant attention given to these special people may create the appearance that the group is preoccupied with receiving attention, with too little attention directed to the effects of ill-conceived decisions and actions. Rivalry for attention within the group may create the appearance of destructive open competition for attention and favors.

Envy

Superstars are good candidates for envy. Their many desirable attributes, their success, their rewards, and their outstanding performances all get attention and merit the admiration of others. Others may wish they could think as quickly, that they possessed as much knowledge or education, or that they received as much attention and were as successful. Envious feelings fuel desires to improve oneself, which is good. However, those who do not wish to make the effort of self-improvement may resort to degrading and limiting the superstar to improve comparative appearances. Rather than accept the superstar or improve oneself, the resort is to minimize or eliminate the source of the unfavorable comparison. As a result, the superstar becomes the focal point of criticism, and management may be scapegoated for fostering special treatment for their star performers and the appearance of elitism.

Synonyms for *envy* include: jealousy, covetousness, invidiousness, and begrudgment.

Provocation. One or more individuals become the focus of a great deal of attention, praise, and rewards. One's contributions and those of others seem to go unnoticed in favor of one or a few individuals and their accomplishments being acknowledged.

Feelings Generated. One may feel left out, discriminated against, ignored, unappreciated, underpaid, unrecognized, hurt, rejected, abandoned, angry, and down on one's self.

Psychological Responses. Feelings from the past of being left out and ignored are rekindled along with the associated anger that was felt when these injuries and injustices occurred. Fantasies may develop where the subject of the envious feeling is replaced, deposed, or conspicuously defeated. Vindictive triumph, it is felt, will be accompanied by sudden recognition for one's abilities and work. Paradoxically, feelings of having been hurt or rejected may lead to irritability and depression that lower performance and the likelihood of meriting the admiration of others.

Reactions and Public Perceptions. Efforts to take advantage of the focal person's notoriety for self gain may appear to be small minded and indicate limited thinking and self-seeking purpose. Rivalrous displays of interpersonal competitiveness accompanied by vindictiveness may give the appearance of being an envious sore loser who is jealous and filled with hate. Sulking withdrawal accompanied by indignation and pronouncements of unfairness may create the appearance that if one can not succeed at getting attention then it is appropriate to give up.

Shame

Feeling ashamed and embarrassed about a real or imagined humiliation can occur at work. An encounter with a superstar can yield an embarrassing outcome which, if not properly handled, can result in feelings of being humiliated both by the superstar and by one's own incompetence. The feelings of embarrassment and shame may be short-lived if the incident is not too attention getting. They may, however, be long-lived if the embarrassment is a major one or if it involves a personal aspect of one's life, unknown to others but of profound personal importance. Avoiding feeling ashamed can become a major organizational influence motivating work if shame is frequently imparted by management.[4] No one wants to feel ashamed. No one wants to be shamed in the same way that may have occurred all too frequently in childhood. However, hierarchical organizations with many layers of authority relations create a setting where being shamed by powerful and influential others such as superstars is likely.

Synonyms for *shame* include: disgrace, dishonor, embarrassment, and unworthiness.

Provocation. One's work and ideas are shown, unexpectedly in the presence of others, to be deficient beyond any reasonable doubt. Similar feelings of embarrassment and humiliation are felt as others hold the poor performance up for public scrutiny and condemnation.

Feelings Generated. One may feel embarrassed, angry and punitive toward one's self and others, frightened and like wanting to run away, helpless, inferior, powerless, hurt, and panicky.

Psychological Responses. Strong wishes arise to undo the damage or to somehow repair it. The psychological defenses rationalization and denial may be pressed into service to help deaden the pain of the humiliation. Feelings of being competitive and vindictive, and fantasies of getting even with those who participated in the public humiliation, arise. Wishes to withdraw from the painful situation may also coexist with feelings of fighting back. One may make the resolution to never have anything like this happen again.

Reactions and Public Perceptions. Courageous resolve to bear the burden may make one appear to be overeager to be martyred to save face by courageously bearing the shame without breaking. Angry and contemptuous responses may appear to be unwise, further demonstrating that the humiliation was merited and that more punishment may be in order. Assertions that the shame is merited may give the appearance of being too eager to acknowledge being no good, thereby justifying the shaming process. Flight from the situation and those who participated in the shaming may be interpreted as a retreat to safety by a bad loser who is unwilling to take it.

Guilt

Guilt may be imposed by others, or perhaps just as often it may be self-imposed. Others make us feel guilty for actions that we may also be ashamed of. Guilt is also often used to manipulate others into action. Equally likely we may have not met our own standards and performance expectations. We may have made the wrong decision or not have possessed the courage to take an action thought to be necessary. Self-imposed guilt may not always be apparent to others, and it may exist out of consciousness. Low self-esteem can become a major contributor to how much guilt is experienced. If feelings of worthlessness abound, feeling guilty for failures is likely to be an outcome.

Guilt feelings can lead to obsessive or ritualistic efforts to make reparation for past failures. Many personal sacrifices may be made to make up for the problem while, at the same time, punishing oneself for failure. Superstars may be especially effective at spotting the failures and shortcomings that make us feel guilty, and they can become feared for the threat they offer in provoking feelings of guilt.

Synonyms for *guilt* include: feeling responsible, culpable, wrong, remorse, and blame.

Provocation. One unexpectedly learns that others have been let down as a result of failing to do a job as expected. As a result, others and the organization have suffered. Losses have occurred and it is made clear that fault lies with the poor job that was done.

Feelings Generated. One may feel depressed, self-hate, like a failure, accused, convicted, humiliated, caught, infantilized, punished, rejected, abandoned, and singled out as a scapegoat.

Psychological Responses. Feelings of shame, fear, and anger associated with being judged and found guilty by others who may not, in all instances, be respected or who have escaped being held accountable for the problem will arise. The setback, it may be felt, must be borne bravely. Silent wishes to undo what happened, transform what happened into something less negative, and deny that it occurred may make the guilt less painful. Fear of abandonment and anger associated with rejection in early life may, however, also well up to make the moment more painful and difficult to manage. Guilt may also arise over feelings of getting even and lead to further controlled thinking and feeling.

Reactions and Public Perceptions. Public humiliation and punishment may be bravely lived with, making it appear that remorse and acceptance of the personal failure must be tolerated to make symbolic amends. Flight, painful humiliation, and feelings of failure may result in withdrawal from others and the organization which others may interpret as abandonment and a lack of personal strength to withstand the defeat. An outpouring of effort directed at repairing the problem or making amends by producing something else of value may seem to be an unwillingness to accept the failure by magically counter-balancing the failure with a success. Scapegoating and angry offensive counterattacks may be considered to be self-centered survival-oriented responses that try to shift the blame to save face. Assertions of being scapegoated and blamed may also make the individual appear to be a sore loser who believes people are out to get him or her.

Admiration

Admiration like love has many positive aspects. However, if it is carried too far, it can become a negative influence. Falling short of the overpowering bond that arises from total devotion, excessive admiration can lead to uncritical ac-ceptance of the admired other. The superstar's qualities encourage admiration. However, if colleagues become too accepting and too dependent upon the su-perstar for work and approval, the work of others may come to have, as a hidden agenda, not producing one's best work or only producing work that is believed will be approved.

Synonyms for *admiration* include: wonderful, excellent, pleasing, approved of, high positive regard, marvel, and esteem.

Provocation. One or more others possess personal attributes and produce work that most people, including oneself, hold in high regard. Most interactions with these people are seen as rewarding. Everyone thinks highly of them and sees them as outstanding role models for all to emulate. At the same time others may wish to receive admiration.

Feelings Generated. One may feel pleased, open, friendly, warm, secure, trusting, positive, elated, and possibly envious and jealous.

Psychological Responses. Everyone projects good attributes onto these individuals, which makes them idolized. Everyone may come to fear loss of their approval and expend considerable energy to ensure positive relations with these superior others. Feelings of elation about these marvelous people may unintentionally create a self-fulfilling prophecy where rising expectations can not be met, thereby leading to their failure and rejection (not unlike disappointing parental figures who, it was found, had many failings).

Reactions and Public Perceptions. Adoration and willingness to blindly follow may create the appearance of uncritical followership, loss of insight, and excessive dependence. Competition for access and approval may lead an observer to conclude the real agenda is to keep others away so that attention and approval are guaranteed. Similarly, noticeable fear of loss of approval, affiliation, and affection may appear to be the result of too much dependency and low self-esteem.

These ten feelings are some of the most common feelings experienced at work. The analyses have provided the reader with many perspectives and much to reflect on. We all experience these feelings from time to time. No one is immune and everyone can gain from a better appreciation of how they impact work. An equally compelling aspect to this discussion is how the negative feelings affect those at whom they are focused.

THE EFFECT OF NEGATIVE FEELINGS AT WORK: SUPERSTARS ARE PEOPLE TOO

The feelings listed above and their negative outcomes, when directed toward a superstar, can have an effect on this attentive and sensitive individual. They may fuel efforts to malign, limit, control, and even get rid of the superstar. Superstars can be expected to respond with feelings of their own—the same ten feelings discussed in the previous section.

Superstars who have a chance to work in a receptive, nurturing setting will be able to shine. Their special talents will be openly acknowledged. Their specialized needs, if any, will be supported by their organization, supervisor, staff, colleagues, and friends at work. Their achievements will be genuinely celebrated, and their rewards will be regarded as fair and reasonable. And, although competitive and envious feelings may arise, they will not become a dominant theme of interactions with the superstar. Others will enjoy working with the superstar and the superstar with them. Regrettably, an outcome such as this does not always arise when a superstar shines. Before discussing reactions superstars may have to the ten feelings, discussed in the previous section, that are directed at them, a few words must be added about how superstars view others under normal conditions at work.

A superstar who enjoys work and finds little that needs to be defended against psychologically will find much of interest in work and others as well as encounter the same frustrations and difficulties we all face at work. The superstar may find it difficult to accept emotionality in others that stifles thinking and rational processes. The superstar may become angry and frustrated over going unheard or being blocked by routine bureaucratic impediments. And, at the extreme, it may be known that the superstar does not suffer fools gladly. People who are conservative, have limited insights, think or reason slowly, introduce off task material in meetings, and generally slow up change may be especially difficult and unrewarding to work with. This is not to say that many others may not have the same feelings as the superstar; however, they may be more apparent in the superstar. Others who are the focus of the superstar's frustration may often, and rightly so, feel rejected and set upon by the superstar who sees them as impediments and experience many of the ten feelings discussed. Superstars may then be understood to key off a process like this in an all too human way that, while not exactly unwitting or unintentional, is without any compelling need to feel good about oneself by being better than others. Given this proviso, we can now return to the more malevolent side of the workplace.

Superstars who become the focus of many of these ten negative feelings can be expected to respond with similar feelings. The provocations are similar. The superstar's ideas and proposals may be subjected to endless efforts to find fault with them. Efforts by the superstar to move ahead may be inhibited by many roadblocks. The superstar may be rejected by some and hated and feared by others. The superstar will experience many of the ten feelings discussed earlier and use some of the psychological defenses defined in the appendix. Hate for others may be sublimated into greater productivity. Anger over disappointing interactions with others may be emotionally insulated against by isolation and intellectualization. Painful feelings of being maligned and limited may be denied. The rejecting and limiting actions of others may be rationalized. Fear of failing may be projected onto others who may then be understood as making their attacks out of desperation. The superstar may fantasize vindictive triumph and better times ahead.

All of these psychologically defensive actions lead to dysfunctions at work which are the subject of the cosmology starting with Chapter 6. It suffices here to mention that highly creative and productive people can be expected to be feared and rejected and to go unacknowledged by others and the organization. It is natural to expect that angry and hurt feelings will result and that psychological defenses will be relied upon to cope with them. It is also important to note that these hostile, unreceptive responses may be fuelled by negative experiences from interactions with others who may resemble superstars but are motivated by compelling needs for security, achievement, and admiration.

THOSE WHO BURN OUT OTHERS

Organizations often have shameless self-promoters who attract attention to themselves although it is often hard to see what they accomplish. There are those who are intent upon having everyone like them, sometimes at a cost to organizational performance. There are those who want to win, sometimes at any cost. Their aim is to defeat everyone who stands in their way. Those who do not idolize this self-important individual may face with some assurance being personally attacked as unsupportive, questioning, and not being a team player. And there are those who always see themselves as better than others and espouse high performance standards for themselves and, more important, standards for others that can seldom be met.

In the first case above, it is felt that narcissistic needs can be met by acquiring the love and admiration of others.[5] Every effort may be made to win over, buy, cajole, and manipulate others into liking the person who may act important and who produces highly visible work with flair. In the second case above, the individual's arrogant pride demands always being right and always being deferred to. In the last case, the individual feels superior. This is perfectly clear because no one can meet the standards this individual sets.

Those who encounter these types of actions in the workplace can expect to have an unrewarding experience. These individuals will also provoke many of the ten feelings discussed as they blindly pursue meeting their compulsive needs to feel important, powerful, and admired. These individuals frequently poison the interpersonal environment for the superstars whom they resemble in some ways: high performance standards, important and visible contributions, and admiration by others. Executives, managers, and supervisors must be attentive to the differences to sort out the sources of negative feelings and the all too human tendency to generalize from negative experiences with some individuals.

CONCLUSION

The workplace is filled with feelings, pathos, and the psychology of the individual. Emotions driven by unconscious processes can be powerful motivators for thinking and acting. This chapter has taken ten very human feeling states and shown how they can be powerfully influenced by early life experiences. The same ten emotions have also been shown to be major contributors to the use of psychologically defensive behavior. An appreciation for this irrational-feeling-filled side of organizational life has also been shown to be a likely contributor to limiting the pursuit of individual excellence. The impact of negative feelings associated with being outshined must be appreciated in order to begin to deal with their limiting and rejecting outcomes.

It is also important to appreciate that superstars and others who are outstanding performers have feelings that may be hurt by others at work. Star performers are likely to be the focal point of negative feelings. They also can be expected to be especially sensitive to being limited and rejected and they can be expected to have the same negative feelings as responses.

5

Understanding Behavior at Work

The search for excellence at work invariably leads to finding ways of encouraging employees to strive for excellence. Doing so also leads to finding ways of understanding people, and a popular approach is to classify them. There are many different types of people, and certain individual and group behaviors occur frequently enough to be described and classified. When behavior is categorized, it can be talked about and changed, if necessary, to another category more consistent with achieving good work. For example, being emotional may be counterproductive when clear thinking is in order.

This chapter begins by bringing to the reader's attention some of the problems associated with using classification schemes to understand people at work. We have all learned to classify people and behavior. We are not, however, always aware of the limitations of what we are doing. However, not appreciating the limitations makes us less effective as managers, employees, and friends. It is also important to appreciate that the cosmology of burned-out superstars, beginning in Chapter 7, also has limitations and its wise use means respecting them.

The second part of the chapter provides an orientation to the theoretical perspectives that are used in the rest of this book to understand the thoughts, feelings, and actions of superstars and others at work. These perspectives are the individual, interpersonal, group, and organizational perspectives which inform us about why we and others do what we do at work. Realizing the complexity of these perspectives and their interactions helps us to appreciate how complex and difficult life at work really is.

LIMITATIONS OF CLASSIFICATION SCHEMES

We classify people and their behavior all of the time. We are not, however, always aware we are doing it, and we do not always appreciate how much it affects others. Because classification is so useful and pervasive, it is important to appreciate the problems that uninformed uses can produce at work. Many classification systems seem to be simple and straightforward; however, they have important limitations which should be understood before managers, employees, and trainers rely upon them for insight to guide their actions.

They Are Abstractions

Classification schemes are abstractions. They do not exist. Labelling does not make it so. A child may see his or her thirty-year-old mother as old in much the same way as the mother sees her own sixty-year-old mother. In this case chronological age does not necessarily make a person old or young. Classifications as old or young, male or female, big or small, one race or another, however, can create injustices which do not contribute to better interpersonal relations at work.

They Do Not Include All Behavior

Categories within a classification scheme are invariably imperfect and incomplete. They do not account for all behavior. A broad classification scheme may try to incorporate most behavior but will usually lack clarity and specificity. A highly detailed classification scheme, which is clear and specific, will usually not be broad enough to explain all behavior.

The Categories Are Not Adequately Defined

Categories within a scheme are often not adequately defined in operational terms. The categories may be grounded in theory but hard to translate into practice. For example, to claim a person is an introvert, one must know what kinds of behavior are associated with being an introvert and what kinds are not.

The Categories May Be Overlapping

Classification schemes often suffer from the problem of whether the categories are mutually exclusive. For example, a person may be labelled a perfectionist because he or she expects others to perform their work perfectly. The person may feel superior because the standards cannot be met. Paradoxically, a person labelled dependent may also feel helpless and incompetent because the perfect standards cannot be met. The individual is simply not good enough and may come to believe that depending on others to get the job done is the only safe course of action.

In this example, the imposition of perfect standards of performance confounds the two classifications: perfectionist and dependent. Perfection is the basis for both labels, but it has different outcomes. In the first case, perfection creates good feelings, and, in the second, bad feelings. Each category has elements of the other. They suffer from the problem of not being mutually exclusive.

They Do Not Fully Explain the Dynamic Nature of Behavior

Another problem of classification schemes is that they do not usually deal with changes in a person's behavior over time and under different conditions. A manager may be harsh in the morning and submissive in the afternoon. Employees also act differently relative to superiors over time. An employee may react cautiously and defensively to a supervisor and, upon thinking about it, react more positively during their next interaction.

People Become Pigeonholed

Classification schemes also lead to unfair and unproductive outcomes. People are complicated and they can change. Assigning a friend or colleague to a category may cause us to see the person in only that way. We may unintentionally pay attention only to those behaviors that fit a category and disregard conflicting information. We may also unconsciously treat the person as though he or she is in the category and encourage him or her to fit into it. Expectations are a powerful influence. A teacher who does not expect a student to achieve will find the student to be inadequate—not because of the student's performance but because of the teacher's expectations. Even when a person clearly fits into a category, we must not forget that other classification schemes could be used to label the person.

In Sum

Six important limitations of classifying people have been reviewed. They are applicable to any type of classification scheme that helps us organize our experience. Simplistic classification schemes belie the ultimate complexity of our lives. The following discussion makes this even more clear.

LEVELS OF KNOWLEDGE

A better appreciation of the complexity and limitations of classification systems can be gained by looking at individual and group psychology. Classifications do not provide insights into why people act the way they do.[1]

There are different ways of looking at people. Each of the following perspectives informs the other, and each helps us gain a fuller appreciation of behavior at work. These are areas that are often filled with mysterious, hard to understand jargon. The following four sections consider some of the key concepts in what is hoped to be an accessible manner.

Individual Psychological Perspective

People have unconscious motivations. For example, a son who was made to feel incompetent by his father may feel threatened by negative feedback from a male superior who reminds him of his father and his father's criticism. The reaction to the criticism will be out of proportion. The feelings of anger associated with being humiliated by the father will surface to fuel resentment of the supervisor's criticism. A reaction like this is all too human. It is an unthinking response to the cue. None of us likes criticism. To the extent that we are overly reactive to criticism, we are in touch with earlier painful life experiences.

Although the above example involves others, it looks at behavior from the perspective of the individual's thoughts and feelings and includes psychological defenses such as denial, rationalization, suppression, and selective inattention. Our thoughts and feelings are influenced by intrapsychic processes and are often not open to too much self-examination or questioning by others. For example, a person who usually dominates others may not be aware of responding to others this way because dominance has been learned as an effective coping response to anxiety created by uncertainty. It is also important to note that questioning the person's motivations may cause further loss of security and increased efforts to control self, others, and the situation.

Individual psychology incorporates elements from the levels of knowledge below. In those instances where elements of this level overlap with those below, they are discussed below.

Interpersonal Psychological Perspective

We live and work with others. We become ourselves as a result of interactions with others which make us feel better or worse about ourselves. Others, in psychological terms, are objects who act on us and we, in turn, act on.[2] When others act on us, they may be "good objects" who nurture us and enhance our self-esteem. When we are treated poorly by other people and when caretaking others are unreliable, we experience them as threatening and unrewarding "bad objects."

Intrapsychic processes are involved. The thoughts and feelings of individuals who experience early life trauma will be influenced by those experiences throughout life. Significant others at work and at home may continue to batter and strip away self-esteem or perhaps provide a nurturing environment where self-esteem and personal integrity can be reestablished. The individual and interpersonal perspectives inform each other. Each provides a unique understanding of why we do what we do. Another important aspect of life is to understand why we act the way we do in groups.

Group Dynamic Perspective

We are all members of groups, and groups have a powerful influence over us.[3] Groups at work have some degree of permanency, purpose, organization, and leadership. They include departments, task groups, committees, and informal groups. Group membership means subordination to a group leader, conformity to group norms, and support of what the group does. We all, at times, fear and resent losing our personal autonomy within groups. Group dynamics include the tensions surrounding membership, leadership, goals, routines and rituals, interpersonal power and authority, influence, control, and group process. These dynamics can be understood from a number of theoretical perspectives.

The Group as a Whole. Group dynamics implies that the group can be understood as a whole.[4] Members of groups frequently act alike or provide tacit support for the actions of others. When this occurs it can be understood that the group acted. For example, group members may spend an hour's meeting visiting with each other and not perform any work on a task. It could be concluded from the meeting that the group's covert purpose or unconscious process was to visit. It must be appreciated that the notion of a group is an abstraction that is made more remote by analyzing group dynamics independent of individual behavior.

People in Roles. People in organizations interact with each other both as people and as people in roles.[5] The individual and interpersonal perspectives contribute to understanding how a person in the role comes to be known by others, how the person comes to know self, and how prior life experiences affect acting out the role. The group leader, for example, is an individual with unique needs and desires and, at the same time, is a person who is expected by others and by himself or herself to fulfill the responsibilities associated with a role of leadership. Within this dynamic lies conflict, confusion, and the tendency to know the leader and the role in a way that is similar to how authority figures of the past have been experienced. Group dynamics place intrapsychic process and interpersonal relationships into a setting where many people may act together to structure events and understanding. Group dynamics may, for example, create an incessant press upon the leader to take care of the group's members.

Individual and Group Defenses. Individual psychological defenses involve a person drawing upon coping mechanisms that have been learned throughout life.[6] A person, when confronted with an unfair outcome, may cry, become enraged, or retreat. These reactions, not unlike those of children, are generally regarded as less than adult. Group defenses are the outcome of shared trends in individual defenses. Group members may become collectively enraged or withdrawn and act hostile or dependent. Groups with members who act like this are described as contributing to developing group defenses.

Unconscious Group Process. Closely related to the above is the notion of unconscious group process.[7] Group actions may be based on unacknowledged, covert, hidden agendas that are so rigorously suppressed from open discussion that these group dynamics can be described as unconscious. An example of unconscious group process is a group of people who participate directly or tacitly in the verbal brutalization of a new member. Members of the group may later not remember what happened. They may remember something very different that is something more acceptable, such as the actions were intended to help the person. Group members may also collude to stifle being reminded that the event occurred.

Another example of unconscious group process is efforts by group members to be alike. Differences in age, experience, position, gender, and race may be ignored as though none of the members have unique attributes. Behavioral norms emerge, norms members are expected to follow. Avoiding conflict, rivalry, and the possibility of some members distinguishing themselves at the expense of other members is expected. Those who deviate are disciplined via such mechanisms as being ostracized, ignored, or dismissed from further group participation. Trends such as these are furthered by selecting new members with conforming attributes.

Fight-Flight Group Dynamics. An example that ties together the notions of group defenses, the group as a whole, and unconscious group processes is the tendency of groups to respond to difficulties in a fight-flight mode.[8] When a serious problem develops, the source of the problem may be attributed to an evil empire in another department. The response may then be to attack the source of the problem. Fighting back has many primitive qualities that defend against anxiety. It also distracts group members from having to deal with ownership of the problem and the need to take action within their group. A second common reaction is for a group to talk about anything other than the problem. The problem is ignored. This response represents a flight from a problem that is too dangerous at the moment to discuss or handle.

Organizational Dynamic Perspective

Organizational dynamics expands the level of analysis to the entire organization. Organizational dynamics are the sum of all the actions of individuals and groups at work. It is focused at the nature of the overall organization as it is known by organization members and groups that work within it. Organizational dynamics includes consideration of the type of organizational structure, management and leadership styles, strategic directions, and information systems; in other words, the organizational culture.

How an organization is structured has been of much interest for many years.[9] Tall versus short and centralized versus decentralized are two of the most common structural considerations. Contemporary structural considerations include matrix organizations, issues of participation and self-managing teams, and qualitative considerations involving individual and group psychology.

How an organization is led has also received much attention. The personalities of top management are an important factor in understanding how an organization operates and why.[10] Values, attitudes, beliefs held by managers, and the degree to which individuals in key top management positions are psychologically integrated have a powerful influence on what work is done as well as when and how.

Organizational culture governs behavior.[11] Members of organizations learn what is expected of them from job descriptions and from explicit and implicit performance expectations which are communicated to them in often subtle ways by their friends and peers. Organization members may not know they have violated a cultural norm until others react negatively and perhaps punitively. "You should know, we don't do that here." Organizational culture ties members of the organization together by providing common language and concepts, organizational and group boundaries, values, rewards, punishment, and ideology.

Important parts of culture are myths about the organization, about its functioning, key individuals, and operating environment. For example, a highly visible CEO may, because of persecutory personality trends, believe that the organization is being constantly attacked by others who do not appreciate it and wish to destroy it. Organization members may then have their attention directed to these threats and develop defensive strategies to deal with them. As a result, the organization may pour much of its energy into advocating the development of legislation to regulate or eliminate the external threat rather than improve its performance.

The organizational dynamic perspective is informed by the other perspectives. The individual and interpersonal perspectives inform organizational dynamics in much the same way they do group dynamics. There are several principal differences: the scale is much larger, making face-to-face contact with all other organization members improbable; the issues surrounding power and authority are more complex; the nature of leadership and organizational membership are more abstract and distant; and intergroup processes occur. Group dynamics contribute to understanding organizational dynamics and are, in turn, influenced by organizational dynamics.

Organizational dynamics affect what individual organization members and groups can achieve by controlling many important organizational variables. Leadership styles, organizational structure, and organizational culture can combine to limit the possibility of achieving anything of consequence by rigidly controlling behavior, thinking, and resources.

CONCLUSION

We have all learned to classify others, things, and behavior. We have been encouraged in this effort by social scientists who examine us and our behavior and then find ingenious classification schemes that presume to reflect reality. Appreciating both the limitations of classification schemes, no matter how helpful, and the extraordinary complexity of individual, interpersonal, group, and organizational dynamics will, hopefully, make us more cautious and sensitive about how we understand and interpret our workplace reality.

The appreciation gained in this chapter for classifying people now leads to considering the cosmology of burned-out superstars in Part II. The cosmology provides a typology for the behavior of unproductive superstars who have been burned out at work by themselves and by being rejected and limited by management, colleagues, and friends.

PART II

CASE STUDIES OF SUPERSTAR BURNOUT

This section introduces a cosmology of once productive superstars who no longer shine. The cosmology highlights the all too likely outcome that outstanding performers may burn out from their own expectations and self-defeating actions, and from the inhibiting, insensitive, and rejecting actions of managers, supervisors, associates, and friends at work—the organization.

The cosmology uses the perspectives introduced in Chapter 5. These perspectives, unlike popular books on excellence, provide psychological insights into what really makes people and people in groups tick. Part II provides stories about the lives of five fictional workers who did not always receive the best of care; individuals who grew up in the school of hard knocks. Each chapter begins with a brief cosmological description of a star type that has properties that resemble the case.[1] A fictional case which provides background on childhood, family life, education, social life, and work is then provided. These cases reflect all too common life experiences.

The cases may touch your feelings. You may identify with some of what is said. This is good. If you acknowledge the similarities you may learn more about yourself. If you have known others with similar backgrounds and behavior, you may become more understanding of what they may have experienced in their lives. Before beginning the cases, Chapter 6 is devoted to orienting the reader to some of the commonalities and theoretical underpinnings in these cases.

6

The Common Denominator

Psychology is the common denominator of Part II as we move from looking at the individual to others, groups, and the organization. Each level of knowledge introduces new perspectives of thinking about achieving excellence at work and new ways of understanding life experience and others.

The individual psychological perspective teaches us, for example, that parents who are hard to please may believe that they are encouraging their children to improve. However, if parental approval is seldom forthcoming and failures become frequent and humiliating, the children will become anxious and overly attentive to their expectations. A child may, for example, become invested in achieving high grades or developing superior athletic ability—whatever the parents desire. The child gives up self-oriented development in favor of conforming to parental expectations to secure approval, affection, and love. The child abandons developing its real-self in favor of creating a false-self.

Superstars are no less vulnerable than anyone else. The cases are designed to show how deeply embedded personality tendencies create the need to achieve or, conversely, why some people who are talented and potential superstars do not shine. The cases underscore the fragility of human nature. The characters react to the distressing case situations with feelings that provoke psychologically defensive responses that are seen to be consistent throughout life. The superstars, while having many desirable attributes, are also found to be very human and vulnerable to the feelings and accompanying personal disorganization described in Chapter 4. It is also worth noting that some of the dysfunctional behavior the characters exhibit is like the behavior of others whom the superstar must work with, which provides further insight into people at work.

The interpersonal perspective informs us that other people in our lives have a powerful effect upon us just as we may have a powerful effect upon them. We live in an interpersonal world which may make us feel good about ourselves or may make us feel despised and worthless.

The group perspective introduces a less personal perspective to understanding work life. We are all members of groups at work. We may be members of a production team, department, section, or plant. We may participate in committees, task forces, performance improvement groups, projects, and programs. We may also be active in informal groups such as a lunch group, a bowling team, or a Thursday golfing group. These groups can be fun to work in, or they may be threatening and punishing and discourage risk taking and the pursuit of individual excellence.

Organizational influences are always present at work. Organizational culture can lead to many diverse and unproductive outcomes. For example, unreasonable demands for performance combined with too few resources, lack of top management support, and no willingness on the part of top management to deal with turf battles between departments may create an impossible work situation. Those working in this organization could be expected to feel angry, confused, used, alienated, and worried about the organization's long-term survival.

In this example those in leadership roles create an organizational culture in which employees feel used and abused, in which leadership is reactive and defensive, in which others are blamed for the lack of the organization's success, and in which everyone feels bad about themselves, each other, their work, management, and the organization. Members of the organization feel frustrated, embittered, and alienated from each other, their work, and the organization. Angry, energy-absorbing, and unproductive interactions develop which further increase work-related pressures and the likelihood of even more alienation.

Dealing with problems such as these leads to considering organizational intervention strategies that encourage individuals to achieve excellence. The following intervention considerations inform the interventions discussed in the cases.

INTERVENTIONS

Preventing the development of a hostile and unreceptive interpersonal and organizational work environment is the key to fostering the pursuit of individual excellence. Prevention is emphasized over recovering burned-out superstars for the simple reason that "An ounce of prevention is worth a pound of cure." Developing a proactive preventive process encourages the pursuit of individual excellence on an ongoing basis. There are no opportunity costs. Superstars are encouraged to shine brightly. The need to recover burned-out superstars must be seen to be the result of an overall loss of organizational performance, something that may, however, occur even in the best of organizations. Recovery can be an arduous, unrewarding, and problematic process. "A wasted mind is a terrible thing." If the superstar is to remain in the organization, rekindling the individual's excitement and risk-taking attitude is important and should be undertaken.

Intervention strategies must be informed by the four levels of knowledge: individual, interpersonal, group, and organizational.

Individual Interventions

Human resource managers and managers who supervise outstanding performers should be attentive to what makes their superachievers tick. An outstanding employee who feels inferior and worthless and who has low self-esteem may be working in a highly productive manner to compensate for these "bad" inner feelings. As an adult this individual may have to achieve and win or otherwise be faced with overwhelming feelings of worthlessness and despair—clearly good reasons to devote oneself to succeeding. This same individual may also have a low tolerance for frustration and may quickly develop feelings of self-contempt for personal deficiencies. He or she may hold in contempt others who get in the way or do not meet the standards learned from parental role models who almost always found fault with others. Those working with superstars should consider some simple questions. Do some superstars seem to be especially attentive and overly reactive to criticism? Do they strike back at others who frustrate them or shrink from conflict? Do they seem to be compelled to have others react to them in a particular way? Do they perform for approval?

There is nothing wrong with these kinds of behavior. We all experience them from time to time. We have all become frustrated in a traffic jam and angry with a service person who was indifferent or ineffective at meeting our needs. Our negative response may also have been disproportionate to the situation and counterproductive, perhaps creating an "interpersonal blast zone." And, we have all felt especially good when someone has complimented us on our work or appearance.

Superstars can be made to work more effectively by gaining an appreciation of the less flexible aspects of their personalities. They should be encouraged to improve their self-knowledge and their intentionality. Managers and supervisors can help superstars with "tough love" by letting them know they care enough about them to take the risk of challenging some of their dysfunctional thoughts, feelings, and actions. Human resource managers can help managers, supervisors, and superstars by providing them with learning opportunities about the psychological side of the workplace. A second alternative is to provide managers and staff access to an employee assistance program and possibly to an in-house consultant who is available to discuss problems with them. Dealing sensitively and meaningfully with the people factor is the challenge of the 1990s. It is very likely the most challenging aspect of the workplace, and it is likely to be the last to be dealt with successfully in any organization.

Interpersonal Interventions

The interpersonal level of analysis leads to considering preventive measures that involve educating organization members about how their feelings are influenced by others at work. These efforts need not be pervasive or seen as a basis to create a program or cultural shift in the organization. Rather these learning opportunities should gradually raise consciousness about some of the underlying motivations for interpersonal dynamics. Easy to understand psychodynamic perspectives are available to inform managers and employees.[1]

Group Interventions

Group dynamics can be fascinating but difficult to understand. The complexities of group dynamics do not permit their management in one minute. Human resource managers should develop educational opportunities that help managers and those who work frequently in groups to better understand group processes. A second potentially productive approach is to employ group process consultants to facilitate group processes and to gradually educate group members on how to process themselves effectively. A third strategy is to rotate group members through the role of a group process reporter. This role may, at the end of each meeting or at the midpoint and end, report to the group the group's observed process. It may be observed that a few members did all the talking, that some of the group members seemed angry, or that the group did not stick to the agenda. Names should be omitted. The behavior of individuals should not be mentioned. No effort should be made to interpret the group's process. If there are group process problems, it is the group leader's responsibility to lead the group in dealing with them. The rotation of the role serves to gradually educate group members about group processes. Using this approach also empowers the group to take care of its own needs rather than to rely on a staff of experts.

Organizational Interventions

Changing an organization and its culture is an intervention of sweeping proportions that can be undertaken only with the utmost care and planning. The contribution of organizational culture to work life and achieving individual excellence is explored here. In particular, organizational culture is examined from the point of view that it is a means of minimizing anxiety about the inside and outside of the organization. Recommendations are provided to help direct anyone endeavoring to change a culture that discourages the pursuit of individual excellence.

The critical dimension of all of the above interventions is who should make them and how? Some suggestions have been provided. An organization interested in dealing with the issues raised in this book must locate individuals educated in individual, interpersonal, and group dynamics. Learning opportunities that will help organization members learn more about themselves, others, and the groups they work with should be developed. These individuals may also lead direct interventions in unacceptable individual, interpersonal, group, and organizational dynamics. Top management must be committed to developing these human resources and also be willing to participate actively in the process.

A WORD ON THE CASES

The next five chapters consider the fictional lives of five outstanding workers who have, despite or as a result of adverse parenting, become superachievers whose ability to contribute to their organization was extinguished. These five cases are formulated from Karen Horney's work and DSM-III-R diagnostic criteria.[2] Horney's theory of solutions to anxiety provides five responses which are briefly described at the start of each chapter. The superstars in the five cases rise to prominence and then burn out as a result of personal limitations and as a result of the fearful, envious, angry, rejecting reactions of those they work with. The five cases focus on the emotional feet of clay all outstanding performers have. No one is perfect. No one is superhuman. Everyone has feelings that can be hurt. The superstars in the cases tragically contribute to their own demise.

In Greek tragedy a character is found to have a fatal flaw that ultimately contributes to the character's demise. The five cases in some way include this element of tragedy. In each case the superstar might have avoided the outcome if he or she had not become psychologically defensive. It is also important to appreciate that the characters might not have excelled as much as they did had it not been for the flaw. We are then left with the all too common paradoxical outcomes human nature creates. The superstars in the five cases contribute to a self-fulfilling prophecy where burnout is inevitable.

This book looks at the impact of not so easily understood emotions on outstanding performance. In particular the interaction of negative emotions such as fear, anger, hate, and envy create unproductive work-related outcomes. This is not to say that people and organizations are doomed to be dominated by these emotions; however, it is important to appreciate and acknowledge that they exist in the workplace and how they can influence it. By attracting attention to these doom and gloom elements of work life, they can be understood, appreciated, and dealt with intentionally.

IMPLICATIONS FOR MANAGEMENT AND ORGANIZATIONS

The five cases and much of the content of Part I either implicitly or explicitly imply that management is poor or missing when negative individual, interpersonal, group, and organizational dynamics develop. However, these outcomes can occur even when members of management are attentive, understand what is going on, and care about the people involved. The cases, however, do point out problems with management that either contributed to the creation of the burnout or did not prevent it.

Much the same can be said for the concept of organization. Once again the reader may come to feel in a reified sense that "bad organizations" use and abuse their employees and that it is to be expected that outstanding people will become disillusioned and burned-out and will leave. Organizations are created by people and maintained by people. So, to be clear, the examination of the role of the organization in this book folds back upon looking at the people who create them—people who are not always rational, fair, and just and who might become frightened and angry at work.

THE IMPERFECT SUPERSTAR

The five cases raise the question of why the characters are superstars when, in the end, they contributed to their own burnout and they came to act unproductively. These observations may be restated: Why were the characters in the five cases not superhuman? Why did they not overcome the problems they faced and win?

Superstars are people, too, people who have feelings that can be hurt. The idea that they should be able to overcome all problems—personal, interpersonal, group, and organizational—sets them up to fail.

Second, the question raises the further question of exactly what aspect of superstardom is being discussed in the cases. If superstars are so good, why are they imperfect? What is being talked about in the cases may be circumscribed as follows. Figure 1 lays out the familial and personal development origins of the burned-out superstars in the cases. The figure provides for a range of family life from good, which encourages the development of adequate self-esteem and self-integration, to poor, which inhibits the fulfillment of these developmental tasks.

Also provided in the cases are the development of many personal attributes that permit people to become high achievers or not so high achievers. These personal attributes are then matched with personality attributes that include provisions for individual variations where lower levels of self-esteem and self-integration may arise from the good end of the family and developmental continuum and higher levels of self-esteem and self-integration may arise from the poorer end of the continuum. The figure also groups those with lower self-esteem and self-integration together to account for the familial and developmental origins of the burned-out superstars in Part II. Provision is also made for an individual whose self-esteem and self-integration is adequate to cope with work-related stress and anxiety including the negative feelings of others without becoming psychologically defensive.

Figure 1
The Familial and Developmental Origins of the Superstars in the Cases

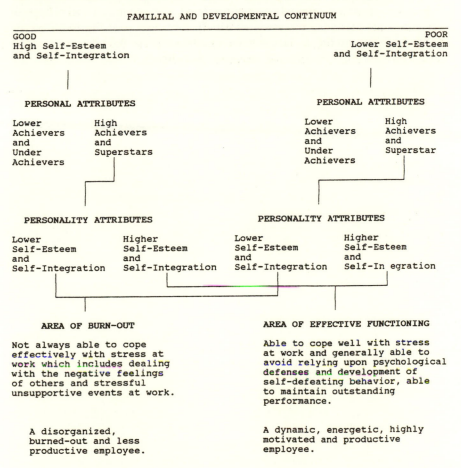

FAMILIAL AND DEVELOPMENTAL CONTINUUM

GOOD	POOR
High Self-Esteem	Lower Self-Esteem
and Self-Integration	and Self-Integration

PERSONAL ATTRIBUTES   PERSONAL ATTRIBUTES

Lower	High	Lower	High
Achievers	Achievers	Achievers	Achievers
and	and	and	and
Under	Superstars	Under	Superstar
Achievers		Achievers	

PERSONALITY ATTRIBUTES   PERSONALITY ATTRIBUTES

Lower	Higher	Lower	Higher
Self-Esteem	Self-Esteem	Self-Esteem	Self-Esteem
and	and	and	and
Self-Integration	Self-Integration	Self-Integration	Self-In egration

AREA OF BURN-OUT   AREA OF EFFECTIVE FUNCTIONING

Not always able to cope
effectively with stress at
work which includes dealing
with the negative feelings
of others and stressful
unsupportive events at work.

Able to cope well with stress
at work and generally able to
avoid relying upon psychological
defenses and development of
self-defeating behavior, able
to maintain outstanding
performance.

A disorganized,
burned-out and less
productive employee.

A dynamic, energetic, highly
motivated and productive
employee.

SUPERSTARS AND THE SITUATION

One last consideration underscores the importance of situational variables. It
is not the intention of this book to limit discussion to the Magic Johnsons and
Donald Trumps of this world. Many people, as the cases will make clear, can
achieve stellar results at work if allowed to do so. To the extent that someone
with outstanding skills is not permitted to use them, there is no opportunity for
this potential superstar to shine. On the other hand, some with good skills may
achieve individual excellence, if only in a limited area, if encouraged to do so.
Everyone might be a potential superstar. The burned-out superstars in the cases
presented serve to acknowledge and illustrate the importance of situational variables on performance.

CONCLUSION

It is not possible to provide an uplifting and rosy picture of the portion of organizational life being discussed in Part II. Organizational life is filled with tragic outcomes. Acting as though tragedies do not occur does not open up this aspect of work life to inspection, learning, and change.

7

The Pulsar

A pulsar is believed to be the neutron star remains of a supernova that are
held together as it rotates in fractions of a second by its excessive gravity.
As it spins it sprays electrons into space from its poles that are detected on
earth as microwave radiation pulses—radio waves.

This case draws on Karen Horney's arrogant-vindictive solution to anxiety. This
response involves a win-lose attitude. This individual's arrogant pride, if damaged, must be vindicated by triumph. Others must be defeated. This individual's
highly competitive nature leads to self-knowledge of being the only one who is
right. However, threats to this worldview always exist and must be constantly
defended against, necessitating a continual vigilance and a readiness to get even.
This response is similar to that of the DSM-III-R (Diagnostic and Statistical
Manual of Mental Disorders) paranoid personality, who fears being exploited,
harmed, and maligned by others; who holds grudges and lacks forgiveness; and
who launches frequent counterattacks. This response is also discussed in Kets
de Vries and Miller's *The Neurotic Organization* as the paranoid type.

In this case, when Bob's arrogant pride is damaged by a group process, he
becomes vindictive in his actions. He wishes to get even for having had his
pride and feelings hurt by hurting others back. Understanding Bob's case helps

us understand the desire we may all have from time to time to get even with others.

CASE EXAMPLE

Bob and his two older brothers grew up as model children and students. Bob's mother, to whom he was very attached, was a homemaker and a community leader who participated in city government by chairing an important civic committee. She had been attentive to her children but she had also been remote. Bob often could not tell what she thought or how she felt. His father set high goals for him which he strove to meet to avoid painful criticism. Bob learned that achieving excellence was critical for success. He also learned that criticizing his parents, or their work and activities, would not be tolerated. They were not to be questioned. Punishment would be forthcoming if he did. Nonetheless he occasionally challenged his parents when his feelings were hurt, and he bore his punishment with resolve.

Bob's father owned his own manufacturing company. He was not around much, but when he was, he enjoyed his family. Bob, as his brothers had, worked part-time for his father when he entered high school. Bob learned a lot about what it took to be a good worker, an effective supervisor, and a good manager.

Bob, who was an outstanding student, decided early to become an engineer, just like his father. He worked hard in high school and participated in student government. He was also an above average athlete and earned letters in football, basketball, and track. Bob managed to receive an academic scholarship to a first-class engineering school where he excelled, and, upon graduation, he was recruited into a major manufacturing company. His first job was to work on a project team.

The team worked for three years on spearheading the changing of an old, cumbersome, and ineffective raw materials inventory and transfer system for a large, single-site producer of agricultural products and chemicals. Bob had been extraordinarily productive as a member of this successful change effort. The team's work, which owed a great deal to Bob's many ideas and hard work, revolutionized the system in thirty-six months.

Bob proved to be an original and resourceful thinker. He generated many ideas that greatly facilitated the project team's work. Versatile and hardworking, he was willing to perform research, make site visits, collect and analyze data, interview employees, screen software applications, review the literature, and contact the faculty of several universities for advice and counsel. Bob also was a thoughtful critic and contributor to the ideas other project team members developed. His many insights were welcomed by his colleagues. Bob proved to be a capable innovator and a good problem solver when implementing team recommendations. Managers welcomed his help and advice.

When the project was completed, Bob's outstanding work was rewarded by his being promoted and reassigned to manage one of the key elements of the new system. During his first year as manager, Bob implemented many of the remaining elements of the new system and gradually built up a staff of informed and dependable supervisors and foremen who enjoyed working with him. When the implementation was nearing completion and the system's performance was stabilized, Bob directed his attention to making more improvements. He began to resolve operating problems in other areas of the plant that negatively impacted the performance of his system.

Bob contributed many insightful criticisms and ideas at meetings; however, they were not always warmly received by some executives, other managers, and some staff. Even so he steadfastly continued to generate ideas and to advocate change. Resistance to his ideas and eventually to himself gradually built up. He began to find himself excluded from key meetings, and he heard from friends that he was being maligned by some of his colleagues.

During one important meeting that was called to discuss a problem that affected Bob's system, a manager unexpectedly blew up and launched a scathing attack against Bob. Bob was condemned for his constant pressure, for his insensitivity to the problems others faced, for his appearance of grandstanding, for his arrogance, and for his being overly energetic and his eagerness to criticize. Other group members quickly joined in on the attack.

Bob anxiously listened and eventually tried to defend himself. He reminded the others that they were there to get the job done. His efforts to refocus on the problem merely aggravated the situation. Bob left the meeting feeling angry, disillusioned, set up, unsupported, and threatened. Days later it seemed to him that it was too dangerous to continue to advocate openly for change. He thought to himself, "If I am going to be treated like this, then I am just going to do my job like everyone else. If maintaining the status quo is what they want, then I can certainly contribute."

Bob began to limit his participation in meetings both in attendance and in contributions. He seldom spoke up, and he allowed some ill-conceived proposals to pass. What was most interesting was that no one seemed to care.

He still encouraged his staff to seek excellence in their work and to improve their system constantly; however, the only changes he considered were those that were limited to his system. He gradually made it clear that he would not agree to make a change that involved changes in any system he did not control.

He also began to play the passivity and resistance games. He resisted making changes in his system requested by his colleagues. He used standard reasons to explain why he could not immediately respond. He made a point of using words and phrases that were frequently heard at meetings when what was really being said was that no action was likely to be taken. "I don't know, Paul, the idea sounds good but it will mean reconfiguring a number of subsystems and I just don't have the staff to handle it now." Or, "That idea will need sign-off at least at the VP level. I couldn't consider it without Joe's OK."

Playing the game, however, was occasionally wearing. At times what was going on seemed unbelievable to him. Ideas and proposals surfaced which had obvious defects that were often minimally discussed before implementation and resulted in predictably negative consequences. He knew that, if he had been included or could have participated as before, the problems and negative outcomes could have been avoided. He did, however, despite his better judgment, occasionally respond to some proposals of people whom he especially detested with thoughtful, well-researched reports that undermined their ideas and held them up for public ridicule. He knew that the responses did not endear him to those he chose to cross; however, it felt good occasionally to "nail them."

Bob adopted a pattern of intense periodic outbursts which were directed at others and their proposals. He used these attacks to vindicate his hurt feelings and pride. His associates responded by continuing to try to insulate themselves from him by limiting the information he had and his participation in meetings. As near as possible they wanted to cut him off from any avenue of getting even with them, although some unconsciously felt they deserved it for having attacked Bob in the first place.

CASE SUMMARY

This superstar, in response to what he felt was a limiting and rejecting work environment, angrily retreated to his office. He was content to perform assigned work in a manner consistent with the expectations of others. Little was seen or heard from him after he shut down except during periodic efforts to get back at those who had rejected him and whom he now held in considerable contempt. His overly energized, periodic efforts to get even reinforced the perception of him as dysfunctional despite the validity of his contributions. In sum, Bob did not like some of his peers and they did not like him. Bob and his colleagues unwittingly created a self-fulfilling prophecy—a self-perpetuating, unproductive, and destructive cycle of interpersonal relations.

Bob, like many of us, contributed to a situation in which he and those around him burned each other out. The result was a lose-lose outcome. Everyone and the organization lost. Bob's good will, innovativeness, and hard work were lost. His peers became defensive and had to invest time, energy, and organizational resources in making sure Bob did not get them. A cold war, difficult to end, had been created. A change in this unproductive outcome begins by examining the contribution that the levels of knowledge can make to understanding the situation. Since the case is fictional, the following analysis is intended to model or illustrate how psychologically informed inquiry can help one understand the workplace.

INDIVIDUAL PSYCHOLOGICAL PERSPECTIVE

A superstar like Bob may have many motivations for his high achievements and his reactions to problems and others. These motivations are rooted in his past life experience.

Bob's life experience had been filled with criticism and rejection and led him to use his superior education, intelligence, and skills to achieve recognition and acceptance at work. Bob was driven by these internal forces to excel and excel he did. Unfortunately, his motivations to achieve excellence ran into resistance from others who were not so highly energized. The eventual blockage of his pursuits frustrated his drive to achieve to receive recognition and put him in touch with his painful early life experiences. Bob, who still unconsciously resented how his father had treated him, transferred his feelings onto others who frustrated him when he was an adult. His response was also unwittingly modeled after the familiar behavior of his father who had found fault with everyone and who had frequently and openly judged others as deficient and contemptible. Bob's response, based on these psychodynamics, was predictable and even irresistible. Bob's thoughts and feelings, which arose from the sum of his prior life experience, determined his behavior.

INTERPERSONAL PERSPECTIVE

Bob's intrapsychic processes, which were in large part determined by deeply held feelings of uncertainty about himself and his self-worth imparted to him by poor parenting, played an active role in his interpersonal world. From his mother, Bob did not learn to tolerate ambiguity well. He wanted to know where people stood relative to him. From his father, he learned to see others in black and white terms. Others were either good or bad; for him or against him. Those who did not help him achieve and did not reward him were bad.

Bob was liked by his subordinates. Sensitive to their needs and always available for feedback, he celebrated their achievements. After all, he wanted to be a good parent. Others deserved what he did not get as a child. However, an occasional employee and others who interacted with Bob as peers or as authority figures did not always fare so well. When others frustrated him, or got in his way, or rejected or punished him, he brought down the hammer—"Yes, but." Bob, in modeling his father's familiar critical and condemning behavior, unintentionally set up the same interpersonal dynamic at work that his father had created relative to him. Other managers and some of his staff were found to be deficient and, in Bob's opinion, had to be pushed to higher levels of performance. However, when a higher level was achieved, Bob did not stop and celebrate their achievements but responded with "Yes, but." "Yes, you did a good job, but you can do better." Or, "Yes, I can see you think you achieved a great feat, but there are many other aspects of your work that can still be improved upon." Or, "Yes, but look at what others have achieved." Or, "Yes, but look at the ideal." And, "Yes, but look at my work." Bob's "Yes, but" response to others, especially those who got in his way, created a familiar and predictable outcome; they did not like him just as he did not like his father.

Those who persistently frustrated him were singled out for more vigorous assault. Bob unmercifully humiliated them whenever he had the chance. He wanted them to know that he could reach out and touch them just as they were limiting and rejecting him.

GROUP DYNAMIC PERSPECTIVE

Group dynamics were important to Bob for it was in a group that the initial blow occurred. The committee setting provided the opportunity and perhaps the safety in numbers for some members of the group, who had arrived at the meeting already feeling angry about having another project surreptitiously terminated, to gang up spontaneously on Bob. The members of this angry subgroup were a sentience group—a group of members who shared similar feelings. When one group member launched the attack, other members of the heretofore unknown subgroup suddenly emerged. Other members actively supported the attack on Bob without really thinking about it. At the same time, the remaining members of the group, who may have shared some of the feelings or none at all, withdrew to the safety of silence. When one of the members of the silent subgroup did speak up to point out that it was unfair to blame Bob for all of their problems, the angry subgroup members unceremoniously ignored the point.

Bob very naturally began to experience membership in the group as punishing and threatening. His continuing role as a member of the group seemed in question. His efforts to deflect the aggression by reminding the group's members of a pressing time boundary for a decision were dismissed by the group. Bob was then further scapegoated for trying to take the group off task. Bob was glad to get out of the meeting alive; later he decided to withdraw from active participation in the group.

Group as a Whole

When members of a group act together, it may be said that the group does something even though, in this case, the use of group is a reification. In other words, saying that a group did something ignores the fact that it was the members of the group who acted which relieves the members of the need to assume personal responsibility for their actions. Nonetheless group dynamics can be seen to be a whole. In Bob's case it could be said that the "angry subgroup" located Bob as the source of their problems and they slaughtered him as a scapegoat. They killed him off as a member. Some members actively participated in the process; others tacitly supported their actions by remaining passive and silent. It was as though the meeting had been called for the explicit purpose of getting Bob; even though this had not been discussed prior to the meeting and was not on anyone's mind when the group entered the room.

It is also noteworthy that no one questioned Bob's silence and his lack of participation at future meetings. It was not as though Bob's changed behavior had gone unnoticed. Those who did not like Bob and his contributions felt relieved. A few members were concerned that Bob's feelings had been devastated; however, no one talked to Bob outside of the group and no mention was ever made of the attack. Bob's retreat from participation in meetings perhaps was not discussed out of fear of resurfacing hostility and bad feelings. The group, it might be inferred, was acting to deny and forget what had happened by not attending to the member it had injured. The group was in flight from collectively held fear about its power and guilt about what had happened.

Individual and Group Psychological Defenses

Individuals and the group acted out their angry feelings on Bob. The group as a whole retreated into a defensive group process. Psychological coping mechanisms, activated by anxiety from group membership, led some members to project their bad feelings onto Bob. It was suddenly easy to see that Bob was at fault. There was no middle ground and no stopping the process. As the regressive trends continued, some members, in order to feel better about themselves, used psychological defenses such as rationalization, denial, splitting, projection, and undoing.

Some group members rationalized by saying that they believed what had happened was necessary; that it contributed to improving the group's work. Some group members denied that the group's actions were as aggressive and hostile as they really had been. Feelings of being afraid of the group's violent power and knowledge of not having the courage to do anything about what happened were split off and dissociated to dispose of them. Those who were concerned that they had not helped Bob later offered him a silent apology to undo their part in the process. All of these unseen intrapsychic processes lead to an examination of the idea of unconscious group dynamics.

Unconscious Group Process

There was an unconscious process at work in creating the angry sentience group that did not like Bob. Members of this subgroup did not know that they were members of a sentience group until a fight leader emerged to attack Bob. Once the attack started, the group's process regressed to locating in Bob the source of all of their bad feelings about themselves, the group, and work life in general. Other unconscious processes in the group served to repress, suppress, or otherwise deny guilt feelings for having attacked Bob and "killed" him off; for having actively or vicariously enjoyed the excitement of the attack; for having feared stopping the attack; and for not subsequently coming to his aid either outside of the group or in subsequent meetings where his feelings and lack of participation might have been discussed but were not.

People in Roles

Using roles to understand behavior at work is helpful. Bob's situation in the group implies that he had roles that were either assumed by him or assigned by the group. Bob initially assumed the role of being a creative, critical, and innovative group member. He could be depended on to contribute. However, his zealousness was not welcomed by some members. As part of the unconscious process of developing the sentience group, Bob assumed the role of a ''bad'' group member. Bob then became the injured member, the defensive member, and ultimately the dead group member. Others in the group may also have had roles, such as attackers, audience members or onlookers, and guilty members. One important set of roles in this dysfunctional group process was that of fight/ flight leader.

Fight/Flight

The group's sudden attack on Bob was initiated by one manager who felt angry at the moment and located Bob as the source of the anger. Attacking Bob was an effort to get rid of bad feelings by annihilating the source of the bad influence—Bob. This manager became the fight leader for the ''bad Bob'' angry sentience subgroup. Later the same member saw no reason to deal with what had happened to Bob or to Bob's injured retreat into silence and nonparticipation. The fight leader then assumed the role of the flight leader, who led the group in flight from its responsibility for its actions and its feelings of guilt.

ORGANIZATIONAL DYNAMIC PERSPECTIVE

The leadership and members of Bob's organization were under pressure to meet pressing performance deadlines. The culture of the organization was one of top management's advocating for the pursuit of excellence but not supporting the idea in the way it acted toward operating areas as compared with its successful project groups. Operating managers were held strictly accountable while those working on project teams were encouraged to take risks. Not understanding this difference greatly contributed to Bob's dysfunctional behavior. This understanding leads to considering how Bob's outcome could have been prevented or how that, now that it had occurred, he can be restored to his former high levels of productivity.

INTERVENTIONS

Timely organizational, group, and individual interventions could have avoided the development of Bob's unproductive actions at work. Avoiding the loss of this superstar's productivity involves intervening in several ways. At the organizational level there was an inconsistency in the organizational culture: a high-control, risk-aversive strategy toward operations and the development of innovative, risk-taking project teams. Group members had to understand how this inconsistency impacted on how they dealt with each other. At the individual level, Bob needed to understand why his behavior was effective in one setting and ineffective in another. However, since he did burn out, the question is how he can be restored to shining once again. A restorative intervention will be difficult. The angry, hurt feelings of all concerned combined with unacknowledged feelings of guilt and trends in suppressing conflict make successful intervention in this unproductive system of behavior, thoughts, and feelings problematic.

Prevention

Preventing the development of the ambiguity that led to the angry and hostile actions, thoughts, and feelings among operating managers had to be the focus of the preventive intervention. Bob's insensitivity to the difference in culture also contributed to the dynamic which he had to learn to appreciate in order to contribute to preventing his rejection.

Individual Psychological Perspective. The individual psychological perspective informs us that, in Bob's case, his early life experience led to the development of compulsive tendencies on his part—tendencies aimed at obtaining recognition through personal achievement and winning. He learned he was not a good person unless his parents thought so.

Bob's need to be a superachiever to receive approval to permit him to feel good about himself should have been gradually challenged beginning by letting him know he was OK as a person. He needed to learn that he was unconditionally accepted by others and that when he was productive and rewarded, he was not being rewarded to help him prop up his shaky self-esteem. In order for Bob to deal with the compulsive pursuit of approval and admiration, he had to surface what were painful and repressed aspects of his childhood. He had to learn to appreciate the unconscious impact of his childhood upon his thoughts, feelings, and actions in the present.

Interpersonal Perspective. Improving interpersonal relations is important and should be continually pursued. In Bob's case he had compelling needs to take care of those who worked for him while those who frustrated him were seen as bad and contemptible. Had Bob been guided in gaining insights about the motivation of his behavior, he might have more fully appreciated why he was so concerned about his staff and so embittered by others. Those who worked with Bob and rejected him by either attacking him or not coming to his aid could have had their actions and feelings challenged by any one facilitating group process which leads to considering the group dynamics involved in this case.

Group Dynamic Perspective. Group dynamics are the dominant aspect of this case. There were a number of opportunities to prevent what had happened. The group attack might have been halted had either a professional group process consultant or reporter challenged the dynamic by also pointing out, for example, that little work was being accomplished on the agenda or that there was a lot of anger in the group. Had the group members who remained silent had their roles in facilitating the attack brought to their attention, they might have owned their personal responsibility for contributing to the group's actions.

A more proactive intervention might have led to the group members being more adept at relieving individual and group anxieties as an ongoing process thereby avoiding a blowup. They might also have been more appreciative of the group as a whole phenomenon such as the emergence of the angry subgroup and the subsequent inability of the group to deal with the member that was sacrificed. Equally important would have been a much better understanding of the regressive group pressures that first led to locating in Bob the collective problems of the group's members and then to their unconscious collusion to avoid dealing with their guilt feelings later. Another important aspect of understanding group dynamics would have been the examination of the roles performed by group members and, in particular, the important roles of the fight/flight leader.

A better appreciation of the organizational dynamic perspective could have led the group's members to a better appreciation of why they were feeling frustrated and unskilled. The culture of the group involved that of the organization. Confusion and anxiety experienced by many in the organization regarding control versus innovation may have led to the formation of operating groups that were expected to solve problems by not taking risks. The group incorporated the problem of a lack of leadership at the highest levels of the organization.

Restoration

The difficult task of restoring Bob to his former highly productive self is also informed by the levels of knowledge. At the individual psychology level, Bob needs to be aided in becoming more self-reflective. He needs to be encouraged to inspect his behavior and motivations. He needs to be asked why he is so angry and withdrawn. Why is he occasionally so contemptuous of others? Answers to the questions should lead to understanding his painful experience in the group—his negative feelings, his disillusionment, and how these feelings and events have important parallels in his early life experience. He has to learn that these feelings are acceptable but should not be permitted to dominate his life at work.

The interpersonal level directs attention to helping organization members to understand their feelings about Bob and how they currently treat him in a way that encourages him to respond in the way he does. They may learn that they are consciously or unconsciously providing him with provocations to attack them so that they, in a sense and ironically so, control his behavior. They make him react. Compassion and sensitivity are important changes that are needed to help Bob restore good feelings about them and himself. Taking these steps will also have the effect of making the organization's members feel better about themselves and that they can do something constructive to change the cycle's self-defeating interactions.

The group dynamic perspective includes rehabilitative steps such as gaining a better understanding of the group processes that may keep Bob in his sacrificed and angry man roles. Reconciling, nurturing, and welcoming Bob back to active and valued participation in the original group and all other groups he may have dropped out of is important.

The organizational dynamic perspective is not as important in restoration; however, it should be clear that the organization values taking care of its members as people. Everyone, it should be known, counts, and the leadership of the organization is willing to invest in resources and programs to help its employees.

CONCLUSION

This case captures the complexity implicit in working with people. Bob was a potentially exceptional employee who was unconsciously motivated to achieve to receive approval to feel good about himself. The compulsive aspects of Bob's personality motivated him to achieve, and, when he was blocked, he resorted to dysfunctional behavior he had learned as a child. Intervening in the outcome of this case has been shown to involve many levels of consideration. Bob is not the only element of the case creating the dynamics, and he is not the only element that needs to be changed. The next four case examples further underscore the complex aspects of this case.

8

The Supernova

A supernova is the brightest of all star explosions where the outer layers of a star are blown off creating a momentary luminosity as bright as a galaxy and billions of times brighter than our sun.

This case draws upon Karen Horney's perfectionist solution to anxiety. This response involves an individual who relies on nearly perfect standards that others are expected to meet. The perfectionist compensates for inner feelings of worthlessness by imposing standards for life and work that no one else measures up to. Others are just not as good as the holder of the standards. At the same time the perfectionist expends a great deal of energy and time to meet the standards in order to avoid having to acknowledge feelings of failure, inner emptiness, worthlessness, and a lack of control. The perfectionist closely resembles the attributes of the DSM-III-R criteria for the obsessive compulsive personality disorder, in which there exists a pervasive pattern of perfectionism and inflexibility. There is a preoccupation with excessive detail and rules, excessive morality, and causing others to submit to this individual's way of doing things. This personality type is further discussed in Kets de Vries and Miller's *The Neurotic Organization*.

It will be observed in Nora's case she never quite measured up to the expectations of her parents no matter how hard she tried. As a result she continued to strive to master perfection as an adult which permitted her to excel at work but, when blocked, to experience a crisis. Understanding Nora's case permits us to appreciate that part of us that strikes back at others by finding fault.

CASE EXAMPLE

Nora grew up in a difficult family situation. As an only child, all of her parents' attention and ambitions were focused on her. Her mother, who worked, was harsh and generally disapproving. Nora had to act, think, and feel like her mother wanted her to or be punished, sometimes with severe beatings. Her mother frequently told her to shape up.

Nora's father was remote and paid little attention to her or to her relationship with her mother. Her father expected her to achieve perfection at everything she did, and both he and her mother were always available to offer her criticism. As Nora grew older she stayed away from home as much as possible, and she became like a new family member to the families of several friends. Nora was very angry about how she was being treated by her parents, but it was much too dangerous to express her feelings. She occasionally broke things in her room and exhausted herself with play; later, she used work and exercise to burn off her many feelings. She also learned from her parents that when she was feeling bad about herself one thing she could do to relieve her feelings was to cut down somebody else. No one was perfect.

When Nora entered college all she wanted to do was to get married so she would not have to go home or depend on her parents who manipulated her through finances and making her feel guilty. Nora married in her junior year, finished college, and started to work. Nora quickly learned that her new husband would not provide her adequate support nor pay her much attention—not unlike her father. She turned to her work and eventually her children to meet her affiliation needs and to maintain her self-esteem.

Nora was a loyal employee who patiently worked her way up to a responsible managerial role in her institution. Over the years she proved to be an outstanding employee; she was acknowledged several times as the employee of the month in her entry level position. Nora excelled at her work. Her dependability, high standards, and willingness to work long hours to finish important projects perfectly and on time were much admired.

Nora's current position combined important work on major projects with managing a large, complicated computerized information system that was frequently impacted by changes in other areas. She had been a highly visible and much respected member of these projects teams and could always be depended on to hold up her end of the work. Her innovativeness, resourcefulness, and leadership skills earned her much recognition and the admiration of many.

A change in supervisors, however, had a negative impact upon how Nora saw herself and how she felt about her work and the institution. The supervisor was remote and uncommunicative, did poor work, and was generally unrewarding to work with. The supervisor's lack of knowledge about work, indifference about meeting deadlines, and lack of willingness to take the time to do a good job led to a number of major problems with Nora's ability to get her work done, which infuriated her.

Nora felt her track record and reputation were on the line. The supervisor seemed to be unconsciously intent on setting Nora up to fail perhaps unconsciously enjoying seeing Nora become anxious and frustrated. Nora's response to her supervisor was to point out to the supervisor the problems being created. However, this tack did not change the supervisor's attitude or performance. Others were also aware of the problems. As time passed the supervisor's poor performance, unpredictable participation and work attendance, and marginal interpersonal skills became a matter for the public record. Even so, upper management did nothing.

Nora felt betrayed by the organization, frustrated and angry about her ineffective superior's behavior, and concerned about what others were beginning to think about her since she was now less prepared than usual because of the supervisor's withholding of information. Nora was also beginning to feel that her long overdue promotion was being threatened by her supervisor who she suspected was enjoying trying to get even with her distancing and judgmental attitude by criticizing Nora behind her back.

As time passed Nora became more agitated and her feelings more mobilized. She wondered, "What the hell is going on? Doesn't anybody care?" To make things worse, Nora's inability to get her work done to meet her high standards had been compounded because she now had to spend valuable time correcting problems created by her supervisor. These problems and her conflictual relationship with her imperfect supervisor eventually led to a less than glowing evaluation.

Not unexpectedly Nora's attitude and behavior began to change noticeably. Nora began to make herself more visible in the project groups in which she participated. She became very careful about what the supervisor was doing or not doing to avoid being blindsided. She began to volunteer for projects unrelated to her area. Nora said she wanted to work with people who were squared away and were fun and rewarding to work with. She began to look for other positions within the organization to get away from her supervisor.

Nora's inability to meet her own performance criteria, her lack of recognition for her hard work and at times dazzling performance, her lack of promotion, and her friction-filled relationship with her supervisor created a meltdown. Nora did not like her work, and her anger led to an explosion. Nora's compelling needs to achieve, to be able to meet her high standards, to work with others who met her high standards, and to receive public recognition for her efforts were frustrated.

Nora's self-initiated change, however, created confusion about her role, and her performance began to lag across the board. Her tremendous work load, the many meetings she had to attend, her lack of support from her area, and her inability to take work home led to her compromising her performance. Negative feedback and complaints were becoming more common. She began to point out to others who withheld their approval that they, too, were imperfect and, by her standards, poor performers.

Nora's feelings were growing progressively more hurt. She felt depressed, overworked, and underacknowledged. Her hard-earned reputation for perfection, dependability, and excellence was being, she felt, unfairly threatened.

CASE SUMMARY

This superstar, in response to being limited and maligned, exploded. In order to feel appreciated, Nora began to contribute to a number of different areas in her organization. As a result, she spread herself so thin that she could no longer shine at anything she did. At the same time she antagonized her less effective supervisor who, in turn, acted to undermine her performance which reinforced Nora's belief that she went unheard and unappreciated. Nora's supervisor and her peers were also aware that she had become frantic to have herself and her contributions acknowledged. This realization made the supervisor and a small clique that supported the supervisor feel better about themselves and provided them an incentive to continue to limit and ignore her productivity.

Nora was in pain from being cut off from the organization, from others, and from the constructive use of her skills and talents. Her response was to seek recognition from others. Her actions were, however, self-defeating. She, in effect, deskilled herself by spreading herself too thin. This superstar's behavior, when combined with the negative reactions of others, tragically produced an unproductive cycle where no one benefited from her energy. This outcome may be better understood from a number of perspectives.

INDIVIDUAL PSYCHOLOGICAL PERSPECTIVE

Nora's superior abilities and performance have their origins in a childhood where she tried to compensate for not being found to be good enough. No matter how perfect she tried to be, she always seemed to be just a little short of receiving her parents' approval. As a result, Nora became sensitive to what she thought others thought of her and, as an adult, she developed compelling dependencies on others for how she felt about herself.

She also learned, as a child, that, when the approval of others was not forthcoming, it was her fault. Certainly, she thought, her parents could not have been at fault for her poor performance and, as Nora grew up, she seldom ever thought that others were at fault for not accepting her. At an unconscious level, Nora had been hurt by her parents and their unyielding lack of acceptance of her. She harbored deeply felt anger and contempt for them and for anyone who was not considerate of her and appreciative of her abilities. This contempt for others became apparent when she made it clear that, when others did not approve of her, she was prepared to cut them down to size. They did not measure up to her high standards. This was especially true in the case of her supervisor who happened to possess a powerful, authoritative role relative to her—a role not unlike that of her parents.

Those who knew Nora knew that she was motivated by lifelong trends of seeking perfection which were aimed at making her feel better about herself. They also knew that when approval was not forthcoming from others she would unmercifully impose her perfect set of standards upon them. They would be found to be grossly deficient and, therefore, not merit her time and attention.

INTERPERSONAL PERSPECTIVE

Nora needed the approval of others to feel good about herself. As a child, she had learned that she had to be perfect to get approval. She tried to perform outstanding work and to be good to others because that is what she expected of herself. Her standards did not permit her to act any other way. Nora also learned to save face by imposing her perfect standards upon rejecting others to dispose of their lack of support and disapproval. When others were not supportive, they were discounted; otherwise, she would have had to face her inability to be perfect enough to merit their approval. Imposing her standards in this way permitted her a silent victory over them. Nora also felt that if she was good to others they would, according to her standards, be obliged to reciprocate. Those around her learned they had to approve of her or be prepared for Nora's scorching disapproval. Most recently, Nora's life at work was dominated by her relationship with her immediate supervisor who both withheld approval and frustrated Nora's wish to achieve perfection in her work. Nora's predictable response, her disapproval, only served to further alienate her supervisor and polarize a small group of the supervisor's friends against her. Nora began to look elsewhere at work for the attention and approval she desired. But she was faced with the possibility that this effort would fail because she was becoming ineffective, which further frustrated her drive for perfection.

GROUP DYNAMIC PERSPECTIVE

Nora was admired by those with whom she worked. Her meticulous attention to performing outstanding work endeared her to her fellow workers. Nora was known for her eagerness to take on new tasks even when they overburdened her, which eventually led to her not being able to handle all of her responsibilities.

Group as a Whole

The members of the groups in which Nora participated were supportive and approving of her. They had negotiated an implicit agreement with her. She was to perform outstanding work; in return, she was to receive their approval and support. The members of these groups usually accepted Nora's sacrifices, which led her to doing more work than others. There also seemed to be tacit agreement that this outcome would not be discussed; after all, if she did all the work, they did not have to work. Naturally she was encouraged in making these sacrifices by rewards of thanks, gratitude, and praise.

A second important group which also acted as a whole is upper management. Upper management's not so benign neglect of a performance problem led to operating problems. Despite considerable evidence to support the conclusion that something should have been done, no corrective action was taken. This lack of willingness to act leads to considering some of the regressive and unconscious aspects of group dynamics.

Individual and Group Psychological Defenses

Nora experienced individual regression because her best efforts at winning approval were failing. She became irritable, moody, and angry. She did not feel that she was being treated fairly. She felt that others were angry with her (the projection of her angry feelings onto others) and taking it out on her. Nora's strategy of seeking approval from others through perfect performance also led her to rely upon several psychological coping strategies—reaction formation, rationalization, and denial. She reacted to her supervisor by developing a reckless and uncaring attitude. She became openly critical and antagonistic with the supervisor from whom she had hoped for approval. She had to think of herself as deserving of approval, and she rationalized her willingness to make personal sacrifices in the pursuit of the perfection. "Someone has to do the work." At the same time, she had to deny the negative impact that her perfectionism had upon her life and feelings.

The members of groups Nora worked with also had to rationalize their excessive reliance upon her. Perhaps it was thought that overworking her was what she needed to develop her career and potential. Or, it may have been thought that the work load somehow benefited her because she desired it. Instances of occasional but intense and uncomfortable interpersonal conflict between Nora and others were denied, and the conflict was occasionally suppressed. "We need to get back to discussing the problem at hand."

Unconscious Group Process

Unconscious group processes developed around Nora's active role in groups. Group members felt something was expected of them in return for Nora's productivity and friendliness. Group members also felt uncomfortable with what occasionally amounted to dumping on Nora who was, it seemed, always willing to assume ever greater responsibilities. It also became important to suppress knowledge of Nora's growing dysfunctional behavior and the problems she was having with her supervisor.

People in Roles

Nora preferred to see herself in a limited set of interrelated roles: outstanding employee, hard worker, keeper of the performance standards, and good person. She also assumed competitive and vindictive roles when someone got out of line relative to her and her rigid performance expectations. Nora's supervisor assumed the role of a bad, withholding authority figure—not unlike the role of Nora's parents. Others around Nora were expected to assume receiving, admiring, and supportive roles that helped her feel good about herself.

Fight/Flight

Nora found herself in the role of fight leader because she felt she had to do something about others who did not measure up to her standards. Nora's drive for perfection and achievement required removing others who were blocking her pursuits. Nora did not tolerate the presence of flight leaders who might have led the group off task or acknowledged Nora's undiscussable but all-out effort to achieve recognition. Group members had to be appreciative, approving, and admiring of her.

ORGANIZATIONAL DYNAMIC PERSPECTIVE

The organizational dynamic perspective emerges as an important one in understanding Nora's relationship with her supervisor. Despite the existence of clear evidence of the marginal performance of the supervisor, the upper ranks of management tacitly protected this individual. This may have occurred as part of an undiscussable process of trying to protect themselves from the results of having made a poor hiring decision or from having to act to correct the situation which would create feelings of guilt. The message being sent to the lower ranks of the organization was that management was willing to tolerate poor performance. The lack of willingness on top management's part to deal with the supervisor may have also provided a model of behavior that discouraged Nora's colleagues from confronting her over her actions and lagging performance. Intervening in processes and outcomes like these is a challenge for anyone. In this case, top management is the key; it was their actions or lack thereof that created the organizational dynamics.

INTERVENTIONS

Intervening to stop what happened in this case requires developing an appreciation for why Nora became dysfunctional as a result of her conflicted relationship with her supervisor. The ineffective supervisor frustrated Nora's need for approval and her need to achieve perfection in her work. Efforts to prevent the outcome and to restore Nora to her former high levels of performance will share much in common.

Prevention

Preventive measures must focus on the ineffective and counterproductive performance of the supervisor who has, in a sense, driven Nora mad.[1] The supervisor and top management entered into an unconscious conspiracy to not deal with the supervisor's performance problem. Nora also needed to become more aware of why she felt the way she did and how her feelings led her to react in a way that assured the further alienation of the supervisor whose approval was so desirable.

Individual Psychological Perspective. Nora's life experience resulted in her having compelling needs to seek the approval and admiration of others by being perfect. She knew that her rejection was the result of her having failed to do well enough; to be good enough. Her wish to be perfect and to accomplish more work than others should have been challenged. Nora had to learn that she was OK even if all of her work was not perfect or if she did not achieve more than others.

A successful intervention strategy would encourage Nora to be more self-reflective. The gaining of self-knowledge would have made her less compulsive, less rigid, and less willing to pursue self-defeating and self-destructive behavior. At the same time her work performance need not have changed. She could have pursued perfection and high levels of productivity, but not for the purposes of receiving approval.

Nora also needed to learn more about her feelings and her reactions to her unrewarding supervisor. The supervisor unconsciously reminded her of one or both of her parents and possibly of other unsatisfactory relationships experienced as an adult. All of the negative feelings associated with these prior relationships were transferred onto the relationship of the moment filling it with hard to manage intensity.

Interpersonal Perspective. Those who worked with Nora and were her friends had to learn about how they could contribute to her efforts to change. Some may have unconsciously preferred her to stay the way she was and rejected her efforts to change. "You used to be so nice." To be avoided would have been anyone playing the role of an armchair Freud by offering counseling. Others might have unintentionally enabled her to maintain her compelling need to seek approval by approving of her actions, actively soliciting perfection, and, equally important, not disapproving of her self-defeating actions. "After all, she might be crushed." It should have been apparent to those who worked with her that they could be part of the solution or part of the problem.

Nora's supervisor precipitated Nora's immediate crisis. The supervisor presented a difficult problem. Nora's behavior was essentially authorized by those she reported to, since they accepted her performance. Regrettably management was not perfect. Given the circumstances, it was unlikely Nora or anyone else could have changed the situation in the short term. Challenging what was going on would have been foolhardy. As a result, Nora needed to be supported in working through her feelings about how she was being treated and how the supervisor's actions were threatening to her.

One possible productive avenue of pursuit could have involved intervention from the personnel department keyed off by Nora's requests for transfer. Nora's problem, when combined with other information, should have encouraged the leadership of the personnel department to advocate a review of the situation by top management.

Group Dynamic Perspective. Nora was a highly productive member of the groups in which she participated. However, Nora's energy and willingness to do the work led the members of these groups to being pulled into a role of dependency upon her. This unacknowledged, unconscious process, if questioned, could easily have led to Nora's becoming anxious, her role being threatened, and her motivations being questioned. Group members could also have been expected to become anxious; their actions and motivations would be called into question. There are, therefore, many reasons why confronting group-as-a-whole dynamics would have been a challenging intervention to undertake.

An intervention could have been expected to key off anxiety and regressive individual and group trends aimed at minimizing or defending against the anxiety. A fight leader might also have arisen to lead efforts to rationalize and deny what was going on. Nora, the interventionist, or some group members might also have been singled out for blame for creating an intolerable anxiety-filled situation. Had this occurred, Nora might have wished to assume all the blame and lead the group in flight from its responsibilities. Drawing the group members' attention to these trends would have limited their development, although they may have surfaced again without warning. Members of the group had to become more aware of some of the unconscious group trends. The leaders of the organization should have made sure that those most in touch with personnel problems had an opportunity to openly communicate their insights and information to an appropriately high organizational level. The organization's leadership should have encouraged this communication even though it was threatening to all concerned.

Restoration

Nora has reached the point where her excessive needs to receive approval, which have been aggravated by her unrewarding and interpersonally punishing relationship with her supervisor, have reached dysfunctional proportions. She is no longer productive, and she has begun to be seen as a problem by others. Restoring Nora to her previous level of functioning can be approached from two perspectives: The situation can be changed, or Nora can change. Both of these avenues of pursuit are demanding interventions. If the situation is to be changed, who shall act as the catalyst since normal channels have failed? Unless the organization has created the formal or informal means of communicating the problem high enough up in the organization to key off change, upper management's intransigence to change what is going on relative to the supervisor's performance may not be challenged. Situations can go on like this indefinitely.

An alternate avenue of pursuit is for an expendable consultant to intervene. Top management must also be sensitive in its response when problems are identified and brought to their attention. For example, an immediate, heated, and condemning confrontation with the upper levels of management of Nora's department, which questions their lack of corrective action and makes them feel defensive, may motivate them to make changes but also may motivate them to suppress conflict and to discourage employees from discussing their problems with human resource managers. In order for change to be effective, defensive and anxiety-ridden encounters should be avoided.

Nora and others are also contributors to the current problem and must become part of the solution. Nora might benefit from an employee assistance professional's attention and perhaps a referral for appropriate counseling. Nora must become more aware of those powerful but unconscious motivations that compel her to seek approval by being perfect.

Those who work with Nora must become more aware of Nora's dysfunctional behavioral tendencies so that they can avoid reinforcing Nora by encouraging her blind pursuit of perfection. The same type of intervention must be made in the groups with which she works. Individuals and groups are unwittingly acting to keep Nora in her role of achieving perfection by rewarding her behavior. Attention must be directed to accepting Nora first and her productivity second.

CONCLUSION

This case is a second illustration of how a mix of unconscious motivations arising from early life experiences can impact the workplace. Nora's compelling needs for perfection almost certainly contributed to the outcome. The problem of the supervisor, one no doubt played out countless times in organizations, can be understood by using all the perspectives used in this chapter to understand Nora's situation. The supervisor may have been dependent upon alcohol or drugs or may have suffered from a narcissistic personality deficit that made being liked and sociable much more important than performing work. Nora's efforts to hold the supervisor's "feet to the fire" would have only reinforced these trends.

Top management's lack of response may also be understood by using the same perspective. Top management may have been in flight from feeling guilty about acting powerfully and hurting the supervisor's feelings. "After all, they certainly would feel hurt if they were treated the same way." In this case, it seems more important that they feel good about themselves than that they have to deal with a progressive discipline problem to improve performance.

9

The Black Hole

A black hole is the remains of a massive star that has collapsed so much that its gravitation is so powerful that escape velocity from its surface exceeds the speed of light and nothing, not even light, can escape.

This case draws upon Karen Horney's resigned solution to anxiety. This response originates from being unable, on the one hand, to reconcile feelings of being powerful and assertive and, on the other hand, feelings of being passive and dependent. The tension between these two modes of thinking, feeling, and action cannot be resolved, and the individual gives up by withdrawing from active social life. Others are seen as invasive and coercive influences who provoke the need to either fight back or give up, both of which are to be avoided. By retreating from interaction, this individual minimizes anxiety. This response resembles the DSM-III-R schizoid personality disorder in which a pervasive pattern of indifference to social relationships develops along with restricted emotions. This DSM-III-R category is also used in Kets de Vries and Miller's *The Neurotic Organization*.[1]

In this case, Sally learns as a child to fit in and to keep a low profile. As an adult she continues to respond to stressful situations by withdrawing from sight and dropping out. Understanding Sally's case permits us to appreciate that a part in all of us sometimes would just like to be left alone.

CASE EXAMPLE

Sally was a foster child who was abandoned by her mother when her father disappeared. Sally was easy to place with several sets of foster parents who invariably found her to be a model child. Sally always seemed to fit in easily. When she was finally adopted at the age of six, she was thankful. Her new parents, however, proved to be dominating and unaffectionate. She once again used her now perfected skills of adaptation to fit into her new family with her older brother. Sally was very bright, always attentive to what was going on, invariably willing to adjust her attitude and to change her expectations and behavior. She was determined to fit in. Sally did not form a strong bond with her parents or her older brother who, she learned, was also adopted. Sally was content to play out a role to sustain family membership. Sally feared being abandoned, and she hated how she had been treated. She also feared being powerless, and she abhorred others who acted powerfully relative to her and rejected acting powerfully herself to avoid making others feel powerless.

Sally was one of those little known honor students in high school. She excelled at her studies, but she did not participate in extracurricular activities even though she was encouraged to do so by some of her friends. Sally did not go to college. Her parents did not encourage her to go and, as usual, she was indifferent toward the opportunity. Sally finally enrolled in a two-year secretarial program at a local community college which she completed in three years while she worked evenings as a waitress and a drugstore clerk. Sally needed to work because she moved out of her parents' home after graduating from high school. Some of her friends thought it was strange she did not see much of her parents, but she seldom visited or called. Sally's few friends found her difficult to coax into doing things together and she seldom dated. Although Sally did not seem depressed, she was listless and indifferent toward others. Nonetheless she was an exceptional student and a highly productive worker who invariably set the standard at whatever was assigned.

When Sally finished her career training she had a number of job opportunities because of her outstanding scholastic performance. She became a valuable secretary to a major executive of a large manufacturing company. She seldom made mistakes and was always attentive to every need. However, during her three years in the position, she remained remote and expressed little interest in moving ahead in her career. Her indifference changed when a friend took an active interest in her and located for her an office manager position. Sally began to shine, and she distinguished herself as an effective supervisor and administrator. The manager she reported to permitted her a great deal of flexibility and autonomy but was always available for support and coaching. She transformed a poorly functioning area into an area that set performance records. As a result, Sally was encouraged to assume more responsibilities by taking in under her wing other problem areas. She ended up with substantial responsibilities, and a major promotion acknowledged her success. Sally's detached and indifferent attitude gradually disappeared, although she still tended to be a loner.

The merger of her company with a much larger conglomerate led to some major changes for Sally. She was reassigned to a department that she knew little about and did not like. She was expected to straighten out massive operating problems keyed off by an ill-conceived and surreptitious reduction in staff, overlaid by a redistribution of work that increased the total work to be accomplished. Her large staff was demoralized, and Sally received little support from anyone. It was "sink or swim." Try as she might, she could not halt the deterioration. She could not improve staff morale or garner more resources. Demands were frequently handed down from on high for work that could not be accomplished, and deadlines were set that could not be met. She resented the demands and the top-down micromanagement and interventions into her areas. Those running the company seemed to make a lot of unnecessary mistakes. She gradually became more attentive to defending herself and her workers from the uncaring and at times hostile operating environment that evolved. She began to feel that she just wanted to be left alone to get her work done.

Sally gradually disappeared. She slowly retreated from active participation. On the one hand, she felt she could do little about the situation; on the other hand, her employment was not being threatened although her raises were suffering. She made sure things did not fall apart, but she gave up trying to improve them. She volunteered for fewer projects and produced less overall work. She did make sure her staff received her attention, but she felt there was little she could do to help them. They did not like their work, and there was nothing she could do to change it. Her participation in meetings fell off to near zero, and she developed few requests or recommendations. Sally essentially dropped out and withdrew from participation in her organization. In its place she began an extensive exercise program that helped her cope with her angry feelings.

CASE SUMMARY

Sally's response to being rejected was to implode. After shining brightly this superstar was undermined, disregarded, and cut off from using her abilities. The change in ownership, management style, mission, values, supervision, and her position alienated her. Sally was resentful of the sudden loss of visibility, approval, and the affection of others. These feelings were further aggravated by the realization that the change very likely came about as a result of other less competent but more numerous and powerful others. As a result, she felt her highly effective contributions had been crushed. Rather than contest what happened, however, she took a familiar path and withdrew from active participation. It was too painful for her to try to continue to work as she had, and she began to fantasize about leaving the organization. Supervisors and peers did not question her withdrawal. Some were thankful because they could avoid the risk of being outshined. No one took the time to take an interest in her. So long as she was able to get most of her job done, who cared how she felt; everybody was under phenomenal pressure. She eventually made it clear that she wanted to be left alone. She was willing to abandon her good feelings, her abilities, and her career pursuits to avoid painful and coercive interactions with more powerful members of her organization. Occasional efforts on her part to try to make contributions came to be seen to be out of role for her, and she was ignored. She began to look to other pursuits, friends, and recreation as outlets for her creative energy and for positive reinforcement.

INDIVIDUAL PSYCHOLOGICAL PERSPECTIVE

Sally's early life experience is the key to how she reacted to her new situation. Sally's parents dominated her which she felt was unfair. She had been coerced into conforming. Her parents had controlled most of her activities, and she had been expected to make A's in school. Sally felt oppressed by her powerful parents but also guilty about resenting their control. Sally learned to hate power and being controlled, but she also learned to feel uncomfortable with feeling powerful enough to assert herself against the control. She learned that, if she did as little as possible and fit in, she might not be exposed to these two sets of powerful but conflicting feelings.

Sally's parents were also remote from her. They seldom did things with her, seldom celebrated her successes, seldom cared for her when her feelings were hurt or when she had problems. They seldom encouraged her to do anything on her own. At the same time, it was clear that Sally was expected to love and respect her parents. After all, they were making many sacrifices for her.

These early life influences were gradually reversed at work when two caring individuals took a real interest in her and what she could accomplish if given the chance. However, the change in the company's ownership keyed off many negative feelings for Sally when she was placed back into an organizational setting not unlike that of her childhood. She was once again expected to conform and perform with little if any attention to her needs. Her angry feelings about being treated like this, fuelled at an unconscious level by her feelings for her parents, led her, predictably, to withdraw and close off her feelings rather than to fight back. Since she unconsciously abhorred acting powerfully, as her parents had, and since she detested being helpless and controlled, she withdrew to not dealing with these issues at all. If everyone left her alone, there would be no problem. Rather than feeling defeated and dominated she began to look elsewhere for satisfaction. Withdrawal from active living had been her silent protest to how she was treated by her parents. Her response was predictable.

INTERPERSONAL PSYCHOLOGICAL PERSPECTIVE

The interpersonal world is an important one for Sally. The two people in her life who were helpful to her and who sincerely cared about her turned her around. She came out of her shell and began to live life and enjoy her abilities and to work to her fullest—a testament to the resilience of people. Her supervisory talents were based on a firm understanding of the delicate balance between control and coercion, between being used and being cared for, and between being nurtured and being oppressed. Her keen intelligence, highly developed interpersonal sensitivities, and industriousness made her a fine role model for others to emulate.

Regrettably, Sally's interpersonal world came crashing down when her role was reorganized by new management. Sally lost everything she had worked for including her much needed interpersonal support. Sally experienced her new job and her new treatment much like her lifelong encounter with her parents, and it was natural that she responded by withdrawing from others the way she had learned to do as a child.

GROUP DYNAMIC PERSPECTIVE

The group dynamic perspective is of lesser importance in understanding Sally. Her participation in groups at work was effective, although she was not a person who particularly enjoyed interacting with other people. She maintained a discreet psychological distance from the members of the groups in which she participated. She was always watchful for group actions that might lead to her being used or rejected. She was a silent member, but she could be an effective representative of her areas when appropriate.

Group as a Whole

Sally's case has some elements that can be understood from the group-as-a-whole perspective. Her fellow workers were a large informal group. Everyone in this group was willing to leave Sally alone. No one was willing to make the personal investment to challenge her loner attitude. No one was willing to take the time to engage her until her friend and her second supervisor intervened to help her. The members of the groups in which she participated seldom tried to draw her out, and she was rarely asked to take on group tasks although her distant attitude occasionally attracted the negative attention of some group members.

Individual and Group Psychological Defenses

The change in ownership keyed off regressive individual and group processes. Members of the organization felt invaded and set upon by a larger, more powerful external entity. They did not know how to respond. Many members, like Sally, were reorganized without any consultation or consideration of their interests, abilities, or ambitions. Their angry, helpless, and alienated feelings were shared by many and created a pervasive need to deny or rationalize what was happening to them. Bad, malevolent feelings were often split off and projected onto the executives of the new parent company. A great deal of energy was consumed in sublimating anger into passive aggressive activities, such as resistance to change, unconscious undermining of work, and occasionally into work to sustain the organization and individual employment.

Unconscious Group Process

The members of the original organization shared many unconscious fantasies of rejecting the takeover company and of defeating or killing off their personnel. Many talked about the good old times, about taking vacations and recreational activities in an unconscious act of escape from the unrewarding situation. Undiscussable, shared images of being attacked and violated existed alongside needs to be taken care of and nurtured by perfect, loving parents.

Members of the executive group from the takeover company also shared an active unconscious life. Their shared fantasy world was one of taking control, dominating the members of the existing organization, and whipping them into shape. At a deeper level, they felt shame and guilt as they understood that they were there to provide financial nurturance to the parent company by stripping off assets and draining the employees and the reputation of the company to maximize short-term profits.

The regrettable part of all of these unconscious thoughts and feelings is that they formed the basis for most of the interpersonal interactions. Hostility, resentment, aggression, alienation, perverse power and dominance motives, and suspicion and paranoid thoughts could not be brought out into the open to be discussed. After a while most organization members understood that it was much too dangerous to tap into this Pandora's box.

People in Roles

The role perspective contributes to understanding Sally's situation. Sally abhorred roles associated with power and dominance. She also abhorred roles associated with being weak, submissive, and vulnerable. These two role sets are the opposite ends of a continuum from which Sally could find no peace of mind. Her solution was to assume another role—that of dropout. She gave up trying to deal with the issues of the continuum. She assumed the role of a loner who avoided as much as possible other people who made the continuum an issue. Others always seemed to have roles containing the threat of being coercive and dominant.

Others interacted with Sally by assuming and assigning roles. Many around Sally understood that their role was to leave her alone. They had to be careful that when they interacted with her they did not make her feel they were trying to control or dominate her. Others rejected this role preferring to ignore her and to avoid interacting with her. Sally's few friends and her supervisor, who had encouraged her to use her abilities, were able to assume or, more important, earn roles of trusted and respected others who had taken the caring and nurturing roles that Sally had always fantasized about.

Sally was also assigned roles by others depending upon how they felt about her and their interaction with her. Some experienced her loner role as rejecting and unfriendly. They attributed to her the additional role of being aloof and acting as though she felt she was above them. Others attributed to her the roles of social isolate, silent member, and the frail or weak member who could not take direct confrontation.

Fight/Flight

Fight and flight issues are important contributors to understanding Sally and her work life. Sally was in flight from herself and her problems related to dominance and submission. Sally was in flight from others including her parents.

The organizational setting and the change in ownership created pronounced tendencies for organization members to fight back against the invaders or to flee from them. The executive group of the takeover company were mobilized to fight and located in the members of the organization all their problems for not achieving more profit.

ORGANIZATIONAL DYNAMIC PERSPECTIVE

A dominant aspect of the case is the organizational perspective. The ownership and leadership of Sally's organization changed. Just when she was beginning to achieve her potential, she was reassigned and left to "swing in the wind" by the invading executive group. The members of Sally's company rapidly developed angry, hurt, and paranoid feelings about the change in ownership and what it meant for themselves and "their" company. The change created an organizational operating environment that was hostile and uncooperative. Resistance was met with force. Some were fired, others left. The immovable object was crumbling in the face of an irresistible force. Having reached a situation like this, the idea of having avoided it or changing it seems remote.

INTERVENTIONS

Intervention strategies to prevent the implosion or to get Sally back to shining are both obvious and problematic. However, preventing what happened in the case of the not so friendly takeover might not be possible. If the actions of the executives of the parent company were not aimed at making the organization effective over the long run, the outcome of the case was irresistible. Sally might have been able to maintain good self-feelings if she had been able to distance herself from her loss of support and from the negative feelings arising from the depersonalization and alienation that were essentially imposed upon her.

Restoring her to her former brilliance is also unlikely if the values of the new management and the resulting organizational culture are not aimed at investing in its people. Sally could, conceivably, live out the rest of her work life in this burned-out, lifeless state.

Prevention

Sally could have taken self-imposed steps to protect herself if she had had enough self-reflective skills and a firm enough sense of self to establish and maintain the needed self-other boundaries. Preventive measures must focus on the predatory culture of the parent organization which was imported intact across organizational boundaries. Organizational development efforts aimed at enabling employees to cope with the new stress will not be effective. The source of the stress is not being acted on directly because most employees will understand that it is too dangerous to challenge what is going on to make work life better.

Individual Psychological Perspective. This perspective tells us that Sally entered the new situation with a pervasive life experience of resolving her internal personal conflicts with power and dominance on the one hand, and with submission and powerlessness on the other hand, by withdrawing from an active thinking and feeling life. When she began to discover the parts of herself that had been lost, such as her talents in leading others and organizing work, her analytical skills, and her ability to take charge, she began to shine. This, however, occurred only because of the support of others, and, regrettably, she did not establish a firm enough sense of self and adequate self-esteem to resist the negative influences of the change. The depersonalization she experienced flooded across her boundary with the rest of the world. Preventing this outcome for Sally would have required her to gain more self-reflective skills, more knowledge of the impact of her early life experience on her thoughts and feelings, and a greater willingness to stand her ground without feeling flooded by feelings of acting dominantly. Much of this work could have been facilitated by counseling and therapy.

Interpersonal Perspective. Sally was a loner who preferred to avoid interactions with others whom she experienced as trying to control and use her. Rather than resist these tendencies in others, she preferred to avoid them. The one time she did receive support, she discovered that she was a capable person who could exercise authority without feeling bad or guilty. However, as soon as she was confronted with the results of the takeover, her ability to regulate her feelings and interpersonal boundaries collapsed. Avoiding this outcome, as mentioned, would have required greater attention to the needs, aspirations, and feelings of the employees of the company. The finance-related mentality of the buy-out company made numbers more important than people, with predictable results.

Others around Sally and her friends could have played a more active role in challenging her interactions with them. They might have called into question Sally's tendency to always think that they were out to get something and that their attention to her was always invasive and coercive. Their "tough love" could have helped.

Group Dynamic Perspective. Groups contributed to Sally's situation. Group-as-a-whole dynamics permitted and possibly encouraged Sally to not take an active role. Leaders and group process facilitators might have tried to deal with her lower than expected or desirable participation. However, they might also have observed that she did contribute when one of her areas of responsibility was under discussion. The group unwittingly acted to assign a role to Sally, one of low participation, to enable other, more active members more "air time" and opportunities to distinguish themselves.

The critical aspects of this case are the organizational values and culture of the parent organization that took over Sally's company. It did not take Sally and others long to deduce from the actions of the new executives that there was a new unannounced and undiscussable hidden agenda implied by their presence in the organization. The predatory nature of the acquisition and subsequent imposition of a new set of corporate values and culture stunned many of the employees. Prevention of this outcome implies looking even further up the "food chain" to the values and goals of the highest levels of the executives of the parent company. Perhaps they are driven by personal greed, unrequited search for fame and wealth, and power and domination over others in an effort to compensate for narcissistic deficits they likewise developed from childhood on. Perhaps their education was also at fault. They had learned that the price/earnings ratio was all that mattered.

Restoration

Getting Sally to shine again might involve only restoring to her sufficient support and control over her work. She has demonstrated that she is resilient. Her strategy of retreat may have protected her sufficiently to permit her to shine again without her carrying forward resentment and feelings of paranoia and vindictiveness. She should be encouraged to examine what happened to her— the feelings that she experienced and how her feelings, the events, and her reaction to them are a part of a consistent system of coping responses that originated in her childhood. She could be assisted in this work by a friend who is willing to assume some risk in confronting her over her thoughts, feelings, and actions or by therapy.

The group level of analysis indicates that it would be important for group members to pay attention to her feelings of abandonment and alienation while reaching out to her to let her know that she is not alone in her feelings. She needs to know that others feel the same way and have just as hard a time coping with them as she. Admissions such as these draw people together, minimize interpersonal defenses, and permit them to act collectively against the adverse trends at work.

The organizational level will require a change in values and culture before Sally will probably be able to return to her former star status. The organizational environment must be turned around to permit members and management of the organization to feel good about themselves, each other, their work, and their organization. Regrettably, when the game is one of buying and selling companies, the people who staff them are bought and sold as well. When only numbers are important, people become depersonalized and are also treated like numbers. Perhaps the change in these values must begin in the business culture.

CONCLUSION

This case may be all too familiar to anyone who has been through a change in the ownership of his or her organization or through a major change in leadership. Sally's unique life experience and personality, when combined with the insensitivities of the takeover, created hurt and confused feelings and a return to her retreat from actively dealing with the conflictual aspects of interpersonal and workplace relationships. Sally is stuck in a situation where her response to others is unproductive for the organization and, more important, for herself. Sally may, as a last resort, need to find a new job, something she may not have the wherewithal to undertake in her burned-out condition. This case also points out the inherent unfairness of expecting employees to make all the adjustments. Even if they can cope with their anxieties, anger, and alienation, it does not make it right; their energy is consumed in coping rather than in making a contribution to work.

10

The Red Giant

A red giant is the coolest of stars. It has most of its mass in its core which is surrounded by an extremely large envelope of gas that permits it to achieve great brightness.

This case draws upon Karen Horney's narcissistic solution to anxiety. This response comes from one who wishes to be admired and loved by others. This individual is not engrossed in self-love, but is highly dependent upon others for good self-feelings. This individual will do whatever is necessary to obtain these much needed feelings from others including changing self and manipulating organizational resources. This response resembles the DSM-III-R histrionic personality disorder in which there exists a pervasive pattern of excessive emotionality and attention seeking which may include preoccupation with appearance, seductiveness, and a ready befriending of others. This response is discussed in Kets de Vries and Miller's *The Neurotic Organization* as the dramatic type.

James, throughout his life, was always hungry for the love and approval of others to reassure him that he was, in fact, loveable; something his parents left him wondering about. His wish to be the center of a support group eventually became the dominant influence in his work life and led him to change his behavior at work. Understanding James' case helps us appreciate that part in all of us that wants to be the center of attention and feel loved and admired.

CASE EXAMPLE

James was outstanding at everything he did. He was a superior athlete in high school and captain of the football team. A popular student, he had run for president of the student council. He possessed disarming intelligence and good analytical skills. James was also intensely interested in his friends. He found them fulfilling, and he enjoyed receiving their attention, affection, and admiration.

James' family was a large one and both of his parents worked. As a middle child he did not get enough attention. No matter what he did, his parents always seemed to say more good things about and do more things with his older and younger brothers and sisters. Despite trying hard and achieving a great deal, he never seemed to be able to access the attention he felt he deserved from his parents. Worse yet his efforts made his fellow siblings competitive toward him. He felt angry about feeling cut off from the warm affectionate relationships he saw others receiving.

As a result, James' many successes in school and a large network of friends did not appease his need for attention. James expended much time and energy ensuring that his friends and the girls he dated were always around him. He was willing to extend himself to bond them to him.

James earned a scholarship to a top-flight business school and a place on the university's football team. He was just as successful in college as he had been in high school. He was the center of a large network of friends and he was popular with the girls. James' high grades, good interpersonal skills, and high energy level enabled him to be recruited to a fast-track executive development program in a large national corporation. He was off to a great start with his career.

James quickly distinguished himself in his first position. After three years he had assumed greater responsibility and had achieved several attention-getting successes. James, it always seemed, was able to come up with the big ideas, and he was usually able to get those around him to help him get them off the ground. He was the focus of a large and active social network, and he had become engaged. His outstanding work was acknowledged by his admission to the second phase of the fast-track executive development program. This acceptance prompted James and his fiancée to get married.

The fast-track program called for James to rotate to a number of areas in the company to ''learn the ropes.'' He was to be exposed to much of the company and its subsidiaries and to have an opportunity to work with and learn from many of its best managers. James reported to work from his honeymoon in a new state to work for a major subsidiary.

James became immediately uncomfortable in his new position. His superior was remote, hard to access, and hard to connect to on a person-to-person basis. In fact, as time passed, the relationship proved to be consistently unrewarding. The supervisor could not be coached into liking James or approving of his best efforts. At the same time, many of those James worked with were similar to his boss. They were hard to get to know and hard to befriend. James also discovered a subgroup of managers who were highly competitive and tried to take advantage of everyone and every opportunity to advance their own points of view and careers. To confound his feelings of isolation, James was shuttled for weeks at a time between the main office and a plant.

James was exposed to a great deal of information and he learned a lot about the subsidiary, but he was precluded from developing his all important network of friends. As a result, his need to receive the love, admiration, and approval of others was frustrated. He brought his unmet needs home and hopelessly overwhelmed his new wife. She quickly learned that, no matter how hard she tried, she could not meet all of James' needs. He was inconsolable, and he held her accountable.

James had a bout with drinking and engaged in several extramarital affairs before he was transferred to a new subsidiary a thousand miles away. James felt the transfer was a new opportunity to fit in better and, of course, he was still advancing his career. This move permitted him gradually to build up a small group of friends who were lost in his next reassignment. James continued to move about within the company for a number of years. He was seldom able to develop his much needed network of friends. His wife eventually left him. He became a social drinker and an occasional recreational drug user. However, he was successful at work; he had an unerring quality of coming up with the big ideas even though he also developed a track record of having problems implementing them. His follow-through and attention to detail were not adequate. His leadership style evolved to being one of delegating many of the details while demanding the attention, loyalty, and devotion of those who worked with him.

James was eventually recalled to the corporate headquarters and given a promotion to assistant vice-president. This promotion was the recognition he had so desperately sought, and he was back among many of those who had been his good friends years ago. His career was solidly on track, and he soon married an old friend who had recently divorced. Children quickly followed. Over the next five years, James' leadership style gelled. In his new role he was in head-to-head competition with his peers for the few higher level positions. Promotions were slower and harder to get. James was initially successful in his new role. His superior skills and abilities, his talent in selling people on his ideas, and his highly energetic work habits all combined to make him a highly visible contributor in meetings and developer of new methods and programs. As a result, he became the focus of the competitive urges of his colleagues who lined up coalitions of higher level executives to limit him. James began to discover that many of his ideas were being picked up by several of the senior vice-presidents who then handed them back down to some of their protégés.

James was silently infuriated when he began to receive less approval and recognition for his work. There did not seem to be anything he could do to stop it. No matter how good his ideas were, many were stripped off for others to develop. Meanwhile, he was becoming socially isolated—something that made him most uncomfortable.

One day in a meeting, James had an idea. This time, his spontaneous response to having the idea was to find a way to draw the idea from one of his colleagues who had said something that had keyed off the idea. He was successful at this attempt, and his colleague felt great about the idea he seemed to have had without realizing it. James was made to feel good by everyone in the group for having helped his colleague with his new idea. Everyone was happy including James.

James began to work consistently with others in this way. He was admired for it, and his circle of friends grew. This style also fit well with his tendency to delegate many of the details and problems of acting on his ideas to others. There was, however, tension around this method. Others knew it was James who had the ideas and that James was essentially manipulating group members into believing it was they who had the ideas. James also occasionally became frustrated when an idea was not being adequately developed. When this occurred, it made for tortuous meetings where James had to pull from others the next steps in the process. However, eventually everyone came to accept the process and James was happy with it because he could continue to think up the big ideas without having to become the focal point for interpersonal rivalry.

CASE SUMMARY

This superstar has learned to avoid being limited and rejected by letting others bask in his glow. James created situations where others received recognition for his ideas and work. This contrived altruism, however, might not burn forever. There was an underlying instability that threatened the balance of interpersonal relationships. Although conflict and negation by others was avoided, everyone knew what was going on. James' abilities were clearly visible, and his efforts to have others benefit were resentfully appreciated by others. The style can be sustained only as long as no one challenges the obvious manipulation of credit for his productivity. This solution to being rejected and limited may collapse at any time.

INDIVIDUAL PSYCHOLOGICAL PERSPECTIVE

James developed his high level of skills to please his parents to get their attention. He later used them to advance his career. He was also familiar with others (his siblings) becoming competitive toward him and acting to cut him off from receiving attention. James did not appreciate that he relied upon his abilities to obtain the affiliation, approval, admiration, and love of others as a substitute for having not received them from his parents and family. James learned to cope with the lack of parental nurturing and affection by replacing it with that of others. James needed to be recognized and admired. He was not always consciously aware that he was willing to do whatever was necessary to receive these scarce commodities. It is also clear that, when he failed to garner the admiration and attention of others, he experienced a collapse of his self-esteem. His anger toward others and toward himself for having failed to control them was then turned inward to create depression and self-defeating and interpersonally destructive behavior.

INTERPERSONAL PSYCHOLOGICAL PERSPECTIVE

James' interpersonal world was most important to him. He was intent upon getting others to like and admire him by outpourings of hard work, brilliant thinking, helping others, and constant attention to trying to control what others were thinking and feeling about him. Those around James did not always understand what his motivations were. At times he seemed happy and at other times inconsolable. His friends did not appreciate how dependent James was upon their feelings toward him as to how good he felt about himself. In particular it was not clear to his friends why he had begun his strategy of helping everyone else at work to shine—a strategy which seemed to be self-defeating. However, his strategy did not threaten them, and his efforts provided him with long sought after approval and admiration. Not appreciated at the time by him or others was the smoldering contempt he held for himself and at times for the others who always risked creating instability in this effective but fragile interpersonal solution to anxiety.

GROUP DYNAMIC PERSPECTIVE

Groups also are an important part of James' life. He enjoyed being social, and his good interpersonal skills made him a highly visible group member. His productivity and leadership were major contributions to groups, and he enjoyed the many opportunities groups provided him to gain recognition.

Group as a Whole

This perspective sheds light on how the members of the groups James participated in responded to him. James needed the approval of others, and most group members implicitly understood that they could depend on him to get the job done. James' strategy of allowing others to glow in his light was a process that had, without discussion, been accepted by all concerned. Group members acted as a whole to accept this process so that they could feel good about themselves and avoid being outshined by James.

Individual and Group Psychological Defenses

Early in James' career he was unable to build up a group of friends to supply him the affiliation, approval, and admiration he needed. As his first wife discovered, without friends he was unable to compensate for his inner emptiness and his feelings of worthlessness associated with his low self-esteem. This led to the eventual disintegration of his first marriage when he located the source of his bad self-feelings in his wife. He also tried to anesthetize his pain by using alcohol and drugs, and he rationalized his pursuit of attention by understanding that he was doing productive work. He also turned inward the anger he held for his work and others just as he had done toward his parents, his brothers and sisters, and others who had rejected him. The members of groups James belonged to also had to deal with their relationships with him. They had to rationalize accepting James' efforts to win approval through hard work and making them shine. They also defended against the knowledge James was, at times, inwardly contemptuous of them by denial and rationalization. After all, weren't they "laughing all the way to the bank"?

Unconscious Group Process

Unconscious group processes in this case closely parallel individual and group psychological defenses. Groups in which James was a member had to dispose of what amounted to his arrogant contempt for them and, to a lesser extent, his manipulative and guilt imparting self-sacrificial approach to interacting with others. No one discussed James' behavior with him. No one challenged the group dynamics he established.

Unconscious group processes had to be at work to deal with the highly competitive interpersonal environment as many executives tried to "claw their way to the top." Everyone involved had to avoid the knowledge that many times their actions were oriented toward self-aggrandizement and were not for the good of the company. The processes that led to these outcomes were not open to discussion.

People in Roles

James needed to find himself in roles where he could distinguish himself and receive attention and approval. These roles often included leader, innovator, strategist, friend and confidant, and in the end, altruist. James also occasionally found himself in the roles of the rejected member and the victimized member, which he associated with his early life experiences. Those around James found themselves in receiving roles as James was intent upon providing everyone with something to earn their affection and admiration. Others knew that it was their role to make James feel good about himself by being his friends, supporters, and mentors.

Fight/Flight

James was a good fighter. He had been fighting for attention all of his life. He was willing to deal with others who blocked him from getting what he wanted; however, he preferred to deal with them by taking covert and socially accepted actions. His strategy of letting everyone share the products of his abilities was a way of fighting back. At the same time, he was also able to see himself as better than others, but he avoided becoming the focus of their destructive envy and competition. James was also in unconscious flight from his repressed feelings of rage and hurt over his childhood. James did not like flight leaders who led others away from him, his ideas, and the work. Flight leaders also periodically emerged to stifle conflict and dissent over James' actions to maintain the delicate balance that had been struck.

ORGANIZATIONAL DYNAMIC PERSPECTIVE

This large, complex organization did not offer much support to its executives and employees other than to provide them with recognition for succeeding. James and others like himself were expected to make do as they were transferred from plant to plant. In the corporate headquarters there was little room for collaboration. Among the upper ranks, interpersonal competition was the norm as the struggle to get ahead became the focus. This setting contributed to James' situation when he found it necessary to avoid threatening and alienating his peers to maintain their friendship.

INTERVENTIONS

Avoiding the outcome of this case involves reconsidering the nature of the organization's culture: the strategy for developing its executives and the creation of competition for promotion. Successfully intervening to restore James to full ownership of his abilities is problematic. Both James and the other group members have worked out a set of relationships that permit them to function effectively and to maintain the illusion that everyone is happy. Not being dealt with, however, is James' self-defeating behavior, suppressed anger, and contempt; the feelings of group members of being manipulated; and the underlying instability created by the combination of all of these undiscussable factors.

Prevention

Preventive measures must focus on James' learning more about his unconscious motivations and his compelling needs for admiration and approval from others. Those who work with him must learn more about why they react competitively toward James, the effect of their competitive responses upon him, and their acceptance of James' excessively altruistic approach to them.

Individual Psychological Perspective. James was unconsciously preoccupied with receiving the attention of others either through personal achievement or through friendships. When he was unable to gain attention, he experienced its absence as painful, and he unwittingly resorted to self-defeating acts. His actions were not disruptive at work although they contained elements of manipulation and implicit contempt for others. James' strategy worked, and it created the desired good feelings toward him. He was willing to risk career advancement to obtain these good feelings.

An intervention would require examining James' unconscious motivations that compelled him to seek the attention, approval, admiration, and love of others. He would have to be encouraged to examine his prior life experience for the roots of his deeply felt narcissistic deprivation and how trying to fill this void had become his unacknowledged quest—one that he had to pursue at even great personal cost.

Interpersonal Perspective. Those who worked with James and his friends knew him to be a highly competent and creative person who was eager to do good work but who was also preoccupied with receiving acknowledgement for his work and the approval of all those around him. Any wavering on the part of anyone attracted his attention and unsettled him. As a result everyone who worked with James learned to be attentive to him. Usually no one questioned his actions for fear of causing him distress. James' compelling needs reduced others to supporting him. His friends and colleagues enabled him to avoid dealing with the source of his compelling interpersonal needs. Preventive measures would have had to surface these undiscussable tacit agreements which could be expected to make everyone anxious. Anyone trying to facilitate or lead these efforts could have expected considerable individual and group resistance. After all, change in this case would have seemed like "rocking the boat."

James' strategy was not counterproductive for his organization; however, it ultimately continued his self-impoverishment. Interventions focused at encouraging James to reown his abilities would have involved encouraging others to confront the sources of James' fears in their adverse reactions to his productivity and many ideas. So long as they became anxious, defensive, envious, and competitive, James would have had to continue to avoid alienating those he so desperately wanted to be connected to by getting rid of that part of him they responded to so negatively.

Group Dynamic Perspective. James succeeded in endearing himself to group members by disowning his abilities that made him the focus of envy and interpersonal competition. Preventing James from continued disownership of his abilities would have required encouraging the group members to look at unconscious group-as-a-whole trends that encouraged James to continue what he was doing. Group members had to be encouraged to examine their unacknowledged motives for accepting James' self-sacrificial approach to working with them.

A number of aspects of the group dynamics could have been inspected as part of a preventive intervention. In particular, unconscious group processes and roles would have been important to examine. The groups involved worked toward establishing an uncomfortable and unstable relationship with James. So long as no one challenged what was going on, no one had to deal with it. Instances where James did challenge others directly were quickly reacted to to suppress or otherwise dispose of the tensions created. Dealing with these important actions, as represented by roles as they appeared, could have made it much more difficult to continue to pursue the process. James' role of quasi-altruist and the roles of being needy and inferior, which he foisted off on others, needed to be scrutinized. The roles assumed by group members of unquestioning receivers also contained important information about what was happening. As these roles emerged, they could have been systematically questioned and held up for inspection.

Restoration

Restoring James to full ownership of his abilities requires James' examining his unconscious motivation for making the sacrifices. Perhaps the most difficult aspect of intervening at the individual level is that James may not see a need to change his behavior. He may not want to see that his actions are self-defeating, contemptuous, and manipulative. His continued ability to function effectively and to receive approval and affiliation are being met without seriously compromising in his mind his ability to do his own thinking.

Changing the group dynamics that have developed around accepting James' efforts can be difficult. It might be asked, "Why rock the boat?" If everyone is happy, why invest a lot of time and energy in changing it? And, given time and resource limitations, it may seem to be imprudent to undertake a change effort. However, if the stability of this strategy should begin to fail and James should begin to experience himself as being used or the group members should become affronted by his silently contemptuous and manipulative strategy, then group productivity might suddenly suffer. It might be at this point, where painful group dynamics come to the surface, that an external intervention might be most successful. The organizational level requires an examination of the effect of current staff development and promotion strategies on the organization's top executives. Being tough and competitive may not be the best way to develop outstanding leadership at the top.

CONCLUSION

The case deals with the fundamental issue that we all wish to be liked and admired; some of us more than others. The case highlights the truly solitary nature of some kinds of executive development programs and, by extension, what it may mean to move, be transferred within a company, or to change organizations. Changes like these put pressure on us that can lead to avoiding change for fear of losing friends, work relationships, and the good self-feelings they provide. Change can then be seen to threaten fundamental feelings about ourselves and may be actively resisted or avoided.

This case also points out that some personal and interpersonal solutions to the experience of anxiety, inner emptiness, and worthlessness can be adaptive but, at the same time, impoverish everyone involved. James, his friends, and his coworkers became locked into a complex set of feelings, psychological defenses, and unconscious group processes which, if questioned, would have threatened their ''house of cards.''

11

The White Dwarf

The white dwarf is a very small, dim, and old star that is in its final stage of its life. It has too little energy to overcome its gravity and has collapsed to a small solid state.

This case draws upon Karen Horney's self-effacing solution to anxiety. In the self-effacing response, acting assertively or powerfully is rejected in favor of assuming a more passive and dependent role. Others are relied upon to take care of the individual and to manage what is going on. In return, this individual is willing to develop extensive and even morbid dependencies upon others who may use this individual to meet their own ends. This response is similar to the DSM-III-R dependent personality disorder and the proposed self-defeating personality disorder in which others are looked to to be in charge, and demeaning and self-defeating behavior is willingly undertaken to secure attachment. In Kets de Vries and Miller's *The Neurotic Organization* this personality type is similar to the depressive type.

Judy learned as a child to depend on her mother and others to keep things under control when stressful situations developed, and she continued this behavior at work. Understanding Judy's case permits us to appreciate that part in each of us that sometimes likes to be taken care of.

CASE EXAMPLE

Judy was an only child who, many thought, was lucky to have reached adulthood. Judy's father, who worked as a salesman, was gone most of the time. He was also an alcoholic who was occasionally violent, frequently unpredictable, and always remote. Whenever she tried to stand her ground, her resolve was crushed by her father's belt. Judy's mother stayed with her father, she said, only because of Judy. Judy depended on her mother to maintain some semblance of order in her life, and together they made it from one day to the next.

Judy avoided her father who was threatening and she eventually came to avoid her mother who was manipulative and made her feel increasingly guilty. She stayed in her room much of the time which she maintained in meticulous order. Her room and her appearance were just about the only things she learned she could control even though her father occasionally disturbed her room and condemned her as an "unsightly slob." Judy felt overwhelmed by the situation, and she was willing to do whatever it took to maintain her safety at home.

Judy was a bright, capable student who was always on the honor role, and she won a number of scholastic achievement awards. Judy preferred to have a few close friends whom she could trust. She was a good group member, but she was not interested in taking leadership roles. She also found it difficult to relate to boys and, although she dated, she developed no close relationships.

Judy's mother was able to help her go to a small private college where Judy studied sociology and psychology. Judy distinguished herself and was thought by several professors to be an outstanding student who worked hard, paid close attention to detail, developed good insights, and possessed creativity. One of her professors urged her to become a psychologist and helped her obtain loans and scholarships and gain acceptance to a prestigious program. She distinguished herself as a student, therapist, and researcher. She continued to have a social life which included only a few close friends who were attentive to her feelings and fears. She remained exceptionally ambivalent about developing a relationship with a man.

Judy was successful in completing her degrees, and she joined a metropolitan clinic which specialized in family therapy and the treatment of alcoholism. A hard worker, she was an outstanding therapist who made many sacrifices for the clinic, the staff, and her clients. She was detail oriented and she was easy to work with although she became distressed when criticized. Judy eventually married a man who proved to be abusive and unreliable; however, she persisted with the relationship because she believed she could reform him.

Judy's many successes at work made her a good candidate to assume more responsibility. It was, therefore, a surprise that problems developed when she was given a chance to manage a new clinic in a nearby community. It was not long after she assumed this responsibility that her work began to deteriorate. Clients complained that she seemed preoccupied. Instances occurred when she balked at making administrative decisions, and she proved to be ineffective at supervising her staff. The new clinic's success was in question, and she blamed herself. She often felt that she should never have assumed this level of responsibility. Her problems were aggravated by two of her male colleagues.

Judy found herself engrossed in two significant interpersonal conflicts: one with an older male therapist in the downtown clinic, who thought he should have had her job at the new clinic, and the second with a young male social worker in her clinic, who challenged her authority and undermined the decisions she did make. She was unwilling to confront either of these men over their behavior, although their aggressiveness toward her had been commented on by others. Rather than deal with their behavior, she avoided them. It seemed that she was willing to suffer virtually any humiliation at their hands so long as they left her alone.

Judy eventually resigned from her position to the relief of all concerned and returned to work in the downtown clinic. After this negative experience, she steadfastly refused to assume any roles that had administrative responsibilities associated with them. Eventually no one considered her for any role other than that of a therapist. Despite her obvious intelligence and abilities, Judy preferred to let others take the heat for running the show and making the big decisions. She proved to be consistently content to make outstanding contributions as a therapist. She uncomfortably accepted the fact that she was unable to advance her career.

CASE SUMMARY

This superstar has settled on a strategy of shining less brightly than she could by achieving in a small area of her work life. Judy made outstanding contributions as a therapist while keeping a low profile and letting others run the show. She, however, honored her commitment to herself by using her skills and abilities for clients and the clinic's best advantage. By assuming a role of dependency, she minimized her exposure to risks, envy, and negation by others. Her peers, although aware of her abilities, were not intimidated by her in her limited role and unconsciously appreciated her self-minimization. Judy's strategy permitted her to shine more faintly so that she could avoid provoking envious and competitive behavior toward her.

INDIVIDUAL PSYCHOLOGICAL PERSPECTIVE

Judy grew up in a family with a remote father who was unpredictable and threatening. Her mother provided her safety but at a cost. Her mother imparted guilt by letting her know she made many sacrifices for Judy. As a result, Judy did not develop a sense of security in dealing with others, especially men. Her behavior at work was motivated by the knowledge that conflict could explode into a violent episode, as it had with her father. To cope with her father's behavior, and by extension the behavior of other men, she learned to avoid being too visible, assertive, or independent. When things got stressful at work, Judy looked to others to take care of the situation. Contemplating taking any position that might attract attention to her was to be strictly avoided in the future—a reaction learned from her father and reinforced by her clinic management experience.

INTERPERSONAL PSYCHOLOGICAL PERSPECTIVE

Judy's friends and colleagues knew her to be kind and sensitive and willing to do anything to help them out. Their training permitted them to understand Judy's thoughts, feelings, and behavior in terms of her background. They, in turn, tried to be helpful to her while avoiding encouraging her to be dependent upon them. It was clear to them that Judy would become anxious about any change in the quality of their relationships with her; the slightest rejection would make her very anxious. Judy's quest for interpersonal security was the dominant influence in her personal and work relationships.

Judy was willing to work hard for others, but she did not want any responsibility. She made it clear that she preferred to depend upon others to take care of the "big picture." She knew she was very capable and was content with this self-knowledge, although she occasionally felt distressed about her self-limiting behavior. These internal conflicts at times left her feeling bitter about compromising herself. She silently resented the advancement of others who offered less but were aggressive self-promoters. Her peers were not threatened by her steady but self-minimizing contributions which improved everyone's lot. Her willingness to receive little recognition provided the opportunity for others to shine while reducing the likelihood of her becoming the focal point of the destructive envy of others.

Some of her work colleagues believed that Judy had overreacted to her negative experience at the new clinic. However, no amount of understanding, reassurance, or coaxing could get her back into a higher level of clinic leadership and responsibility. Judy steadfastly refused to deal with interpersonal power and authority issues, preferring to act helpless and dependent upon others.

GROUP DYNAMIC PERSPECTIVE

Judy was liked by her colleagues and was considered to be an outstanding therapist. She proved to be ineffective at coping with anxiety-provoking situations especially those that dealt with issues of power, authority, conflict, and control. Judy avoided being put into a position where she had to deal with others in any capacity other than a collegial one. She was a willing but cautious participant in the work groups in which she was a member.

Group as a Whole

Judy was a member of a therapeutic group which functioned on a professional collegial basis. This group welcomed her as a therapist but rejected her as a leader. It had also been ineffective at reengaging her to be a more productive member of the clinic by encouraging her to take on additional administrative responsibilities. The group also contributed to the conflict Judy experienced with her two male colleagues by not discussing the obviously negative impact of their actions. Judy also succeeded in imposing her expectations upon the group; namely that she be permitted to function only as a therapist.

Individual and Group Defenses

Judy's childhood created a world filled with many perceived threats that had to be defended against. Instead of acting to meet these threats she preferred to be passive and dependent—behavior she learned of necessity from her relationship with her parents. She also learned to rationalize her behavior and to deny that her actions were self-defeating. She repressed thoughts of being able to act on her own behalf for fear she would get into touch with the "bad" feelings of being powerful that she abhorred in her father. She was willing to make many personal sacrifices and suffer humiliation to develop and maintain dependency upon others who were expected to care for her in return for her devotion. Those who worked with her tried to undo the harm of her experience in the new clinic and may have eventually intellectualized her nonparticipation as the best available course of action for her.

Unconscious Group Process

Unconscious group processes arose, in this case, relative to the lack of a reaction to how Judy was treated by her two male colleagues. Group members unconsciously understood it would be hazardous to try to intervene. Thinking and talking about it made them anxious and fearful. Their lack of a response led to feelings of guilt over what had happened to Judy which they collectively suppressed from group consciousness. Unconscious group processes also led to ready acceptance of her resignation and to the clinic personnel's receptiveness to Judy's wish to have no responsibilities.

People in Roles

The role perspective contributes to understanding the dynamics of this case. Judy preferred a role of dependency. Her negative experience in a role of power and authority, which provoked the envy and competitiveness of two of her male colleagues, created an intolerable situation for her: one not unlike her relationship and role with her father. Those in roles of clinic leadership also contributed to

Judy's situation by assuming passive and helpless roles when they failed to intervene to stop the competition and aggression directed toward her. The two males had assumed roles of aggressors to Judy and others in the clinic.

Fight/Flight

The roles of fight and flight add many insights for understanding the dynamics of this case. Judy was in flight from interpersonal conflict, guilt, and uncertainty and felt anxiety ridden and stressful. She was unable to defend herself against aggression, and she was unwilling to assert herself against others. She was in flight from taking charge of any administrative responsibilities that involved the wielding of power. Those who were willing to lead the group in overcoming problems (fight) were supported by her. The two aggressive males were fight leaders who marshalled forces against Judy and eventually defeated her. Clinic members, as a group, were in flight from the aggression of the two males and from their guilt over not intervening when it became obvious that Judy was in trouble.

ORGANIZATIONAL DYNAMIC PERSPECTIVE

Judy's clinic was a small, professional organization where professionals assumed managerial roles they were not well prepared to handle. The wish for peacefulness and collegiality was not fulfilled when power and authority issues were under consideration. A second important attribute of the clinic was the fact that many of those who worked in the clinic, as a result of their professional training, were aware of the internal conflicts they possessed and were especially attentive to interpersonal and group processes. The clinic as an organization was filled with sensitive people who, because of their own issues with power, authority, conflict, and aggression, were ineffective at dealing with interpersonal conflicts and rivalries among themselves. Members of the clinic were unwilling to confront the two males over their aggressive behavior, and opportunities to enable Judy to be more effective were not seized.

INTERVENTIONS

Avoiding the outcome of this case is important because, once Judy rediscovers how dangerous the world is, it may be very difficult to coax her back into assuming the risks associated with self-assertion and the assumption of personal responsibility. Successfully intervening in this case to turn around what happened involves providing Judy with sufficient support to gradually reassume increasing responsibilities.

Prevention

For these mental health professionals, avoiding the outcome of the case would seem to be easy. After all, they should have understood what was happening. Regrettably, however, even the most informed individuals may balk at intervening as a result of their being just as afraid as Judy.

Individual Psychological Perspective. Judy was reduced to complete dependency upon her mother to protect her from an unpredictable and occasionally brutal father. She had been bullied and intimidated all of her life. It was reasonable that, when the going got rough at work, she was unable to cope with the anxieties created.

Judy understood much of what had happened to her as a child as a result of her training. However, even the best of understandings did not permit her anxiety-free functioning. Judy needed to learn to confront others who, like her father, might attack her. She also had to overcome the dread of acting on her own behalf. She had to appreciate her feelings of guilt about self-advocacy, which arose from her relationship with her mother who had made it clear that Judy should accept what she had because of the major sacrifices her mother was making for her. These internal conflicts need further work in therapy to permit Judy better functioning as a person and employee and also as a therapist who must understand her own problems before she can understand those of her clients.

Interpersonal Perspective. Judy's colleagues had to be encouraged to be more sensitive than they were to her plight and more willing to assume personal responsibility regarding the actions of her two protagonists. Judy might have succeeded if she had received the support of her colleagues and staff. Judy was sent out to the new clinic to fend for herself—something she was not prepared to do without additional training in administration and not without supervision and mentoring.

Judy's work life did not need to be as negative as it was. It is likely that Judy's vulnerability to male aggression was implicitly known to her two protagonists, and they unwittingly acted on it to "get even with her" or to make themselves feel better about being subordinated to her. Judy's predictable response encouraged them to continue their assault when they felt that she might not last much longer. Regrettably, no one at the clinic was willing to intervene. Stopping the aggression would have been a major factor in helping her to succeed and realize her abilities.

Group Dynamic Perspective. Groups are an important aspect of this case. Judy worked in the downtown clinic group. She was placed in control of a new clinic. Judy needed to maintain liaison with her colleagues downtown when she moved to the new clinic; however, she was cut off. Downtown clinic group members acted as though she was no longer one of them; she had come to symbolize the other clinic. A successful intervention would have involved drawing the group's attention to how they had developed the idea that Judy was somehow no longer one of them. Judy might have also reacted to this process by acting as though she were, in fact, different from them.

The group of people she supervised at the new clinic did not respond well to her uncertainty and her lack of administrative experience. When a male subordinate began to criticize her and act on his own, other members of the clinic either actively or tacitly supported him. Judy gradually became isolated, discredited, and eventually disregarded which made efforts on her part to lead and to supervise difficult. These group dynamics could have been vigorously challenged by Judy with the help of a mentor or an interventionist. Judy needed this support because she was not able to act effectively on her own behalf. Working through the actions of the two males and the group's willingness to tacitly support their behavior would have been important.

Judy's small group of friends supported her and sympathized with her, but they were not able to provide her with any useful advice because they had no administrative experience. The more disorganized Judy became, the less they wanted to be around her. As a result, just when she needed their support most, it was withdrawn. Support from the leadership of the downtown clinic could have made a major difference in how Judy experienced and dealt with her problems.

Restoration

Judy's hard-earned self-confidence has been shattered. Restoring it sufficiently to permit her to accept more administrative responsibility will be difficult. Judy must gain a better appreciation of what happened to her and why. She needs to renew her understanding of how her childhood determined much of her behavior when she is confronted with male aggression and uncertainty. Those who work with her need to come to her aid. They need to own their responsibility for not having acted to help her and acknowledge their unwillingness to intervene. In particular the two male aggressors need to understand their motivations and make amends with Judy. Group activities need to be attentive to the processes aimed at excluding Judy or victimizing her. Care must be taken to encourage her to assume small amounts of additional responsibilities. When she does, she must be supported, and her efforts must be acknowledged and appreciated.

CONCLUSION

This case illustrates how powerful an influence unacknowledged, undiscussable, tacit individual and group dynamics can be. Judy was unconsciously set up to fail by the leadership and members of both clinics. Her leadership contribution was killed. The case also underscores how powerful an influence unresolved individual and group issues regarding power, authority, aggression, and conflict can be. These are attributes of daily work life that are so threatening that they are seldom if ever discussed and are usually shut out of consciousness. Modern hierarchical organizations are filled with all of these "bad" attributes, and, if they are dealt with in the same way as they were in this case, the painful and unproductive outcomes should bear a resemblance. Perhaps the best games-men and jungle fighters will always inherit the organization.

This case concludes the in-depth discussion of how outstanding people at work do not always get the chance to shine.

12

Individual Excellence in the Workplace

This chapter recaps the contents of the five previous chapters: the cases of the pulsar, the supernova, the black hole, the red giant, and the white dwarf. Despite their complexity, the five cases, their analyses, and the suggested intervention strategies share many things in common. The cases underscore the importance of understanding ourselves, others, groups, and organizations from a psychological perspective. This understanding is amplified in this chapter. Two additional psychological concepts are provided to further our understanding of the individual psychology of the cases: the development of self-esteem and the development of self. The chapter then summarizes the content of the cases associated with interpersonal, group, and organizational dynamics. The chapter concludes with a last look at the construction of the cosmology of superstars by providing several additional types of burned-out superstars and examining some of the limitations of the cosmology.

OVERVIEW OF INDIVIDUAL PSYCHOLOGY

Each of the five cases draws upon common types of family settings and life and work-related experiences. The superstars, when looked at from the individual psychological perspective, share in common psychological attributes that can be organized around two basic elements of development: the development of self-esteem and the development of a real-self versus a false-self. These two important psychological concepts explain how we experience ourselves and others. These concepts underlie our motivations, thoughts, feelings, and actions. They are the basis for who we are and how we feel about ourselves.

Development of Self-Esteem

Self-esteem is how we feel about ourselves.[1] An individual who learns to feel unattractive and undesirable will very likely maintain these feelings regardless of any amount of evidence to the contrary. Parents, siblings, and others throughout life who say, "You look like you have put on weight," are not helping to create and maintain self-esteem.

People who have adequate self-esteem have a realistic understanding of their strengths and weaknesses and have no compelling needs to achieve to compensate for perceived weaknesses. Self-esteem permits effective functioning and relatively defenseless reality testing. Although stressful events provoke anxiety they do not create so much anxiety that one's self is experienced as threatened, crushed, or humiliated. Adequate self-esteem permits coping without the loss of the ability to understand what is going on and to deal with events intentionally.[2] It is also important to appreciate that self-esteem is not an absolute quality. It varies according to the situation. For example, an executive who functions effectively in a high-stress job may find the visit of a mother-in-law or a parent's disapproval stressful and hard to cope with.

Low self-esteem was a common denominator in the five cases. Each superstar suffered from not having developed good self-feelings as a child. Low self-esteem made it necessary to develop compulsive and overdetermined coping mechanisms. For example, some of the characters compensated for their low self-esteem as adults by trying to earn the approval of others at work in the mistaken belief that the approval would compensate for negative self-feelings. Rather than deal with the internal origins of the low self-esteem, a Band-Aid solution was used to compensate. Once begun, however, these compensations must be constantly maintained in order to avoid the dreaded feelings of low self-esteem. Each of the characters in the cases suffered from some degree of low self-esteem and each developed defenses against the feelings. The psychologically defensive processes described in the Appendix emerge to cope with the anxiety created by the feelings of low self-worth and undesirability. The coping mechanisms that were found to work best during childhood were seen to have been adopted for use throughout life.

The cases illustrate that many aspects of family life, parenting, and subsequent life experience interact to create and perpetuate low self-esteem. Parenting will be discussed below, but the same considerations apply to others such as spouses, lovers, and close friends during adulthood. It is important to appreciate that, once low self-esteem is created, it will probably be reinforced by subsequent life experiences. Low self-esteem can become a self-fulfilling prophecy where psychological defenses combine with self-defeating behavior to ensure that the individual and others will not find the individual of value.

In sum, low self-esteem leads to compulsive behavior where the freedom to choose is often missing. Self-limiting and self-defeating behaviors are acted out in a process of compulsive repetition, and contemplating changing these inter-personal dynamics is often just too painful and threatening. Thinking about changing calls into question a lifetime of poor adjustment that is painful to accept.

Low self-esteem can be seen to be a major influence in the cases. Bob's parents did not help him to feel good about himself. His mother's feelings were hard to determine, and his father usually criticized his performance. Bob learned to feel that, unless he outperformed everyone else, he had failed in the eyes of his parents, which caused him to feel despair and rejection. As a worker Bob initially felt good about himself when he won the approval of others. When his behavior was challenged in a group, however, he knew he had lost and he retaliated by taking pot shots at others. If he could not have it his way, he would drop out and get even.

Nora had little opportunity to develop self-esteem. Both of her parents were very critical of her. She learned she was deficient, inadequate, and undesirable. No matter how perfect she was, she never received their love, affection, attention, and approval. Her anger toward her parents she experienced as dangerous to hold, and she repressed it from her awareness. Nora did not gain adequate self-esteem throughout the case although she was an outstanding performer. Her conflict with her supervisor resurfaced the feelings she had held for her parents: her feelings of being helpless, unwanted, and deficient and the need to act cautiously on her anger. Furthermore, Nora lost the one thing she had learned to value most—being perfect.

Sally was a child who had carved out some self-esteem, after all, she had survived. Sally was, however, always alert for problems of being controlled too much and acting too controlling on her part. Her inner strength, she felt, allowed her to function well without others. She learned not to look to others for self-esteem. She found there was peace and contentment in just being alone. At work she proved she shined in working with and leading others if given the chance.

James missed the opportunity to gain good self-feelings from his family. No matter how hard he tried or how successful he was, he did not receive his parents' love. He also learned that his achievements provoked destructive rivalry from his brothers and sisters. Despite being a highly productive employee, James was dependent upon others to make him feel good about himself. Without a close-knit support group, he was lost. James eventually sacrificed his career pursuits in favor of maintaining good feelings about himself.

Judy grew up avoiding her threatening father and her controlling and manip-ulating mother. She gradually learned not to trust herself. Judy developed a fragile sense of self-esteem that could be easily challenged by others. If things were not quite right, she would immediately retreat to letting others take care of things. Judy's fragile self-esteem was closely tied to her false sense of self and her poorly defended self-other boundaries, which introduces the second aspect of individual psychological development.

Development of Self

Self is that part of us that permits us to experience ourselves as distinct from others—as individuals who may act autonomously.[3] The concept of self, or how we think about ourselves, is associated less with feelings than in the case of self-esteem. Self arises from learning to become socialized and not always being able to do what we want. We cannot always act with perfect autonomy, and we cannot act without regard to the thoughts and feelings of others. However, if parental expectations are pervasive, a child must learn to conform to these expectations or be punished and rejected. The child must learn to be someone the parents will approve of or else face their loss. In order to feel wanted, the child unwillingly transforms self into the false-self desired by the parents.

The concept of self implies that we are able to establish, monitor, and maintain interpersonal boundaries. Two key interpersonal fears affect boundary management: the fear of being engulfed and the fear of being abandoned.[4] Parents may be too concerned about a child and overwhelm it with attention, smothering its self-development, its ability to find areas of autonomous behavior, and its eventual ability to separate from the parents. The child is engulfed by its parents and later in life may avoid others for fear of being engulfed once again. In contrast, other parents may be unconcerned about the child and provide inadequate attention, assurance, and security. This child learns to fear being separate and alone and experiences developmental problems associated with fears of abandonment leading to separation anxiety.

In either of these cases, the mix of parenting is inappropriate and stifles the development of the child's ability to be accepted for itself. Anxiety created by parental figures is experienced as flooding across the child's interpersonal boundary. As an adult this individual fears alienating others by imposing interpersonal boundaries and perhaps feels guilty about imposing what may be felt to be a selfish, self-centered construct into relationships. In contrast, this individual may also feel fearful of being engulfed if boundaries do not exist and guilty of not looking out for self should engulfment occur. A spouse's or supervisor's slightest discomfort may signal disapproval and loss of attachment or threatened domination and engulfment, creating excessive and hard to control anxiety. As a result the false-self emerges as a dominant life force to cope with this conflict. An individual may, for example, always be willing to conform rather than to live life assertively.

The concept of self is an important factor in these cases. Bob developed a false-self focused on winning and achieving at everything he did to obtain scarce parental approval. He won the approval by overcoming every obstacle including others. At the same time, he learned that he should not question authority figures and that if he did they would punish him. Bob grew up quickly and learned to do what his parents expected of him. As a child and young adult he was always serious and competitive. Bob did not have a chance to explore other aspects of his personality. He did not have much fun. He seldom developed nurturing, supportive relationships with others; he always felt he had to compete against them. He was not very spontaneous; he preferred to plan and think ahead about what he had to do next to win and stay on the good side of his parents.

Nora learned that she had to be perfect to maintain any good feelings about herself. The expectations of her parents had to be met, and she focused her energy on achieving perfection at things her parents valued. She might have, at times, felt she had changed her self into a lifeless machine intent on mastering her studies and her work. Like Bob, Nora experienced early foreclosure of her childhood and play. She seldom had the opportunity to be autonomous, spontaneous, or playful. As an adult her false but perfect self dominated her life and she avoided questioning her pursuit of productivity and perfection in lieu of living her own life.

Sally learned to alter herself to fit into new situations by being quiet and withdrawn. She feared abandonment and was willing to give up personal pursuits to secure herself a family life. She learned that the best way to fit in was to make few demands, to make good grades, to be industrious, and to act autonomously with care. She felt best alone. As an adult and a manager she was able to shine when she was given the opportunity. She always knew she could, but she did not have such a goal for herself and she seldom advocated for herself. However, underlying her success she was prepared to abandon her real, competent self in order to disappear into the background. This is what eventually happened at work. Being used, ignored, unsupported, and abandoned were feelings she was familiar with and which she had learned to cope with in the past by withdrawing.

James did his best to earn the love and attention of his parents. He was always attentive to them and he distinguished himself in school. However, he did not learn that he was loveable. No matter how hard he tried or how much he changed himself, parental love and approval did not seem to be forthcoming. When he started to move around at work he was unable to get his affiliation needs met; they were lacking just as they had been lacking at home. When he rejoined the home office, he was determined to avoid having that happen again. He gave up career pursuits and self-advancement, things he had worked hard for and had come to value, in favor of maintaining his group of friends.

Judy had little opportunity to develop the safe and caring parental relationships she desired. Her threatening father and manipulative mother left her feeling helpless and dependent. She responded to others by looking to them to control and fend off a threatening interpersonal world. She learned that letting others run the show was better than having to deal with anxiety-ridden problems and conflicts. Judy's false sense of self led her away from feeling secure and effective and toward dependency. She felt she had to depend upon others to take care of things when the going got tough.

The self is a critical aspect of how we relate to others and work. If we do not know who we are, if we are unable to just be ourselves, if we are unable to establish and maintain interpersonal boundaries, and if we are not able to act intentionally, then much is lost. The cases clearly illustrate this eventuality.

OVERVIEW OF INTERPERSONAL DYNAMICS

The interpersonal perspective was also important for understanding all the cases. This perspective underscores how important other people are in our lives, beginning with our parents, brothers, sisters, and friends. They can have a powerful effect on us which influences how we think and feel about ourselves. In each of these cases, parenting was less than optimal; in several of the cases, it was devastatingly poor or absent. These early interpersonal life experiences were shown in the cases to influence behavior relative to others at work in many ways.

Bob learned that he had to win out over others. At work he continued to try to achieve and win. Nora learned that she had to be perfect. As an employee she continued to strive for perfection and when she could not achieve it, she became furious, just as she had as a child, and sublimated her angry feelings by trying to achieve even more work. Sally learned that, in order to be wanted, she had to fit in. As an employee she was willing to do what was expected. When she was given the chance to use her abilities, she shined. However, when the company changed hands, she retreated to her old coping method of keeping a low profile and just fitting in. James learned that, no matter how successful he was, he could not get the affection he wanted. The executive development program further frustrated his need to develop a support group. When he was finally able to locate a group of friends, he was willing to do whatever worked to maintain their friendship and he would not risk alienating them by using his abilities. Judy learned that others had to be depended on to take care of her and any major problems that arose in life and at work. Her response, when the going got rough, was to look to others for help. Her negative leadership experience reinforced her beliefs and feelings that she was unable to deal with tough problems and had to depend on others at the clinic.

The cases illustrate that childhood and subsequent life experiences are part of a continuum that can create an internally consistent, self-sealing system which becomes rigid over time. The cases show that how we relate to each other is part of an unconscious and often unacknowledged system of coping with anxiety. The cases underscore the point that how we relate to others and how others relate to us at work are greatly influenced by how we feel and think about ourselves and others and, conversely, how others feel and think about themselves and us. The cases draw attention to the regrettable fact that we may have been set up by our parenting and subsequent relationships to experience problems later in life related to others at work. The ability to work effectively together in the 1990s can be improved by understanding the impact of these kinds of unconscious interpersonal trends at work.

OVERVIEW OF GROUP DYNAMICS

Groups are an important part of the workplace. Groups contain within them many hard to understand and hard to manage dynamics. Learning to work more effectively in groups and learning to make groups work more effectively are major challenges for the 1990s. The cases illustrated various dynamics that may arise in groups. Bob learned that groups can be different within an organization. Behavior that one group approves of may be toxic to the members of another group. Bob found out that unconscious group dynamics can create a violent lynch mob mentality, which could even kill him off as a productive member.

Nora learned that groups could be an uncertain setting for her to locate approval for her outstanding performance. When she found her performance questioned by members of some groups, she became anxious and increased her efforts to achieve more. She also learned that some groups, like top management, may tolerate poor performance preferring to maintain a hidden agenda aimed at keeping everyone feeling good rather than getting work done.

Sally and the members of her organization became engrossed in the group dynamics involved with the takeover. The new managers changed the organization's culture into an autocratic one that tried to dominate and use people to make money. So long as everyone did what they were told, they had a job. This intergroup attitude generated a predictable response from the members of Sally's organization who felt used and abused. These two large groups deflected creative and productive energy into the perpetuation of dominance and control issues and active and passive aggression.

James learned that his participation in groups, starting with his own family group, could be unrewarding and leave him feeling unloved. His feelings of being left out were reinforced by his experience at work when he began to move around. He finally reached the point where he was willing to contribute his abilities to group process without owning his abilities. He was willing to give up a part of himself to maintain good feelings toward himself. The group members, in turn, were thankful that he helped them to shine and they responded by liking him.

Judy wanted to be taken care of. She participated in groups but primarily as a dutiful follower. Her worst fears about assuming responsibility were realized when she became the manager for the new clinic. The unsupportive and even cruel group dynamics that developed around her leadership confronted her with a scenario similar to that of her childhood. She was just as unable to deal with the problems and conflicts in her new setting as she had been in her past setting.

Her predictable response was to retreat to the safety of the familiar role of therapist and let her colleagues take care of things.

The cases illustrate the complexity of understanding and managing group dynamics. Groups often take on a life of their own. Groups can foster individual and group excellence or create hostile and unrewarding dynamics. A number of unconstructive group dynamics occurred in the cases. The cases illustrate that being able to spot unconstructive group dynamics and being able to understand them from the different perspectives can facilitate the group process. A number of different group dynamic perspectives were explored in the cases: the group as a whole, group defenses, unconscious group process, roles, and fight/flight.

The group-as-a-whole perspective was seen to be an important perspective in each case. The group as a whole killed Bob off as a member, and the group then acted as a whole to avoid dealing with the guilt felt by its members. In Nora's case, most of the members of groups she worked in learned to accept her willingness to do much of their work while members of upper management, as a group, avoided having to deal with the poor performance of one of their own. In Sally's case, her fellow workers constituted a group which left her alone and which occasionally ridiculed her as a "stuck-up loner." For James, membership in a group where its members acted to make him feel good about himself was of paramount importance. If there was no group or if the group did not fulfill his needs, James was in trouble. Judy learned that groups can set up a member to fail and then not come to that member's aid.

Individual and group defenses against anxiety were found to have important explanatory power and to help anyone working in a group to better appreciate that much of what happens in a group is more felt about than thought about. In Bob's case, group members disposed of guilt by rationalization and denial while Bob reacted to their actions by insulating himself emotionally and dropping out. Nora developed a reaction formation toward her supervisor and had to deny the self-destructive effects of her perfectionistic approach to working with others in groups. Members of groups she worked in disposed of their feelings of using her by rationalizing that letting her work so hard was good for her. The unfriendly aspects of the takeover, in Sally's case, created many anxieties and much anger that had to be defended against. Organization members were seen to project their bad, malevolent feelings onto the new group of executives, permitting them to see themselves as good people set upon by an evil external force. Anger and hostility were changed into passive aggressive actions and occasional bursts of productivity. The members of the new executive group insulated themselves from negative feelings about their actions, and they were powerful enough to have the luxury of overtly acting out their aggressions on the members of Sally's organization by firing rebels. James tried to cope with his inner emptiness by filling it up with good feelings from his friends which he felt he had to maintain at any personal cost. James worked hard to deny the self-defeating aspects of his behavior while those around him rationalized receiving from him and denied that they were vulnerable to being manipulated by James as a result of their own self-centered career interests. Judy disposed of the dangerous inner anger she felt over how she was treated by denying, suppressing, and repressing it as she always had. Those who worked with her rationalized and denied their inaction when they neglected to help her when help was clearly in order. The males involved in the attack upon Judy denied and rationalized their actions: She was not fit to lead; all they did was expose the fact.

Unconscious group process was also seen to be a way of understanding what happens in groups. Many things that happen in groups result from heretofore unforeseen dynamics. Unexpected and seemingly unexplainable things happen in groups, but when they are seen as part of a process, to which group members are unconsciously contributing, they become understandable.

In Bob's case, the angry sentience group suddenly formed as a result of bad feelings about management and recent events. Angry, helpless feelings suddenly surfaced and were focused on Bob whose actions were more like those of management than like those accepted by the group. In Nora's case, the unconscious group process was focused on negotiating Nora's self-sacrificial role and the roles of receiving group members who were then expected to befriend her and give her their approval. Unconscious group life was seen to have an active role in Sally's case. The hostile takeover keyed off in Sally and her fellow workers primitive images of being attacked, violated, and dominated. Images of triumph, dominance, and perhaps rescue abounded on the part of the executive group from the takeover company. These powerful, unconscious images proved to be too threatening for anyone to deal with in the open. Much of what James did was out in the open at the start. However, unconscious group processes were at work in negotiating James' role of promoting the careers of others, which was implicitly linked to being liked and accepted by his friends. Judy's organizational situation was filled with unconscious group dynamics. She was set up to fail without anyone being aware of it. She was virtually excommunicated from the downtown clinic and did not receive coaching or mentoring by senior management. Nor was she helped in dealing with aggressive male employees when she needed help. When she was finally killed off by her male aggressors, mutually shared guilt and anxiety over what had happened resulted in the membership of both clinics avoiding dealing with their part in the painful outcome.

The use of roles was also found to provide a window through which to look at group dynamics. The idea of a role is easy to understand, but it is somewhat difficult to apply in practice. The cases provide examples of how roles can be used to understand group dynamics.

Bob acted out the roles of being critical and creative, which were acceptable in one group and unacceptable in a group of fellow managers. Group members came to have angry roles and acted out the roles of attackers, onlookers, and eventually guilty members. Nora acted out roles associated with outstanding performance and roles of judge and jury in relation to others meeting her standards. Those who worked with her were expected to accept roles of letting her do the work and admiring her. Sally assumed the role of loner; others assumed the role of leaving her alone. She was also able to assume the role of being an effective manager which she was unable to continue to act out when she was surreptitiously reassigned. James acted out the role of a nurturing person who was worthy of being liked. Those around him learned that their role was to receive what James had to offer and to be his friends and support him. Judy learned that a role of leadership was painful and filled with threat. She preferred the safer roles of therapist and of being dependent. Those around Judy were reduced to the roles of observers of an attack, attackers, caretakers, and guilty members—not unlike the case for Bob.

Groups can also become filled with anxious group members who either feel like fighting back or fleeing from the situation. These feelings can, if not harnessed in a positive direction, lead groups away from work on tasks. These fight and flight group dynamics were illustrated in the cases.

In Bob's case, a fight leader emerged to lead the heretofore nonexistent angry group in its attack against him, and, eventually, this same individual became the flight leader who led the group away from dealing with its guilt. Nora was often the fight leader in the groups she participated in because many things seemed to threaten her standards of performance. As the fight leader she could also be expected to be opposed to anyone leading the group away from its work and achieving perfection. Sally was in flight from others who did not support her. The buy-out created many fight tendencies on the part of both sides as members of both organizations became locked in a battle for control. James was in flight from his abilities which, if fully displayed, would, he feared, make him the focus of rivalrous attention. Underlying this process was James' flight from his inner emptiness, which he tried to fill with good feelings from his friends. Those who worked with him were in flight from the knowledge that they were being reduced to receiving and were, perhaps, at times, being contemptuously manipulated by James. Judy was in flight from responsibility, and her negative leadership experience made this clear. In contrast, the two men who led the attack against her were the fight leaders who toppled a powerful female authority figure.

ORGANIZATIONAL DYNAMICS

The organizations we all work for have many attributes that we are not always aware of. These attributes can make us feel good about ourselves, others, and the groups in which we work. We can feel like we belong and that we are valued and important. Organizations can encourage us to be ourselves; they can respect our needs for autonomy, to think and to reflect, to question the status quo, to try new things, and to take risks. They can provide us with a bandage if we fall down.

Organizations can also have a culture that is harsh, punitive, risk aversive, high control, uncaring, and unrewarding. They can be filled with managers who are authority oriented, remote, unapproachable, unsympathetic, defensive, anxious about their status, and anxious about dealing with poor performance and discipline issues. We saw many of these negative trends develop in the cases.

Bob learned that an organization's values, precepts, and culture need not be uniform. To be avoided are management practices that are espoused but not always followed in practice. Bob's organization sent out mixed signals about innovation and the pursuit of excellence. Even though innovation was encouraged in some areas and much talked about throughout the organization, the crushing sense of control and accountability in operations was inconsistent with innovation, risk taking, and the pursuit of excellence.

In Nora's case, top management of her organization was willing to tolerate poor performance in their ranks, which set an example for others throughout the organization. The management culture, by avoiding interpersonal confrontation, protected people rather than promoting outstanding performance. Similarly, no one was willing to confront Nora over the change in her behavior and her growing performance dysfunctions.

Sally's case is a good example of the radical transformation that often results from changes in leadership. Her organization and its values, as represented by those who encouraged her to achieve excellence in her work and who provided her with opportunities to test her abilities, were cast aside by the management of the takeover company. The change in management returned her to a setting where she found she was not valued as a person. The predatory and dehumanizing attitude of the managers from the takeover company penetrated all parts of Sally's organization making everyone feel they were being taken advantage of.

James' case illustrates the impact of constantly moving executives around in a presumed process of developing them. Even though James had overdetermined needs for affiliation and approval, what he experienced could be expected to put most personalities under stress. The organizational culture that James eventually returned to, one of competing for a few top spots, did not encourage collaboration and the development of close friendships. James solved this problem by giving up, for the most part, his career pursuits in favor of not being seen as threatening and therefore likeable.

Judy's professional organization had a culture centered on collegial working and interpersonal relationships. This culture, however, was not effective at self-management, and it was unable to deal with interpersonal and intergroup conflict when it arose. The culture was one in which aggressive behavior was tacitly rewarded. It was predictable that the most aggressive clinic members would succeed in clawing their way to the top.

The unconscious but pervasive and powerful aspects of organizational culture will be discussed further in Chapters 13 and 14.

OVERVIEW OF INTERVENTION STRATEGIES

The intervention strategies mentioned in the introduction and discussed throughout the cases were informed by psychology. If the idea is to work with people rather than to manage human resources, then efforts to make change must be informed by the "people factor."

Individual Interventions

Individual interventions are the most invasive and touch upon an unaccepted aspect of our society. Mental health is still in the closet. It is not acceptable for a man to be sensitive and a woman to be assertive. It is even more unacceptable to acknowledge that we all have within us some neurotic trends that affect our behavior. In the 1990s, a more enlightened approach to working with and managing others will be to understand that we can all have compulsive and rigid elements in our personalities that may or may not be adaptive to the workplace.

Another important aspect of dealing with people as individuals is whether dealing with individuals is cost effective. How cost effective can it be to help one person in thousands to better understand the impact of highly idiosyncratic personality distortions upon the ability to do good work? However, if it is appreciated that employees may, at the minimum, suffer, from time to time, from some degree of personal disorganization, then an investment in a people orientation can pay off. Employee assistance programs are an acknowledgment of this equation. This consideration is especially important in the care of superstars.

Individual interventions are obviously the most invasive for they deal with the psychology and personality of each of us as an individual. People who become disorganized at work and have their performance suffer can benefit from a referral to an employee assistance program. The professionals who staff these programs will help locate mental health professionals in the local community who can be of assistance. All it takes is for the employee to be open-minded enough to accept such help. Management and fellow workers must also accept that it is all right to seek help for disorders ranging from mild episodic neurotic dislocations to major problems with alcoholism or schizophrenia. Regrettably, however, our society has often made seeking this help taboo.

A less invasive method is for the supervisor to confront employees about performance problems being created by personality dysfunctions. Employees should be encouraged to be self-reflective. They should, as a part of the confrontation, be encouraged to understand how they are feeling, how they came to feel that way, when they have felt this way in the past and what they did about it, how their feelings are contributing to the behavior in the present, and how their behavior has become dysfunctional. Friends and supervisors are in a unique position of being able to give the employee "tough love."

Part of caring about others in this way is being able to identify some of the coping mechanisms discussed in Chapter 4. How many times have we spotted someone using rationalization to explain away behavior or relying on denial to avoid having to deal with something that is obvious? How many times have we watched someone pouring energy generated by anger into work to sublimate its energizing effects into something constructive? How many times have we observed someone act out their aggressions by attacking back, working even harder to compensate for a weakness, or developing a nonadaptive reaction formation? Less easily understood and spotted are instances of projection, displacement, and emotional insulation which take more patience to learn about and apply in the workplace.

Interpersonal Interventions

We work and live with others. We have to learn how to cope with the influences others have upon us. And we have to learn how it is we influence others and to what end. The interpersonal world raises the important question of motivation. Why are we being treated the way we are by others, and what did we do to deserve the treatment? These two questions may also be asked of us by others. Understanding interpersonal dynamics is complex; it involves many of the coping mechanisms mentioned in Chapter 4.

Working with others can be a rewarding experience, and it can be a frustrating, unrewarding one. Each of these cases emphasized how potentially frustrating, unrewarding, and even dangerous working with others can be. Bob found out the hard way. People who he thought were his friends and wanted to work with him killed him off. Nora discovered the hard way that it was important to have a good supervisor. She also gained an appreciation for the fact that others might be more concerned with maintaining good feelings than confronting others over their poor performance. Sally found out that coworkers can be nurturing but that the workplace can change overnight, which happened to her when she was reassigned without any discussion. James found out that it was better not to be too good; otherwise, he would risk alienating those he wanted to have as friends. Finally, Judy learned that, when people are threatened by an authority figure, they may become angry, aggressive, and vindictive. She also learned that it was easier to turn her head away from dealing with interpersonal conflict with men rather than confront it. Each of the characters found out that people are people; sometimes they are good, sometimes bad.

Intervening in the interpersonal dynamics of the cases can be managed by supervisors, colleagues, friends, and external change agents such as group process consultants. Supervisors and those in higher management positions may be able to intervene where interpersonal dynamics have gotten out of hand and have become organizationally dysfunctional. However, what is required on the part of all concerned is a willingness to deal with conflict—something that often is unpleasant and can result in even more intense feelings and the possibility that the supervisor or interventionist will be scapegoated. However, supervisors are in the best position to act and should be educated and encouraged to do so to avoid the loss of valuable productivity for their organization. Routine and special performance appraisals are good mechanisms for dealing with interpersonal issues if the performance appraisal format encourages it. Otherwise, daily supervision should include informed interventions into energy-draining dysfunctional inter-personal dynamics.

Group Interventions

Group dynamics is one of the most challenging aspects of getting work done through people. The workplace is filled with many kinds of formal and informal groups which can take on lives of their own that may not always be on task. Working in groups can be a rewarding and productive experience, or it can become outright dangerous as Bob and Judy discovered. The five cases illustrated the darker side of group process and were not intended to be reflective of all groups, although many groups contain some of the dynamics of the cases at some point in time. Dealing with dysfunctional group dynamics is the respon-sibility of the group leader and to a lesser extent the members of the group. Group leaders must be able to spot the development of dysfunctional group dynamics and then be able to intervene to change them. Group leaders should be educated about group dynamics and have opportunities to practice managing group dynamics in "safe training harbors" provided by workshops, off-site training, and organizations that provide experiential learning opportunities.

Intervening in dysfunctional group dynamics takes knowledge and courage. Group leaders, when confronted by aggressive group members and opposing subgroups and coalitions, do not always own up to their responsibilities. They may prefer to work around them than face the danger of openly confronting others over their behavior. It is also possible that a group leader, who may bring to the role dysfunctional personality attributes, may actually induce dysfunctional group dynamics. A group leader who has to control everything or who is laissez-faire can be expected to lead the group in the development of dysfunctions. In either case a second tier of response is for the members of the group to assume some responsibility for acting to remedy these dysfunctional outcomes. This may be done within the group or perhaps in the safety of an out-of-group process in which a few members of the group discuss the dynamics and decide to act together to try to stop what is happening.

A third tier of response is to invite a group process consultant into the group to help group members deal with unresolved interpersonal conflict and other dysfunctional group dynamics. To be successful, this strategy requires the group as a whole to be ready to acknowledge that a problem exists. It must be willing to deal with it—not unlike an alcoholic who must first admit that he or she has a drinking problem before he or she can seek help.

Organizational Interventions

Intervening in organizational dynamics can be highly problematic for anyone other than top management. Unless the organization's leadership is committed to making a change, a change that often implies that they have been less than effective or have inadvertently contributed to an organizational dysfunction, no change is likely to occur. For example, a group of top-level managers who are highly competitive, who always want to be in control, who do not want to hear anything but good news, and who are remote will not be receptive to employees who advocate change. Similarly, the espousal of a group of managers toward making the organization warmer, friendlier, more open, and more risk taking is not likely to succeed unless top management is willing to look at their contribution to the organization's dynamics.

Organizational interventions can, many times, be effectively facilitated by external consultants who are able to say and do things members of the organization cannot, such as confronting top management over their behavior. Organizational change may involve efforts to change the organizational culture, such a sweeping idea that the next two chapters are devoted to describing what it means to change an organizational culture.

THE DEVELOPMENT OF A COSMOLOGY

The five cases discussed do not exhaust the many possibilities provided by human nature and work-a-day situations. The cases and discussions have provided the reader with insights into how to observe self, others, groups, and organizations. It should be apparent that gaining self-reflective skills is a critical factor in understanding one's self and others. Three additional examples of burned-out superstars are provided to promote additional thinking about patterns of knowing, thinking, and acting at work.

Neutrino

A neutrino is a subatomic particle that is so small it can pass through matter without touching the other subatomic particles that compose it. A neutrino can, for example, pass through the earth without touching another particle; without touching the earth.

As a personality type, the neutrino is a person who works in an organization without really being known by others or making a mark of any kind upon others, work, groups, or the organization. Taking risks and being known at work are either avoided as an undesirable, self-centered pursuit or as a threat to becoming the focal point for undesirable attention. This employee is one of those "survivors"; no matter what happens, the person always seems to stay out of trouble. For many supervisors and managers this employee might constitute the ideal employee, a person who follows instructions and does not question what is happening. However, behavior and attitudes like this may be the result of the individual's having found a successful and rewarding life outside of work as might be the case with a child whose parents were dominating, demanding, controlling, unsupportive, unrewarding, and punishing and forced the child to look for love outside of the family.

Solar Wind

The solar wind is a stream of charged particles that radiate from the sun. These particles have measurable force which, if harnessed, could conceivably propel objects through space as a wind powers a sailboat across the water.

As a personality type, the solar wind exerts a constant but hard to detect influence upon others, groups, and the organization. This individual does not seek recognition or reward for outstanding achievements and is content to work in the background.

A likely location for a person with these attributes is at the top of an organization where the ability to influence many aspects of work exists. Such a leader may set challenging goals for others to meet and celebrate the success of others in achieving the goals. This individual may be motivated by a legitimate wish to help others and the organization to shine. An attitude such as this might arise from an early life experience where modest and even stoic behavior is modeled by parents and encouraged in their children. Actions such as these, the child learns, are for a greater good and are admirable.

Binary Star System

A binary star system involves two stars that orbit each other. One star is usually bright and more massive while the second is smaller and less visible. Each star's mass influences the other's mass, just as the gravity of the moon influences the earth's oceans to create tides. In the binary star system the more massive star gradually pulls mass from its companion in an irresistible process of becoming larger, brighter, and more massive; eventually, it extinguishes its smaller companion. The binary star system introduces the interpersonal aspect into the cosmology where two star performers interact with each other. The interaction may have competitive or collaborative aspects.

In the competitive aspect, each star performer tries to outshine the other in a win-lose dynamic. The competition may stimulate a great deal of rivalry and productivity, but the win-lose dynamic means that one must eventually lose. A somewhat similar outcome may arise as part of a parasitic mentoring process where an established superstar takes an active interest in a rising star, but, instead of being helped, the rising star is used merely to bolster the superstar's brilliance. A binary system may also be created when the two stars are more balanced and, although competitive trends may exist, they complement each other in a highly productive process of collaboration where the full output of both stars is harnessed for the good of the organization.

THE LIMITATIONS OF CLASSIFICATIONS

Chapter 5 posed some problems for classification schemes that should be revisited before concluding this chapter. How many of the limitations noted in Chapter 5 did the cosmology encounter?

They Are Abstractions

The cosmology is not intended to be a serious classification scheme. It was noted that the basic personality types depicted in the five cases were derived from the work of Karen Horney who hypothesized the existence of three solutions to the experience of anxiety: the expansive solution, which includes perfectionist, arrogant/vindictive, narcissistic; the self-effacing solution; and the resigned solution. These abstractions helped her to organize her clinical experience. The cosmology's foundations are based on abstractions of reality like all other schemes.

They Do Not Include All Behavior

The cosmology does not include all behavior at work; however, because it is based upon a comprehensive theory of coping with anxiety, it provides a thought-provoking look at how people cope with anxiety at work and their motivations for working.

The Categories Are Not Adequately Defined

The solutions to anxiety are well defined and have been operationalized both in the cases in this book and elsewhere.[5] The five solutions offer a compelling theoretical perspective for understanding the compulsive pursuits of people at work who do not usually stop and ask themselves why they do what they do. The five solutions are sufficiently concrete to avoid the assertion that they are not well defined and operationalized.

The Categories May Be Overlapping

The three solutions are part of a tripartite classification scheme that avoids many of the problems associated with overlapping. The three solutions—moving toward others (self-effacing), moving away from others (resigned), moving against others, or expansive (perfectionist, arrogant/vindictive, and narcissistic)—are mutually exclusive. Moving toward someone as though to hold them precludes moving away from them or against them as though to attack or to control. Moving away precludes moving toward or against others. And moving against others precludes moving toward them or away from them. The cosmology avoids many of the pitfalls associated with overlapping classification schemes.

They Do Not Fully Explain the Dynamic Nature of Behavior

The cosmology demonstrates that people can change over time. Each superstar developed, maintained, and changed behavior in a manner consistent with his or her unique solution to the experience of anxiety keyed off by the rejecting and limiting actions of others. The superstars also exhibited more than one type of behavior depending upon the situation. Karen Horney's theory of solutions to anxiety permit assuming one response at one time and a different one at a later time—whatever works to minimize the experience of anxiety. The cosmology, therefore, includes the dynamic nature of behavior.

People Are Pigeonholed

The cosmology is a helpful scheme for understanding unconscious motivations for behavior at work. To the extent that it is helpful, it should be used; however, the warning in Chapter 5 that classification schemes can be unfair to others and unproductive at work must be headed. The rigid use of a classification relative to someone may be a better indicator of a problem with the person imposing the classification than a fair assessment of the person being classified.

In sum, the cosmology is a sophisticated look at the unconscious motivations of people at work and, although not perfect, provides many good insights and a platform for learning.

CONCLUSION

The state-of-the-art space telescope promises cosmologists a better view of the universe from its position far above the distorting influence of the earth's atmosphere. The cosmology of superstars in this book offers a more sensitive and insightful view of people and the world in which they work. The cosmology of superstars avoids the distortions and self-delusional aspects of the world of how managers are taught to take a minute to manipulate others into achieving greater performance levels. The cosmology makes it clear that people, people in groups, and people in organizations—people at work—are much more complex than a one-minute manager's understanding of human nature and are much more deserving of respect than apparent in the implicit self-serving and self-centered aspects of transformational leadership. The search for individual excellence begins with understanding people and their stories.

PART III

IN PURSUIT OF
INDIVIDUAL EXCELLENCE

The five case studies presented in Part II provided many insights into the interactions among superior achievement, rejecting and hostile work settings, and the psychological defenses that superstars and others may exhibit. The cases tied together and operationalized much of the content of Part I. Superstars were found to have personal attributes others may find disarming. Superstars were found to be imperfect; they may not have had the most favorable of prior life experiences. Superstars were, like everyone else, found to be sensitive to being limited and rejected by others. The superstars in the cases responded to these outcomes by defending themselves in psychologically defensive ways. The focus of the book thus far has been on the psychology of individuals and individuals in groups and the individual's encounter with organization. The superstar, it should be clear, needs a support system in which to work. This leads us to consider how organizations can be changed to provide the support necessary to foster the pursuit of individual excellence.

Part III introduces an overarching perspective for organizational life. Organizations can be understood to be a culture in which people live and work. Organizations are created by, led by, and staffed by people, all of whom have deeply held and, for the most part, unconscious preconceptions of how they are, how others are, how leaders should act, and how an organization should work. These elements, when taken together and set into place, constitute the basis for the culture of organizations. Those in leadership roles have the most influence in determining the culture. Their implicit value systems have a powerful influence in determining what it is like to work with them and by extension within the organization. It is also important to appreciate that workers are not powerless; they also act to determine organizational culture. This occurs in day-to-day give and take where leaders are accepted or rejected, where some people stay and others leave, where some people follow the rules and others do not, where some people are good to others and other people are not. There are many important ways in which all the members of organizations act to create the culture. The term leader is used in Chapters 13 and 14 to underscore that it is not just management who creates organizational culture. Management cannot impose culture, it must be learned; in order to be learned, it must be accepted; and to be accepted, it must be found to be adaptive. Even in the harshest, most unilateral and autocratic organizational culture, some members may find some of their needs met. Some people prefer to be told what to do or tell others what to do. Some people can identify with autocracy and paternalism; after all, it might be just like home, and the leader just like themselves. In sum, organizational culture is the outcome of the interactions of people at work.

Chapter 15 offers some final reflections on achieving individual excellence at work.

13

Toward an Organizational Culture of Individual Excellence

This book has thus far been devoted to looking at the psychology of individuals and relationships with others, groups, and the organization. Thinking and feeling and their relationship to action at work have been brought into focus. The first five chapters explored the relationship between prior life experience and how one feels, thinks, and acts at work. These individual, interpersonal, and group dynamic perspectives are critical to understanding the true origins of behavior at work—to understanding oneself and the people with whom one works. This chapter balances out the importance of these individual, interpersonal, and group dynamic perspectives with that of the organization and its leadership. The organization, it was noted, has been the focus of most of the books that advocate searching for excellence; what is advocated is changing structural, leadership, and philosophical elements of the organization as a whole. This chapter is devoted to defining organizational culture and describing it, its origins, and the management of cultural change aimed at the pursuit of individual excellence at work.[1]

WHAT IS ORGANIZATIONAL CULTURE?

In order to presume to manage or transform the culture of an organization one must first have a clear idea what organizational culture is and how it is created in order to know how it can be managed. Edgar Schein defines organizational culture to be a pattern of basic assumptions—invented, discovered, or developed by a given group as it learns to cope with its problems of external adaptation and internal integration—that has worked well enough to be considered valid and, therefore, to be taught to new members as the correct way to perceive, think, and feel in relation to those problems.[2]

This definition includes a number of important elements. First, organizational culture is a pattern of basic assumptions which exist, for the most part, out of awareness. They are, like Douglas McGregor's Theory X and Y, the implicit beliefs and feelings people hold about human nature, assumptions not particularly open to inspection, and which at work must be deduced from what is happening.[3] For example, an organization founded upon the research of one or a few individuals may have an organizational culture of waiting for more great ideas to come from these same individuals rather than encouraging everyone else to experiment and innovate. Conflict, volunteerism, and lateral communication may be stifled by the deeply held culture element of waiting in awe for the great founding members to produce new ideas.[4]

The definition also emphasizes that culture is learned from what works. Culture unfolds from experience. It is dynamic. It permits change and adaptation relative to the open system in which it exists. If it does not work, it will not be adopted. More problematic is changing or deleting elements of the organizational culture which, once adopted, are no longer functional. It is at this point of organizational change that the irrational side of organization life may perpetuate an unacknowledged theory of practice that is inconsistent with the changing operating environment. If, in the example of an organizational culture which waits for the products of a few great individuals, it becomes obvious that these individuals can no longer produce the needed ideas, the leadership of the organization might well develop more research facilities staffed by new talent to generate more new ideas. However, if the ideas are always brought back to the great individuals for review, assessment, and approval, nothing much has really changed, and the organization remains strangled by its "great man" culture. The cult of these great individuals still dominates the organization, and the espoused theory of diversified, decentralized research does not, in effect, exist in practice. The culture has gone unchanged.

The definition also includes a linkage to the focus of this book in that it emphasizes that unconscious, unacknowledged basic assumptions shape perception, thinking, and feeling. Organization members come to understand, out of conscious awareness, what basic organizational assumptions govern how people are to relate to each other, how they are to understand the nature of other people, what motivates people at work, and what are the relationships of the organization to its operating environment. For example, the culture of an organization may value its employees highly in the belief that they are good productive members of a community who, if given the resources, time, and encouragement, can overcome great obstacles and produce outstanding products by working together in a conflict-free happy family. This same culture may, however, encourage organization members to see grave threat from an operating environment filled with vicious competitors, unsympathetic legislatures, and paranoid journalists. The mixture of possible basic assumptions about these variables is open ended. The question is what are the governing assumptions of the organization and possibly those of the subcultures within the organization? How do they make one organization or organizational subculture different from others? What makes things work, and what things are not going well and why not? What makes one feel good and what makes one feel bad at work? Are there double standards? Are there gaps between what is actually done and what is desired? Are there internal conflicts between the basic assumptions that are the organization, and do they create and perpetuate unconstructive and unresolvable conflict? Is the pursuit of excellence espoused but not achieved in practice? Are individuals encouraged to achieve excellence but then made to feel helpless and ineffective by others and the leadership of the organization? These are important questions to consider while reading the rest of the chapter. The answers to the questions lead to the means of changing the culture.

THE FUNCTION OF ORGANIZATIONAL CULTURE

To grasp the concept of organizational culture and its underlying basic assumptions, it is necessary to develop a conceptual map or model of how culture develops, how it operates, and to what end. Why is a concept as fundamental as the culture of an organization so hard to understand? This section deals with the question of how organizational culture arises, evolves, and changes or does not change. More important, it asks what purpose organizational culture serves that makes it so important that it is created by the individuals who "people" the work groups and organization.

The basic premise of this section is that people create culture to reduce feelings of anxiety that arise when people are confronted with incomprehensible complexity, uncertainty, or the risk of having to act without certain knowledge of what the outcomes will be. When was the last time you wondered what you should wear to a work-related function at a club or someone's house? If you were uncertain, you were also anxious. You worried about it. You knew that, if you did not fit in, you might be ostracized and feel rejected and humiliated. You did not want to leave the impression that you did not know what you were doing; that you did not have the common sense to dress properly. You might even have worried that your social faux pas might lead to a major problem with your friendships, your career, even the rest of your life. If getting dressed might involve this much anxiety, consider for a moment how anxiety might arise relative to the much greater daily complexity and dynamics of work-a-day life. Being anxious should be the norm given complex internal and external operating environments, pressing time lines, conflicted interpersonal and group dynamics, and the narcissistic aspects of the personalities of powerful executives. One mistake, you might feel, could end your career. This much anxiety must be reduced to tolerable levels in order to avoid becoming emotionally overwhelmed, frozen, and unable to act. Schein believes, as I do, that organizational culture contributes to making work life more predictable by shaping thinking and feeling and by filtering out extraneous variables.

Limiting Inside Anxiety

Organizations are composed of people who relate to each other by performing roles and by accepting the role performances of others. A manager's role must be acted out but must also be accepted before followership occurs. Soldiers or oil rig workers must trust others in the performance of their roles in order to be able to function without becoming overly anxious about their safety. The soldier must believe that the fighter pilot will deliver on target the napalm strike ordered by a superior officer. Working inside an organization can be just as threatening, risky, foreboding, and unpredictable—in short—anxiety ridden. The organization could be experienced as filled with warmth, caring, and trust. More likely, it may be somewhere in between. Schein speaks of the problems of internal integration, the problems of getting everyone on track and working together to minimize anxiety. These problems include (1) common language and conceptual categories, (2) group boundaries and criteria for inclusion and exclusion, (3) power and status, (4) intimacy, friendship, and love, (5) rewards and punishments, and (6) ideology and "religion."

Managers and employees deal with these problems every day, but usually they do not think about them or talk about them in Schein's terms. We all need to come to a common understanding of what is happening—what is being said and done—and we must be able to arrive at some level of consensus as to what we are to do and how we are to do it. To achieve this understanding. It helps if we share common knowledge, language, and communication skills.

Members of groups and organizations must also understand where their organization ends and where they, others, and the operating environment begin. Confused and internally inconsistent statements about mission, the scope of projects, and the tasks of work groups combine to create hard to resolve internal conflict that drains off valuable creative and productive energy. Clear statements of purpose, goals, and methods; clear organizational boundaries; and clear criteria for membership increase predictability and minimize ambiguity, risk, and anxiety.

Organization members must also understand how power and authority are allocated and how they will be used. These are scarce and many times dangerous, or at least threatening, organizational commodities that are important to conserve and use wisely. All organization members would like to feel assured they will not become the focal point for their aggressive or destructive use. Organization members also have needs to feel powerful, wanted, and even loved. Organization members need to feel authorized, empowered, and instrumental in order to avoid feeling dependent, infantilized, and cut off from being effective. Affiliation and intimacy needs draw people together; suspicion, anger, shame, and doubt drive them apart. The leaders of organizations must make friends of their employees and encourage mutuality, nurturance, and teamwork.

Rewards and punishments must also be understood and wielded in a fair and predictable manner. They must be arranged to support organizational basic assumptions and discourage actions, thoughts, and feelings that are antithetical to the organizational culture.

Last, organizations need stories and myths to develop and maintain the ideal image of the organization. The idea that the organization is more than the sum of its parts and holds a great deal of meaning for others (meaning that directs thinking and feeling) is a form of ideology which is an undervalued aspect of our organizations today. Who are the heroes? What are the great feats that have been accomplished against all odds? What have been the great victories? And what have been the tragedies and defeats that organization members have suffered through to rise once again?

All of these factors contribute to making participation less anxiety ridden and, therefore, less likely to provoke the psychological defenses mentioned in the Appendix. The inside of an organization should be warm, friendly, predictable, safe, and nurturing. At the same time, it should not be expected to be all knowing, without fault, and, in short, a perfect womb where life is without effort. These impossible fantasies, which employees may wish for and which managers may wish to provide, must be discouraged in favor of reality testing. The inside of an organization should make its members feel realistically good about themselves, others, their work, and the organization. Naturally this desirable state is hard to achieve, and for many organizations it must be acknowledged that the reality of the meaning of the inside falls far short of these ideals.

Limiting Outside Anxiety

Organizations must be prepared to cope with their operating environment, which is usually filled with aggressive competitors, hard to reach consumers, and the limiting actions and "red tape" of public and industrial regulators. The survival of organizations necessitates the consideration of how to acquire more resources than are used in production, in the case of for-profit enterprises, and how to acquire continuing if not increasing public support, in the case of not-for-profit enterprises. Schein also speaks to those elements of an organization that permit it to cope with the potentially threatening world beyond the boundaries of the organization. These elements include (1) mission and strategy, (2) goals, (3) means, (4) measurement, and (5) correction. Managers and employees must deal with these organizational variables on a daily basis; after all, the variables strike at the heart of what everyone is supposed to be doing, how, with what, and toward what planned end.

Before discussing these variables it is important to understand that the division of organizational life into an inside and outside—sides of work life that are both filled with anxieties—is but one way of thinking about organizational life, one way to look at what is going on. These two perspectives are experienced as a set of interrelated variables which are both interlocked and constantly changing. They are parts of a whole that are thought about and felt about as a hard to understand complexity that must be broken down into its constituent parts before it can be described, analyzed, and managed. The inside/outside perspective of organizational life is a good way to look at organizational life.

The owners and leaders of an organization invest it with a purpose or mission that is expected to direct the attention of organization members to what is envisioned for the organization and inspire organization members to pursue the mission. The mission, if understood by all, promotes the development of a shared understanding of what work means, which influences thinking and feeling. Likewise, strategies that operationalize the mission further instruct thinking and feeling and guide managers, administrators, and workers in their actions. The mission and strategy are further operationalized in the form of internally consistent goals and congruent objectives. This rational process of boiling everything down to the essentials, however, can break down when organization members who, motivated by personal values, thoughts, and feelings, not always consistent with those supported by the leaders of the organization, begin to create off-task political, power-oriented outcomes.

Even more individualized and, therefore, more open to manipulation by managers for their own egocentric needs are the means of getting the work done to meet the objectives aimed at goal achievement. Means, including resources and methods, really begin and end with the overwhelming influence of the wielding of interpersonal power and authority. Feeling powerful and acting powerfully are believed to be overlaid with biological imperatives to control and dominate, which are then heavily influenced by life experience and socialization as illustrated in the case studies. People who feel they have to be in control to feel good about themselves (to be doing their job as they see it) can be depended upon to strive for power which they then unconsciously wield to meet their own needs.

The last management concern is that the results of work should be measured and those responsible for the work should be held accountable for the quantity and quality by upper management, which may then lead to corrective actions being mandated to achieve the desired outcomes. These two steps, monitoring and corrective action, include the many bad feelings most employees have come to associate with being held accountable by a parent or organizational superior. Accountability carries with it the feelings of being powerless and dependent, and the possibility of being punished for not being good enough. Accountability, performance evaluation, and rewards and discipline are filled with negative feelings associated with guilt, shame, power, and dependency and are, as a result, often not carried out in a meaningful way by managers.

It may be observed there is a circularity to these outside oriented processes that begins and ends with top management, but which, most important, includes others who are depended upon to act responsibly, professionally, at times impersonally, devotedly, and altruistically—factors often only minimally realized in American enterprises. These considerations lead us to consider the underlying fabric of our organizations—their culture—for it must be asked what shapes the formation or creation of the above anxiety-limiting aspects of organizations.

THE CONTENT OF ORGANIZATIONAL CULTURE

Organizational culture exists without clear knowledge of it. It reduces the experience of anxiety at work by making work life more predictable, less complex, and less threatening. Organizational culture includes those processes, ideas, and ideologies that help us feel as though we belong while, at the same time, not making us feel as though we are being taken over by the organization and are losing our identity. Before discussing the nature of leadership and the connection of organizational culture and leadership to achieving individual excellence, it is necessary to consider a higher level of inquiry.

Organizational cultures evolve from fundamental assumptions or philosophies held by those who own and control the organization, those who lead the subdivisions or groups that develop their own subcultures, and those who work within the organization. Consistent with this book, it must be noted that the assumptions, philosophies, and worldviews held by each of us have been heavily influenced by our life experiences, which have created unconscious and, at times, compulsive motivations that then distort our thinking and feeling. These distortions then fuel or inform the assumptions held about ourselves, others, our organizations, and the world—assumptions that also unconsciously influence what we sense, think, and feel. They are how we know the world, and they seem to us to be absolute reality—not open to inspection or change. These systems of unconscious thinking and feeling constitute the "precultural" elements of organizational life. They are how we have to be to survive independent of cultural considerations. They are us, and they influence the society and culture we create.

Schein notes that a number of important philosophical aspects of existence at work are shaped by our intrapsychic existence: (1) our relationship to nature, (2) our own human nature, (3) the nature of human activity, (4) the nature of reality and truth, and (5) the nature of human relationships. It is these philosophical considerations that make the true nature of management much more than merely the science of finding the most cost-effective way to produce a product, to generate a positive cash flow, or to create a high return on investment. Everyone who works holds assumptions about these aspects of life which are critical to acknowledge.

Relationship to Nature

The world is all around us. Understanding the world means being able to define who we are. This permits us to tell ourselves from others, and it defines our organization (as indicated by its mission statements and goals) from other organizations. We also have to be able to discriminate which parts of our environment are the most important. To do so we must make assumptions about our relationships to others and to the world, and we must do the same for our organizations.

We form beliefs about how nature is in order to live in it. These beliefs can be highly informed and realistic or, more likely, these beliefs may suffer from some degree of personal psychological disorganization. When owners, leaders, and managers hold unrealistic beliefs about themselves, others, the organization, and the world, beliefs which arise from unconscious aspects of their personalities, organizational cultural basic assumptions will become disorienting, pathological, dysfunctional, and nonadaptive. Organization members will live and work in a setting that increases rather than allays their anxieties and provokes rather than discourages the use of psychological defenses. Leaders of organizations must appreciate that the basic assumptions they hold about the nature of the world are important and that they should be open to self-reflection and examination. If they find the world to be threatening, their paranoia may be the norm that governs decision making and work.

Human Nature

We all have beliefs about how we are and how others are based, in part, upon what we have learned from life experience. An example of a set of consistent beliefs is that people are inherently lazy, untrustworthy, inconsiderate, unthinking, and, in general, "bad." These beliefs may be held for only certain types of people and for specific kinds of organizations. In contrast, it may be believed that people and organizations are inherently "good," trustworthy, thoughtful, and hard working, and that organizations are socially conscious and highly productive. It is most likely that all of these beliefs are held and that the ones that emerge depend on recent experience, how we feel at the moment, and the situation at hand. The assumptions we hold about how we are, how others are, and how organizations are come back full circle to influence unconsciously our perceptions, thinking, and feelings and by extension how we work with others. Organization members and leaders must be aware of what they are thinking and feeling about others and be able to inspect their actions for implicit assumptions about human nature. Making a highly detailed and organized list of tasks for someone to perform, for example, includes an implicit assumption about human nature.

Nature of Human Activity

We also all hold beliefs about the nature of our actions relative to others and the world. We might, for example, see ourselves and our organizations as powerful and instrumental and able to change others and the world. In contrast, we might see ourselves and our organizations as helpless, dependent, and ineffective; unable to take action or, at best, able only to react to changes in the environment. Depending upon which beliefs are held, the leaders and members of an organization may feel that they can act proactively and instrumentally, or they may feel that they must always collect more information while waiting to see what will happen. Influences such as these can be easily spotted in work groups and organizations where these basic assumptions lead to feeling valued and influential or frustrated and helpless. How leaders feel about themselves and the organization is the critical variable in how organization members come to understand themselves, each other, their work, and their organization.

Nature of Reality and Truth

Understanding what the facts are can prove to be elusive even for scientists and philosophers. The question we have to ask ourselves and our organizations is how is reality determined? Are the facts based upon hard evidence, or are they the result of a subjective process and layers of filtered (possibly face-saving) reporting? Is reality dictated by the personal biases of a few powerful people at the top? How should we determine what the truth is when rationality is bounded by the cost of obtaining perfect information and the time it takes to get it?[5] Organization leaders must be careful about what is put forward as truth and how much effort is expended in uncovering objective facts about absolute reality. Balances must be struck, but care must be taken that subjective reality does not take over.

Nature of Human Relationships

Finally, people can develop many different assumptions about the nature of interpersonal relationships, assumptions that originate at birth and continue to develop throughout life. Relationships include the issues of autonomy and control. A child may feel controlled and experience little autonomy which, if not eventually changed, infantilizes the individual. The nature of our relationships to powerful superiors at work can also infantilize us when we are confronted by autocratic, paternalistic, manipulative, and control-oriented behavior as employees. By comparison, our relationships can also be liberating when powerful others provide meaningful delegation, empowerment, and participation, and they respect our autonomy. How the relationships are imposed from above and reacted to from below, as illustrated by the cases, can be dominated by unconscious processes that can lead to unproductive working relationships. Organization leaders must be sensitive to how their actions, informed by their beliefs, impact others.

The natures of the world, of humans, of work, of reality, and of working together are the basic assumptions of organizational culture. They are hard to detect and even harder to call into question and change. Their management, however, is a critical aspect of achieving individual and organizational excellence.

LEADING CULTURAL CHANGE

Organizational culture has been described as including well-worn paths for thinking about and feeling about work which often go unacknowledged and which implicitly include the above basic assumptions about ourselves, others, and the work world. Organizational culture has also been described as a meaning that is shared by organization members, which, if disturbed, creates uncomfortable anxiety that will usually be responded to by avoidance and by renewed efforts to make the organization and its culture work better.[6] Seldom questioned will be the need to change the organization and its culture fundamentally. Anyone who does so is taking a serious risk. Now we come to the leaders of organizations and their relationship to organizational culture.

Cultural change is predictably threatening to organization members, and it can be expected to fall to the leaders of an organization to intervene in deeply embedded, unconscious thinking and feeling processes. The intervention will create anxiety as the old ways of thinking and feeling are openly challenged and new unfamiliar ways are put forward in their place. Organization members must give up what is familiar and safe. They must give up some of their skills, relationships, and treasured systems for something new and different. They quickly understand that they will have to (1) learn something new, (2) work through a period of transition from the old ways to the new ways, (3) work out and perfect the new ways, (4) cope with fears that they might not be able to learn the new ways, and (5) cope with their shame about how they let their old systems fail. In short, they must do more work for an extended period of time. They must work through their anxieties, fears, shame, and anger; and they must work through planning and implementing the change while keeping the organization running.

Leaders can help the members of the organization work through their feelings and work harder for a while to make the changes that are needed. Leaders can (1) point the way, (2) stand steadfast in the storm of problems and difficulties created by making the changes, (3) be demanding and hold high expectations, and (4) bandage the knees of employees who fall down along the path of change. If the leader sincerely cares, points the way through uncertainty, coaches and coaxes, and rewards and celebrates the successes while minimizing the fault associated with problems and failures, the leader can hold the people of the organization together. Leaders, according to Schein, help contain the fears and anxieties and absorb or deflect the anger of organization members.

These are indeed weighty responsibilities for leaders to assume. Assuming them is facilitated when leaders understand and appreciate the following list of leadership criteria and cultural change elements.

1. The leaders of cultural change must be able to maintain objectivity in the sea of conflicting feelings and distorted thinking that will be generated by those who are the subject of the change. Objectivity will be aided by the ability to develop keen insights into the dynamics of the organization's culture and the dynamics created by the change effort. The leaders must be decisive in sorting out the important from the unimportant and then be able to prioritize problems with a certainty that assures others.

2. The leaders of cultural change must be willing to challenge, break down, and unfreeze the culture—a process that will be experienced by its members as painful, disorienting, and anxiety ridden. The leaders must be able to communicate the challenges and the need for change without alienating followers who may consciously or unconsciously collude to block and reject the change agents. The leaders must be willing to put the organization's interests before any personal needs to be accepted, liked, or admired. This selfless and possibly altruistic act is an essential aspect of leading a shift in organizational culture. In the process of making this sacrifice, the leaders will instill feelings in others of compassion, understanding, and devoted dedication while they lead the way on a long, uncertain journey that requires courage, sacrifice, and perseverance.

3. The leaders of a cultural change must possess enough inner strength to withstand the many stresses and anxieties that will develop as organization members become fearful, angry, confused, uncertain, and, to some degree, paranoid and obstructive. The leaders must have a realistic and strong sense of self-esteem to minimize the experience of anxiety and to avoid the sense of becoming personally disorganized, doubtful of the course of action selected, and feeling every battle must be won and every protagonist defeated. The leaders must be willing targets of the anger, aggression, and personal attacks inspired by individuals, leaders of subunits, and coalitions within and outside of the organization or section involved. The leaders must be prepared to persist, to remain caring and understanding, and to avoid the temptation to counterattack even when, in some instances, progressive discipline is warranted. Such factors require a constant show of support and confidence by governing board members and CEOs if less than the entire organization is involved.

4. The leaders of organizational change, both during and after unfreezing the culture, must be able to lead their members to a new set of basic assumptions that have to be artfully developed and inspirationally presented in a message that becomes a constant press. The new basic assumptions must be espoused frequently, in many forms, to many audiences; and the leaders must be good models of the new assumptions and pay attention to those aspects of organizational life that have been emphasized. Everyone will watch; double standards or inconsistency may cripple the change effort.

5. The leaders of organizational change must be able to create a climate in which meaningful participation is permitted and encouraged. The leaders must be good listeners and willing to work alongside those who are experiencing the change. The leaders

must be willing to delegate and empower subordinates to act to fulfill the change goals. Everyone must become actively involved in the change process, and everyone must be enlisted in the effort by the leaders.

6. The leaders of organizational change must be effective manipulators of symbols and goals. To do so, the leaders must be able to understand the meaning of the old basic assumptions in order to effectively remove them and replace them with a new set of assumptions consistent with the organization's mission, history, and type of work. For example, a new incentive system, which provides a monetary reward for every new idea generated, may alienate some who are creative because it is their nature to generate new ideas. Being rewarded for something they enjoy doing to encourage them to do more may anger them, may make them feel they must be manipulated to be creative, and may alienate them from themselves, each other, their work, and the organization.

Leadership of organizational change involves many major considerations, and it is a demanding role that can be punishing to assume. However, the question remains, what are the basic cultural assumptions that are needed to instill in an organization a pursuit of individual excellence and avoid some of the outcomes and burned-out superstars of the cases?

TOWARD A CULTURE OF INDIVIDUAL EXCELLENCE

The leaders of organizations are responsible for developing, fostering, and nurturing the cultures of their organizations. It must always be appreciated that any fundamental change in an organization will involve the basic assumptions that constitute the culture and allay anxiety about the organization and its operating environment. Developing an organizational culture aimed at freeing up the pursuit of individual excellence is one of the keys to success in the 1990s and beyond.

The next chapter uses the content of this chapter to describe the elements of an organizational culture that promotes the achievement of individual excellence. The basic assumptions that must be held by leaders of cultural change will be described and related to the anxiety that will be felt about both the "inside" and the "outside" of the organization.

14

The Search for Individual Excellence

This book is about executives, managers, supervisors, and workers who, many times, unconsciously act to limit and undermine others who make outstanding contributions—the superstars all organizations have and need to keep productive. Many aspects of organizations, of work life, and of individual, interpersonal, and group dynamics have been discussed. The cases made the abstract nature of the dynamics more concrete. Chapter 13 provided a window of opportunity for those who are willing to lead their organizations, divisions, and departments in the pursuit of an organizational culture that seeks out individual excellence. This chapter provides guidelines for organizational leaders to follow to establish a culture of individual excellence.

The chapter begins with the basic assumptions that form the culture of individual excellence. The basic assumptions are examined for the meaning they contribute to the pursuit of individual excellence. The chapter continues by reviewing the organizational elements that allay anxiety about the ''inside'' and the ''outside'' of the organization. Steps for developing the culture as well as possible pitfalls are provided. In some ways, these recommendations come full circle, back to the work of Tom Peters and others who make many recommendations about how to restructure the workplace to facilitate productivity and creativity. Some of the recommendations may be similar to those of Peters and others—back to the basic, commonsense approaches to empowering people to think and work. However, what is important to appreciate is that the recommendations of this book arise from a different origin—from insights into people and into the meaning of the unconscious world of work.

A note on leaders must be added before continuing. Superstars, as the cases illustrated, may be anywhere in an organization and may shine at any time. And so it is with leaders. A leader need not be an executive, manager, supervisor, or group leader. Leadership can be provided whenever someone has something to contribute. The pursuit of a culture of individual excellence is everyone's responsibility; therefore, everyone can provide leadership.

BASIC ASSUMPTIONS OF INDIVIDUAL EXCELLENCE

The basic assumptions of individual excellence are those aspects of organization, which, when instilled by leaders, become the fabric of the organization, department, or group—the part of work life that is taken for granted and is not readily known, understood, or open to questioning. The key element of the pursuit of individual excellence is knowing and managing organizational culture. It is important to understand that, from the start, this chapter questions the nature of the unconscious, unknowable aspects of organizational culture—the basic assumptions. To be managed, they must be known and understood. They must be open to inspection and change.

Relationship to Nature

"At the organizational level, do the key members view the relationship of the organization to its environment as one of dominance, submission, harmonizing, finding an appropriate niche, or what?"[1]

In order to be able to function, everyone has theories about how the world works, theories that are so ingrained that they are unconscious. Objects, if dropped, always fall. A part of this understanding is our own unique way of dividing up the elements of our world into us and everything else and a way to make discriminations among what is left—different people, different work, and different organizations. We do this without really thinking about it. At work, the organization and its leaders may, for example, be thought of as submissive. Operating strategies may be consistently reactive rather than proactive. The reasons for the passiveness are not known and not questioned—passiveness is part of the culture.

Basic Assumptions. The culture of individual excellence is created by the following basic assumptions about the nature of the world:

1. The world is filled with change and opportunities to succeed as well as the risks that some efforts will be less than successful. There is a constant need to monitor the world for any change that will impact performance, for any change that will provide new opportunities to achieve excellence. The challenge of achieving excellence is everywhere.

2. The world is receptive to new ideas and new ways of doing things, although Mother Nature will keep reality testing at the forefront of the achievement of individual excellence.

3. The world provides more than one way of "skinning a cat." Some ways are better than others, but there is not always one best way. There is room for different ideas, all of which will have some merit.

4. The world is filled with diversity. Others will hold different worldviews and cannot always be expected to be fair, reasonable, and supportive. Perfect justice does not exist. Those pursuing excellence must be prepared to persist.

5. The world provides everyone with information about oneself, others, and reality. Listening is important to keep in touch with oneself and the world around one.

Pitfalls

1. Gloom and doom often develop when problems and change are encountered. They are not a part of the nature of the world of excellence. The world is always ready for success. Negativism and obsessive fears of failure, rejection, and perfectionism are antithetical to the pursuit of individual excellence. Outstanding work can predominate.

2. Success and achieving excellence come only with taking risks and hard work. Having great thoughts without testing, perfecting, and advocating them usually will not lead to the achievement of excellence.

3. Some individuals know the world to be threatening, and they carry within them needs to compete, dominate, win, and control. Their personal struggles can be adaptive to the pursuit of excellence, but they can be equally nonadaptive. Rather than encouraging adaptive actions motivated by this struggle and discouraging less adaptive actions, it is wiser to challenge the individual's worldview of having to dominate.

Human Nature

"What does it mean to be 'human' and what attributes are considered intrinsic or ultimate? Is human nature good, evil, or neutral? Are human beings predictable or not?"[2]

We all have theories about ourselves and what makes other people and the organization tick. These theories, based on lifelong learning, are so much a part of us that we are not always aware we hold them. These theories exercise a constant and powerful influence on how we think we are and how other people and the organization are and should be dealt with; "Top down is the only thing that people seem to think will work around here." Those who have a leadership role and especially those in the highest positions must hold realistic and sensitive views of the diversity of human nature and its variability over time and from situation to situation. Interpersonal understanding and sensitivity are critical aspects of a culture of individual excellence.

Basic Assumptions. The culture of individual excellence has prerequisites about the basic assumptions of human nature.

1. The diversity of people is good—up to a point. Too often the unconscious goal of groups is to make everyone alike by selection and by subsequent training and peer pressure. Some who do not fit in may be trying to make important contributions, but they may go unheard because what they think, say, and do are different. Listening carefully to dysfunctional group members can yield insights about thinking and feelings associated with what is happening. However, if, in the end, there is no salvaging the situation, the diversity becomes destructive and its source must be removed.

2. People enjoy being productive. Others can enjoy their work, can be productive, can be innovative, can be successful—can achieve individual excellence—if permitted to do so.

3. Others, groups, and organizations can encourage people to feel angry, powerless, and alienated. People who have a bad attitude and who are destructive and dysfunctional may not, in fact, wish to be outcasts. They may have learned from others to be "problems," and they may be able to unlearn their behavior if they are helped by those same others. Everyone has something positive to contribute.

4. People influence others and may not always act like themselves. People and groups may prefer to keep a person in a dysfunctional role—better him or her than me. Some people may be especially vulnerable to being set up to fail or to being scapegoated. In this case, the individuals may learn to accept the role and continue to act it out as a part of an unconscious group process.

5. Compassion is a must. Everyone has an unconscious life which contributes to determining what is thought, felt, and done. Everyone has suffered forgotten pain and humiliations. Everyone has learned to adjust to less than ideal treatment by learning coping mechanisms that, when combined with the level of threat perceived, influence everyone's daily lives.

Pitfalls

1. Not everyone with dysfunctional behavior is salvageable. People can be very resistant to learning about themselves, facing their problems which often means dealing with painful prior life experiences, and changing how they think and feel about themselves and others. Everyone suffers from problems to some extent; however, some individuals are too disorganized to be able to be dealt with effectively at work and should be referred to an employee assistance program.

2. Leaders of groups cannot always manage what is happening. Group dynamics can, for example, create a dysfunctional member who is seen to be the "problem" with the group's performance. This is a very powerful dynamic that is difficult to spot. It can be difficult for leaders to distinguish between individual dysfunctions and group dynamics–induced dysfunctions. Leaders of groups have too much to do. Leaders who believe that this kind of group dynamic is at work should consider availing themselves of a group process consultant who can help sort out who is doing what to whom.

3. Actions that are caring and sensitive must be sincere and flow naturally from the leader and, just as important, from others. However, all too common are artificial, superficial, manipulative efforts to make others love and admire the leader. Unauthentic words, actions, thoughts, and feelings are easily sensed by others unless they have an unconscious reason to filter them out. Leaders must be authentic to avoid developing

and perpetuating a culture in which everyone looks behind what is going on to find out the true meaning—where what you see is not what you get.

Nature of Reality and Truth

"The linguistic and behavioral rules that define what is real and what is not, what is a 'fact,' how truth is ultimately to be determined, and whether truth is 'revealed' or 'discovered'; basic concepts of time and space."[3]

Reality in the workplace can be both real and fabricated by those who lead and work within organizations. Absolute reality exists in the form of walls you cannot walk through. Reality is the fact that you have a job and the notion that an organization exists. These aspects of work life are better understood than the more shadowy, interpersonally subjective world of organizational hierarchy, power, authority, and working relationships; the other basic assumptions discussed here; the ability of managers to lead, direct, and order and the ability of others to question and follow. How these realities are defined and by whom is an implicit part of this chapter. Who should decide what is or should be?

Basic Assumptions

1. A culture of individual excellence is based on the assumption that there is more than one reality when it comes to performing work, working in groups, and working within an organization. Everyone forms his on her own conception of what work is and what the organization is like. However, in order to work together, there must be some common organizational reality. Organizational culture encourages organization members to see themselves, others, and the organization in a certain way. However, a culture of individual excellence must include a constant questioning of this negotiated reality. Leaders must not feel so powerful and omnipotent that they believe they can master organizational reality. It is not management's role to implant "their" reality in the hearts and minds of "their" employees. It is their job to provide leadership that draws everyone to a common understanding of the basic assumptions that are to be heeded within the organization—assumptions that may or may not be agreeable to all concerned but are accepted.

2. Many aspects of organizational reality are subject to manipulation or control. What may seem like a fact is often the product of one person's mind. For example, what is the problem? It may seem obvious that a flat tire on a car is a problem. If the flat tire is defined to be the problem, it is a matter of exchanging it with a spare. However, a person who does not know how to change a flat or who does not wish to change a tire will define the problem a little differently. The flat keeps the car from running; the problem is to get it fixed. There are many other ways to look at the problem. Perhaps the flat creates the problem of getting somewhere on time; the solution might be to abandon the car and take alternate transportation. Perhaps the problem is the lack of a spare tire, or the blocking of a lane of traffic. Those who have the power to define the problem define reality. A cash flow crisis might be the result of too many expenses (cut the budget) or too little income (increase sales). The problem can be defined either way. The subjective nature of the problem, which then directs attention

to working toward solving the problem, must be open for questioning to achieve excellence. Appreciating what exactly is subject to definition is critical—organizational reality is subjective.

3. A culture of individual excellence means reality should be "negotiated" among organization members and not dictated by the most powerful organization member(s). Reality is not a top-down process; it is created by the members of the organization. What is perfectly clear to a CEO may be much less clear to a middle manager. Reality, thinking, and feeling must be validated by others in a process of consensus building, if time permits. In some cases, when time is short, reality may have to be dictated.

4. Reality testing must be of paramount importance for achieving excellence. Individuals and groups can become involved with group thinking processes that become divorced from reality as illustrated by the space shuttle disaster and the Bay of Pigs incident. Leaders striving to achieve excellence must constantly seek out opportunities to test thinking and work against reality.

5. It must not be assumed there is one best way to discover or test reality. The scientific method of hypothesis testing does not always work. Survey and statistical analysis, computer models, and artificial intelligence do not always reveal the truth. There is no one right method for knowing reality. Method should not supplant substance and good judgement.

Pitfalls

1. The idea that it is management's responsibility to define organizational reality must be avoided and seen for, in part, what it is—a self-centered worldview that may conceal needs to feel powerful and in control or in the center of the universe. The seductive nature of being and acting powerfully must be appreciated in order to avoid it.

2. Reality, however defined, is not static. In addition to reality testing solutions to problems, it is critical to keep testing the correctness of the definition of the problem relative to a changing world. To be avoided is a personal investment by management in keeping the problem defined in one way—making the best buggy whip or the largest cars may not always be appropriate in the marketplace.

3. Everyone need not agree upon the nature of reality; however, the definition being used must fit within an area of ambivalence that is unique to each member of the organization. Others may not fully agree with the definition, but they should not be strongly opposed to it. If some members are unequivocally opposed, they should be given a full hearing before being disregarded or possibly replaced; they may have something to contribute.

Nature of Human Activity

"What is the 'right' thing for human beings to do, on the basis of the above assumptions about reality, the environment, and human nature: to be active, passive, self-developmental, fatalistic, or what? What is work and what is play?"[4]

Working is a way of life in organizations. Work can be exciting, demanding, and challenging or repetitive and boring. Workers can experience themselves as in control of their work and instrumental in making a product or delivering a service, or they can feel cut off from feeling instrumental, effective, or good about their work. Organization members can feel good about working with others or experience others and management as indifferent, hostile, unilateral, aggressive, uncaring, and controlling. In sum, members of organizations can feel respected, valued, and instrumental relative to their work, or they can feel alienated from themselves, their work, others, and the organization.

Basic Assumptions

1. Excellence can be achieved by individuals. It does not necessarily have to fall to groups, departments, experts, consultants, and management to achieve excellence. People can do it and should be encouraged to do it.

2. Work, innovation, and change are something to master, a challenge to be overcome. It should not be assumed that something cannot be done or should not be attempted.

3. The achievements of some will not upset the apple cart. Outstanding performance of superstars should not be regulated out of fear of creating interpersonal imbalances that will lead to bad feelings of being outshined.

4. People can enjoy their work if they are allowed to. Incentive programs are not needed if it is believed that everyone can enjoy his or her work. In the place of incentives, rewards should be provided when outstanding performance occurs.

5. People will support each other if they are allowed to do so. If employees believe that they are rewarded only for individual achievement, their attention will be focused on competing, not on helping others. Everyone should be encouraged to coach, counsel, and help others, and to abandon self-aggrandizement that is so often the hidden agenda. After all, we learn from the first grade on that we are graded as individuals. This culture of individual accountability can be damaging to a culture aimed at achieving individual excellence. It is ironic that, in order for individuals to achieve excellence, everyone needs to work together.

Pitfalls

1. Incentive systems may promote productivity, but they are based on the self-centered assumption that people must be manipulated by management to work. Even more distressing is that many incentives promote work in ways or on tasks that may actually be counterproductive. An incentive to increase output will, for example, inevitably encourage cutting corners on quality and safety.

2. Because executives and managers may wish to feel powerful and authoritative, they may unconsciously discourage individual initiative which they may experience as stealing their thunder, recognition, rewards, and promotions. Managers must overcome the fear of letting go, of delegating, of empowering, and of enabling others to work.

3. People may be motivated to do a lot of good work to compensate for inner feelings of low self-esteem and worthlessness and to receive a constant supply of approval.

They may constantly sacrifice to help others succeed. All outstanding work is not necessarily good. Organization members who have compulsive achievement needs may, for example, ruin their health, friendships, and family life if they are not constructively confronted over their behavior.

Nature of Human Relationships

"What is considered to be the 'right' way for people to relate to each other, to distribute power and love? Is life cooperative or competitive; individualistic, group collaborative, or communal; based on traditional lineal authority, law, charisma, or what?"[5]

Do members of the organization and management believe that they must dominate or submit to others; try to harmonize their attitudes, beliefs, feelings, and thoughts with each other; or do they expect to be in conflict with others in the organization until just the right type of work comes along? Organization members must be alerted to the possibility of assisting each other in the pursuit of excellence. It must be felt to be safe to distinguish oneself and to help others distinguish themselves without feeling humiliated and threatened.

Basic Assumptions

1. People enjoy working together. It is not necessary to motivate, manipulate, or manage people into working together. People and superstars can be exciting, stimulating, and fun to be around and work with. People will find ways to make work into play if left alone to do so and permitted ownership of their time, energies, talents, and work.

2. People enjoy their individuality and autonomy, and they enjoy working in groups and with others who respect them as individuals. Everyone has his or her own story and something unique to contribute to work. People can also be resistant to change and even to minimal levels of needed conformity. These individuals can see others as threats and find working with others and performing work intolerable. Not everyone has redeeming work-related qualities; prompt recognition and remedial action must be taken to avoid the appearance of double standards, which can be demoralizing.

3. People will voluntarily cooperate with each other to a degree that cannot be mandated by management. People are self-initiating, self-directing, and self-managed if management lets them be that way. People will figure out what it takes to get a job done if they feel they are respected members of the organization. To achieve this, those in charge must share information and problems, ignore any needs to feel powerful and in control, and avoid handing down predefined problems and solutions.

4. Feeling competitive and being competitive are two different things. Working in an exciting, open, supportive setting stimulates everyone to achieve more and develop new ideas. Feelings of competing against outside competitors and achieving high standards for performance can be exhilarating and create an atmosphere where excellence is the expectation. A sports team that reaches the play-offs includes members who, as individuals and as members of a group, are highly motivated by the sense of competing against and defeating other teams. The excitement of this kind of achievement feeds upon itself. However, just being competitive as individuals or subgroups

within a larger organization can be destructive and drain off energy into unproductive and counterproductive interpersonal and intergroup rivalries. People and groups who are pitted against each other will invariably create a few winners and many losers. Strong competitive urges will offend, frighten, and alienate others. A team member who wants to score all the points or who may be a hopeless self-promoter can be a divisive element on a team. Understanding what it means to compete can avoid those fragmenting and centrifugal forces that can pull people and groups apart.

5. Working together means that some will lead and many will follow. There is no one right leadership style. Leadership must vary based on the people involved and the situation. Those who are effective leaders in one situation may not have suitable leadership skills in another situation. Those who lead should be encouraged to develop self-reflective skills to assist in monitoring their own compulsive tendencies. Leaders must not, for example, experience their roles as something that, if lost, will crush them. Followership can also be understood to be a set of skills and attitudes toward authority figures that can facilitate cooperation and avoid the resistance often associated with bad prior life experiences with authority figures.

Pitfalls

1. Individual autonomy should not be glorified. Although individuals need freedom and support to be creative, they still need each other and the organization. A constant press by an individual to be left alone to be creative is inconsistent with the interpersonal world of individual excellence.

2. Superstars have no license to be uncooperative, abrasive, aggressive, underhanded, deceptive, unilateral, or interpersonally competitive. Many people who achieve a great deal may be motivated, as illustrated in the cases, by inner needs to try to feel good and to receive attention even if much of it is negative. Organization members must not be expected to tolerate or submit to these kinds of abuses. Accommodating them should be viewed as encouraging them and creating a self-fulfilling cycle of continued defenses against any rejection of the superstar.

3. There is no one ''right'' way to work with others, and leaders should not presume to mandate one way. People who care, who are free to help themselves and each other, and who are encouraged to do the right thing will invariably find the right way.

LIMITING ANXIETY

Limiting anxiety at work is the central purpose of organizational culture. The pursuit of individual excellence requires a culture that is safe, supportive, open, and nurturing. The culture of individual excellence will flourish in a world which holds many of the following assumptions that limit anxiety. There are assumptions about the ''inside'' impersonal world of organizations where the following elements dominate work life: organizational structure, policies, and procedures; physical layout of offices, facilities, and equipment; and the organization and safety of the work. There are also assumptions about the world ''outside'' and what it holds for the organization. Is the world threatening or friendly, one that encourages growth or one that frustrates it?

Limiting Inside Anxiety

Organizational leaders must develop those organizational aspects of the inside of the organization that make employees feel secure about the impersonal elements of their world at work: communication, membership, power and status, relationships, rewards and punishments, and unpredictable problems and opportunities.

Communication. "If members cannot communicate with and understand each other, a group is impossible by definition."[6]

A common language and a common way of thinking about others must be developed, one that makes it acceptable to shine or to be outshined. The written and spoken word must include ideas about the pursuit of individual excellence. Policies and procedures must not be written in such a way that discourages the pursuit of excellence either explicitly or, perhaps more important, implicitly. For example, does protocol call for many layers of approval that lead to a risk-aversive outcome that separates those with the ideas from the product of their own imagination?

Possible pitfalls include the following:

1. Possibly of greatest concern is the giving of lip service to the pursuit of individual excellence. There may be few aspects of organizational life that are more disheartening than hearing the party line knowing those who speak it do not believe it or follow it.

2. The wording of important statements must not sound condescending or self-serving on the part of management. Managers must not presume that their efforts achieve excellence; rather, their efforts set the scene for achieving individual excellence.

3. Many aspects of the work environment may inhibit the pursuit of individual excellence. Are training and education consistent with the pursuit of individual excellence provided? Do policies and procedures make it difficult to deviate from the norm? Does the layout of space inhibit the free flow of interaction and communication that so often lead to the generation of new ideas? Is everyone kept informed of new developments and research? Is time provided for employees to explore new ideas about solving old problems or developing new opportunities?

Membership. "One of the most important areas of culture is the shared consensus on who is in and who is out and by what criteria one determines membership."[7]

Group boundaries and criteria for inclusion and exclusion must make clear where the organization ends and the rest of the world begins and, just as important, what it means to be a part of the organization and a member of some of the many subgroups that may exist. Clear organizational structure and statements of purpose and scope for work groups minimize confusion about who may act relative to whom and in what manner. Understanding what is going on helps organization members to coordinate their work voluntarily, a level of coordination that no amount of mandating by top management can achieve. Feeling a part of a group that is treated respectfully by others and by top management is in part the result of identifiable and secure group boundaries and a clear understanding of what constitutes membership. The pursuit of individual excellence needs structure to succeed but will also put pressure on structure for more flexibility or fluidity.

There are three pitfalls to consider:

1. Efforts to explain and clarify should avoid compulsive needs on the part of leaders to feel in control and to avoid conflict by taking care to specify every conceivable interaction. Both outcomes can be rationalized as constructive and the job of management, but they often conceal unconscious paternalistic motivations to feel powerful, needed, and in control and maternalistic motivations to avoid or suppress conflict and to make sure everyone feels good, is treated fairly, and is taken care of. The pursuit of individual excellence will be limited by both of these outcomes that control thinking and creativity.

2. The specification of organizational space, resources, power, and authority should avoid unconscious but not often concealed tendencies to protect one's turf in the form of maintaining tasks, staff, space, and other resources or access to future resources. Careful explication of boundaries and purpose may conceal an unconscious collusion to protect everyone's turf which may also have the benefit of suppressing rivalry and conflict. Individual excellence disrupts the status quo and threatens others and their turf.

3. A call for change in the established patterns of boundaries and work may conceal the unconsciously motivated pursuit of power and empire by an individual or a group. There is nothing inherently wrong with permitting a successful individual or group to acquire more resources as long as they are used creatively and productively. However, to the extent that the motivations are inspired by unconscious needs to feel powerful and to dominate others, the tendency must be resisted in favor of confronting the unconscious motivations.

Power and Status. "Every organization must work out its pecking order, its criteria and rules for how one gets, maintains, and loses power; consensus in this area is crucial to help members manage feelings of aggression."[8]

Power and status are organizational elements that individuals hold. It must be clear how they are acquired and how they are to be used. It must be safe to act powerfully relative to others, and others must understand the limits to which power may be used in order to feel safe. These threatening and foreboding aspects of formal organization must be wielded in a predictable and just manner in order to make all concerned feel safe in their presence. Superstars in particular must be assured that they will not suddenly become a target for someone with power when they suggest or achieve something that is threatening.

The pitfalls to power and status are as follows:

1. Power and status are so often pursued by individuals for their own sake to compensate for inner feelings of powerlessness and worthlessness that they have become dangerous words often banned from open discussion. Power and status are "bad" male attributes associated with dominance, submission, and destruction. Making them safer means being able to talk about them. Outstanding performers will often unintentionally challenge power and authority or possibly, more likely, threaten those who possess them. Being able to talk about what is happening and about what people are feeling is critical to avoid retreats to wielding power and authority as defenses to anxiety.

2. Power and authority may provoke bad feelings associated with prior painful experiences. They may have been used to bully, threaten, intimidate, control, and humiliate. A natural and unconscious process may result in a resistance to those with power and authority and even efforts to dispose of or replace them. Superstars may be especially vulnerable to feeling controlled, intimidated, and threatened because they have felt limited by others all of their lives. Awareness of the likelihood of these feelings is critical on the part of superstars in order to avoid reacting to them to everyone's detriment.

3. Power, authority, influence, organizational politics, and status are concepts that are often very poorly defined in practice. They have only recently become legitimate topics for academics. In order to anchor an open discussion of what they are and how they will be wielded and by whom, they must first be defined, and it must be clear how one can discriminate between them. In fact, they may be more felt about than thought about. However, in order to work through the problems that arise, talking about them is essential and making sure everyone agrees on definitions is critical to achieving a healing communication.

Relationships. "Every organization must work out its rules of the game for peer relationships, for relationships between the sexes and for the manner in which openness and intimacy are to be handled in the context of managing the organization's tasks."[9]

The nature of the relationships among organization members in terms of intimacy and friendship—the feelings of being wanted and of providing for others—requires some prudent limits but must not be inhibited by formal organizational elements. Formal organizational elements should not, for example, make employees feel helpless and infantilized or unwilling to support each other. Attention must be directed to how members of the organization feel and think about each other and those in formal positions of authority.

The following pitfalls must be taken into consideration:

1. Position descriptions, organization charts, patterns of hierarchical organization, egalitarianism, paternalistic or materialistic leadership styles, poorly managed matrix organizations, and many more aspects of organization can conceal unconscious motives to make others ineffective in order to feel needed and in control. Formal structure is important, but it should be inspected for its unconscious uses.

2. Those striving for excellence must feel supported. Formal organization is one way of explaining what an organization is and how its members are related to each other.

However, it is but one way to map relationships at work. No matter how well it is done or how forcefully it is presented, organization members will create their own divergent maps—some motivated by unconscious needs to feel in control or to not be controlled. There are limits to how far formal organization can be expected to have meaning. Individual excellence is achieved as a result of shifting and constantly redefined concepts of the organization, problems, and working relationships. Management cannot make this happen.

3. Formal elements of organization must not be relied on to the exclusion of independent thinking during stressful times. A flight back to the safety of hierarchy may occur when the question is asked, "Who is in charge here?" Who is responsible? While it is important for managers to help absorb any anxiety associated with risk taking they should not be too eager to contain all of it as a "macho move." If everyone participated in creating the problem, the responsibility should be shared and, in particular, superstars should feel responsible for their thoughts and actions.

Rewards and Punishments. "Every group must know what its heroic and sinful behaviors are; what gets rewarded with property, status, and power; and what gets punished in the form of withdrawal of the rewards and, ultimately, excommunication."[10]

The nature of formal rewards and punishments must take into consideration unconscious needs to control, dominate, and manipulate others and needs to avoid feeling guilty when confronting others over their "bad" behavior. Formal evaluation and disciplinary processes should be written down in clear and easy to understand terms that are not subject to too much interpretation. They, however, need to be flexible enough to provide for judgement in their application. Performance evaluation formats that include self-evaluations, for example, provide a formal mechanism for opening up communication and help to contain anxiety by creating a process. Employees also need to know what their rights and privileges are, and they must understand how they will be dealt with regarding their performance—good or bad. It should be clear how outstanding performances will be identified and rewarded.

Possible pitfalls include the following:

1. Supervisors, managers, and executives all share in common anxiety about having to confront an employee over poor performance or misbehavior. No one likes to do it, although many learn to own the responsibility. Psychological flight can undermine the best of systems. Superstars may be disheartened to see others get away with "murder."

2. A similar outcome involves grade inflation—everyone is excellent or outstanding. All the members of the "family" are good and must be treated the same. Galloping egalitarianism can quickly undermine the meaning of being rewarded for superstar performances.

3. Another chronic problem with these systems is budgeting that is inconsistent with achieving excellence. Many times the first things lost in a wave of budget cutting are rewards and raises for outstanding performance and support for innovative projects.

There may be no quicker way to end the pursuit of individual excellence than to say it is valued but not reward it when it is accomplished.

Unpredictable Problems and Opportunities. "Every organization, like every society, faces unexplainable and inexplicable events, which must be given meaning so that members can respond to them and avoid the anxiety of dealing with the unexplainable and uncontrollable."[11]

The nature of unpredictable problems and opportunities that befall organization members must be understood in some way. Was a fatal accident an act of God, the fault of "them" or some scapegoat, or everyone's fault for not being safe? The organization must provide rituals, stories, and fantasies that explain the unknown, give meaning to painful events, and permit the healing of wounds that are self-inflicted or inflicted by competitors. The best ideas may fail. Those who strive for excellence must be aided in understanding problems and failures, and all organization members must be prepared to help heal the injuries and move on to "climbing another tree."

Several pitfalls are related to this assumption:

1. Attribution theory tells us that we often take credit for successes and attribute failures to others. Flight from facing some negative outcomes can be facilitated by creating processes that locate causes outside of the group or organization. A process such as this must, however, be used with care or else failure can become too easy.

2. Pain and anxiety associated with difficult problems may be psychologically defended against by rationalization, intellectualization, and denial at the individual, group, or organizational level. Psychological defenses such as these can magically transform bad outcomes into good ones or make them disappear altogether, erasing them from consciousness and memory. If relied upon too much, magic can shut out reality testing.

3. If the threat is too great, those in control may suddenly look to others to take charge and help them out. An outcome like this can provide opportunities for others to lead and also to be scapegoated. However, when leaders do not lead, dependency needs are frustrated and confusion will reign. The situation may be so uncertain that no one is willing to step forward to provide leadership with the effect of "kicking the group or organization into neutral" where no response is a response.

Limiting Outside Anxiety

Those who have a leadership role in the organization, especially those in the highest positions, must provide an identifiable and meaningful structure that minimizes anxieties about the "outside." Understanding permits organization members to identify with the aims of management, which limits internal conflict while promoting ever better clarification of the mission, goals, and objectives of the organization. In particular, top management must develop thoughtful and internally consistent goals and objectives for the organization and promote their understanding. Management should model the appropriate behavior by trying to accomplish the goals and objectives and not arbitrarily overruling them or developing different ones. Superstars are particularly dependent upon having a clear idea of what is going on and what is expected. Their innovativeness and productivity need structure to keep them from getting off task. It is equally important for them to see that their efforts yield positive outcomes for the organization.

There are several pitfalls to be considered in relation to this assumption:

1. Top management must be attentive to the possibility that, in developing a mission statement and setting goals and objectives, they do not unintentionally incorporate unproductive implicit and sometimes explicit basic assumptions about the world, reality, and human nature. Leaders and managers must monitor themselves and others for basic assumptions that are inconsistent with those of achieving individual excellence. There must be a willingness to confront others over inappropriate assumptions they hold.

2. Members of upper and middle management must model behavior aimed at achieving excellence. They must try to accomplish the goals and objectives that have been set rather than arbitrarily or covertly overrule them by developing different ones more consistent with their personal aims. Uncertainty, inconsistency, and arbitrariness will be quickly picked up by superstars and by others who may see these actions as frustrating, deceitful, and counterproductive, or, perhaps, as a license to do their "own thing."

3. Goals and objectives may be used to manipulate people and their work. It is possible to establish easy to reach goals that permit everyone to be successful. Similarly, impossible goals can be set, which also sends an important message about performance. Yet another possibility is that so many goals may be set that few are achieved, or a few goals may be set to the exclusion of other important possibilities. The setting of goals and objectives can be managed to allay excessive anxiety rather than to create a healthy amount of motivational stress and anxiety.

Leaders and managers must also be prepared to monitor results, supervise, and evaluate and provide feedback to those who are working on tasks aimed at fulfilling objectives. There must be a willingness to confront poor performance without stripping employees of self-esteem. There must also be provision for celebrating and rewarding the many successes that will be achieved.

Several pitfalls exist in conjunction with this assumption:

1. Monitoring results usually means accounting for work, reporting, and measuring; most of all, it means personal acccountability. But who wants to be held accountable? Perhaps management is suspicious that everyone is cutting corners and not achieving as much as they could. Monitoring can become divisive and create paranoia. Monitoring systems must be thoughtfully developed, implemented, and managed in order to avoid creating undue stress about who is being watched and why and what is being done with the information. Superstars attract a lot of attention to themselves and are especially vulnerable to feeling watched.

2. Taking corrective action is also an anxiety-producing situation that many managers and employees collude to avoid or to change magically the inevitable into something

more palatable. Superstars are often more prepared than others to accept bad news and move on. They may feel frustrated when the taking of corrective action is "spoon fed" or postponed until the right moment for everyone.

3. Once a change has been made, it is important to watch to see how it worked. It is usually more difficult to make changes work than to conceive of them, plan them, and implement them. Everyone needs to be prepared to persist and to pay close attention to the effects of the change. Those who "drop their pearls" and leave to others the problem of figuring out how to make the change work will not be regarded as supportive of those who are trying to achieve excellence.

CONCLUSION

Creating a culture that promotes achieving individual excellence has many prerequisites that are demanding to develop. Those listed above are some of the major ones; however, any list such as this is hopelessly incomplete. Anyone striving for a culture of individual excellence will find many opportunities to create many more cultural elements that lead to the path of excellence.

15

Looking Ahead to Achieving Excellence

This chapter is devoted to capturing a few final reflections looking ahead to the future. Writing this book led to many discussions and much thinking about the pursuit of individual excellence. The cases, in which the actors contributed to their own problems by not dealing effectively with their feelings and by not rising above the culture of their work setting, provoked much consternation on the part of some of those reading drafts of the book. This process led to additional reflections worth noting. Also provided are ideas of what the agenda for the 1990s should include if the pursuit of individual excellence is to be achieved. In particular the content of this book points toward new criteria for staff development and higher education and to new organizational intervention strategies that include consultation to the psychodynamics of organizational life.

AVOIDING SUPERSTAR BURNOUT

During the final phases of the preparation of this book, some ideas of how star performers can be more proactive at avoiding burnout came to light.

Many questions were asked why, in the case examples, the actors gave up, quit, or withdrew. This question leads to a larger question: How do many people who achieve excellence at work avoid becoming burned-out? It was not the intent of the book to deal with this second issue, but addressing it does provide some important perspective.

Those who have succeeded in achieving excellence at work, perhaps by overcoming great odds and many difficulties, may well regard Janet Evening and her colleagues in the case studies as wimps, sore losers, and quitters. It may be thought that, if they were not tough enough to make it, they were not really superstar material. What then can be learned from star performers who succeed in avoiding becoming burned-out? Some of the nonorganizational factors that emerged from reading, observation, and discussion are adequate self-esteem, resilience, tenacity and stubbornness, politics, self-presentation, and modeling of behavior.

Adequate Self-Esteem

Self-esteem was discussed in Chapter 12; however, its importance in understanding people cannot be overstated. Feeling good about one's self, one's skills, and one's performance translates into less likelihood of becoming anxious about events and about how one is treated at work. Greater security leads to fewer emotions, negative feelings, and psychological defenses. Less threat will be perceived in the events of the day and in the actions of others. Less threat and stress results in fewer anxieties. The characters in the case examples, as pointed out in Chapter 12, lacked adequate self-esteem to regulate the experience of anxiety, which contributed to their burnout.

Resilience

Personal resilience is an important factor. A person who takes risks at work will inevitably encounter problems, failures, and interpersonal conflict. The ability to bounce back after a negative experience is important in being able to continue to strive for excellence. The characters in the cases, it was found, needed the support of others and lacked adequate personal resilience to bounce back from adversity by themselves.

Tenacity and Stubbornness

Tenacity and perhaps outright stubbornness can be contributors to avoiding some defeats and overcoming some problems. The unyielding pursuit of a goal can take on the dimensions of a quest to overcome all odds. A difficult balance, however, must be struck to avoid burning out everyone else in the process. Stubbornness, it may be found, can become mixed with contempt or indifference for others which, if perceived, can further increase the likelihood of burnout. The stubbornness of some of the characters in the cases created this toxic mix and provoked the wrath of others.

Politics

Shrewd interpersonal and political maneuvering can be factors in avoiding burnout. Being people and organization smart can help get things done and avoid taking too much heat in the process. Knowing when to back off, when to go around people who are blocking progress, when to seek the help of others, and when to make appeals for support can all be effective in getting work done. Organizational politics and influence wielding are all too common. However, once again, there are limits to how far a person can push this approach until he or she is seen by others to be deviously pursuing a personal agenda. The characters in the cases demonstrated a naïveté about interpersonal and organizational politics.

Self-Presentation

Shrewd self-presentation can also help. A person who understands interpersonal and group dynamics can use this knowledge to coax, coach, and steer others into desired courses of action. People who are effective and self-assured presenters in meetings can, for example, sway decision making simply by the force of their self-presentation. The characters in the cases were often tuned into what was going on but did not use this understanding to help them change the outcomes.

Modeling of Behavior

Modeling behavior that is supportive of achieving individual excellence may encourage others to model the same behavior in return. The characters in the cases were often supportive of others and did, in several of the cases, influence behavior relative to themselves. They did not, however, succeed in changing how they were being treated relative to their work and were preoccupied with how others made them feel.

There are of course other factors at work that can account for the success of superstar performers. Those discussed above are, however, some of the major ones. It is important to appreciate that burnout is not inevitable; a highly effective performer can do much to avoid or overcome the rejecting and limiting actions of others. The cases, however, point out the side of life where star performers are often all too human and become personally disorganized and unable to cope effectively.

LOOKING AHEAD—WHAT THE FUTURE HOLDS FOR THE PURSUIT OF INDIVIDUAL EXCELLENCE

This book has examined problems that people create for others and themselves at work. The 1990s will hopefully become the decade where an in-depth understanding of people is combined with a meaningful understanding of the work-place and the pursuit of individual excellence. Should this occur, one of the biggest problems will be how to teach people more about themselves and the psychodynamics of the workplace. Staff development, based on reading, cases, and lectures, although informative, seldom provides more than a cursory exposure that has a short half-life in practice. What is needed are improved teaching models that, in addition to providing lectures, cases, and reading, provide experiential learning opportunities that operationalize learning. Classroom teaching must be expanded to include group experiential learning opportunities. Instances where these methods have been tried have led participants to important and even revelational insights into self, others, and group dynamics. What is called for is an approach to teaching that facilitates developing self-knowledge and an understanding of others under stressful conditions similar to those found at work. For this to occur, the safe harbor of the classroom is needed. Classroom experiential learning models, which include the study of how people respond to stress, are currently being developed by a few faculty members who are interested in developing these teaching methods to bring to life for the student the nature of what psychoanalytic theory has to offer.

A second major area of development for the 1990s is the use of psychoanalytically informed organizational consultation. Throughout the book, mention has been made of the advisability of employing observers of interpersonal, group, and organizational dynamics who are knowledgeable about organizational dynamics.

Organizations are filled with many stressful moments about the inside and outside of the organization that encourage their members to feel anxious and to become psychologically defensive. Organizational culture cannot avoid or contain all the anxiety that arises. Managers and employees cannot be fully prepared to deal with themselves, each other, groups, and the organization. This will be especially true under stressful conditions. There naturally arises a need for expert consultation when work is just not going well. A psychologically informed consultation can be the answer. This type of consultation includes consideration of many workplace variables, for example, the apparent culture of the organization and area within the organization, comparison of the observed culture to the espoused culture for inconsistencies, observation of group processes for dysfunctional leadership and interpersonal dynamics, and the contribution of other factors such as lack of a clear mission and goals and missing resources such as staff or time. There are many more. These consultants are also sensitive to the presence of psychological defenses that often go unobserved and undiscussed and, therefore, unquestioned. These defenses, as have been pointed out throughout this book, can involve the individual, the interpersonal world, and group and organizational dynamics. Understanding them can be facilitated by an observer who is informed by psychoanalytic theory and psychology.

In sum, understanding people, relationships between people, people in groups, and people at work can no longer be avoided if excellence is to be achieved.

It should be clear that understanding the psychology of people in the workplace is critical and all too often overlooked, perhaps because of its hard to understand complexity. However, achieving individual excellence in the 1990s is going to depend on it.

APPENDIX

Psychological Defenses at Work

Psychological defenses are interactive and mutually interdependent and may arise in a sequence. The following definitions describe behavioral categories. It is maintained that, although they are mutually exclusive, they may be acted upon simultaneously, and they may form a system of behavior commonly associated with an individual.[1]

ACTING-OUT

Acting-out is the most direct means of reducing anxiety, frustration, and tension. The wish is acted upon. Felt anger may lead to an actual attack upon the person who is the subject of the anger. Acting-out may include self-defeating behavior. For example, if one person is being unfair or unethical, the response may be to act unfairly and unethically in return. Acting-out at work can be dysfunctional. Many social inhibitors block acting-out in favor of more socially acceptable defensive responses.

COMPENSATION

When we feel deficient or inferior, one response is to work harder to improve ourselves. We may compensate by trying harder. Compensation is usually an organizationally and socially adaptive response to threats to our self-esteem. Compensation may, however, become excessive and compulsive for individuals who have very low self-esteem. For

these individuals compensation may lead to self-destructive tendencies, constantly mobilized feelings, overly energized behavior, and competitive efforts aimed at defeating
others.

DENIAL

Denial is a simple defense to use. An unacceptable or disagreeable aspect of work or
oneself is ignored. A poor decision may be denied. Unpleasant topics such as an employee's poor performance may go unacknowledged and undiscussed. Becoming engrossed in one's work shuts out reality. Paying attention to only those aspects of our
work that fulfill our wish to see ourselves as effective and desirable avoids reality.

DISPLACEMENT

We do not always feel secure enough to respond directly to a person who is frustrating
or hurting us such as a supervisor. Feelings of anger, humiliation, and hate may be safely
discharged by directing them toward another, safer person or symbolic object. A subordinate or spouse may become the focal point of the animosities. Displacement has
socially adaptive value and enables the holder of the feelings to discharge them thereby
reducing internal conflict and tension. If stress is frequently experienced as a result of,
in part, low self-esteem, displacement may become dysfunctional. Important feedback
may be lost to the supervisor.

EMOTIONAL INSULATION

Suffering from disappointment is part of life at work. We do not always get what we
want; others do not always act as we would hope. These disappointments encourage us
to form realistic expectations which take into account the less than perfect world in which
we live and work. By so doing, we insulate ourselves from hurt and disappointment. At
work, emotional insulation is an adaptive defense unless it is taken too far and we become
passive and resigned to poor outcomes. Less adaptive forms of insulation are isolation,
intellectualization, and dissociation. These defenses split apart feeling from thinking and
compartmentalize life. The central element of the defense is that, when one would expect
to have feelings, there are none. A major catastrophe may evoke no feelings of fear,
anger, or guilt. In the case of isolation, loss of market share may be attributed to a strong
dollar and no pain or fear felt. Intellectualization, which may involve rationalization, is
a response whereby adverse events are recast into something more acceptable. Loss of
market share may be seen as a new opportunity. Dissociation permits the holding of two
conflicting attitudes or feelings without conflict. A dishonest executive may be a pillar
of the community.

FANTASY

We may not only deny reality, we may create an alternate reality in fantasy. Productive
fantasies motivate achievement and foster imagination. Unproductive fantasies are disconnected from reality and are not ultimately adaptive. Two common wish-fulfilling
fantasies are the hero and the martyr. Anger is safely dissipated through fantasies of the

hero defeating all who stand in the way. We do not have to act to correct the problem. The martyr suffers at the hands of others where inferior performance can be denied. We do not have to deal with the possibility that it is we who have failed. Fantasies that are obsessive serve to block out reality and can become delusional. An employee who is frequently reprimanded may, upon being terminated, still believe that his or her performance was outstanding.

IDENTIFICATION

A sense of identity may come from many things—our house and cars, our college, our position title with its associated prestige and power, and our organization. True identity, however, develops from being successful as a person. To the extent that we do not possess adequate self-esteem, we may look to other people and other things to secure self-esteem. This process may impoverish the real self. Identification is an important part of the traditional organizational reward systems, such as titles and carpeted offices. To the extent that employees pursue these status symbols in lieu of adequate self-esteem, their efforts are organizationally adaptive but personally dysfunctional.

INTROJECTION

A sense of identity may also be developed by taking into oneself the values and images of others, organizations, and institutions. We take into ourselves (internalize) social values that permit us to function in the presence of others. We locate others who are admirable and take them into ourselves to become us. To the extent that a weak sense of self exists, taking in what goes on around us may be our only means of achieving identity. If we work with an outstanding individual who achieves excellence, we may become like that person. If we work with someone who is predatory, unethical, and dishonest, we may become like that person rather than condemn him or her, which is unsafe and threatens rejection.

PROJECTION

Projection involves blaming others for our problems and attributing to others our negative feelings. Others, fate, and bad luck may explain a failure. "It wasn't my fault." Responsibility for our failure is projected onto others or onto abstractions. A less apparent defense is to attribute to others one's negative and unacceptable feelings and desires. Others may be seen to be like us which may seriously inhibit reality testing. An extreme projection may involve attributing to others our unacceptable impulses. Anger felt for a low raise may be attributed to the supervisor who is seen to be angry and getting even by giving a low raise.

RATIONALIZATION

Rationalization helps us justify past and present actions and to soften painful disappointments by invoking self-deception. No learning occurs from mistakes and problems. Rationalization involves thinking of reasons that justify behavior. Obvious inconsistencies and contradictory evidence may be ignored. Rationalization may involve scapegoating, development of self-righteous and unchallengeable attitudes, development of complex strategies to avoid problem recognition, and lack of need to try to achieve good performance. The rationalizer may become defensive and angry if a rationalization is challenged.

REACTION FORMATION

Reaction formations are behavior that is opposed to repressed feelings. These exaggerated and compulsive reactions serve to keep away painful life experiences and socially unacceptable urges. The development of a reckless and uncaring attitude toward a supervisor may serve to conceal deeply held wishes for approval and affection. Exceedingly productive employees who are willing to work many long hours may harbor dreaded feelings of failure. A female victim of childhood incest may see sexualized threats to avoid the possibility of any type of intimacy with male colleagues.

REGRESSION

Regression involves a behavioral response to frustrated needs and anxiety that is usually associated with childhood. An adult may, through a temper tantrum, sulk and withdraw and appear to have hurt feelings which may have, during childhood, encouraged parents to respond as wished. Implicit in regression is that it may be unfair to hold the adult responsible for the regressed behavior. Supervisors and colleagues are expected to respond as wished for and to obligingly tolerate the regressed behavior without taking offense or striking back, which would be unfair to a child.

REPRESSION

Repression involves the exclusion of experiences, thoughts, and feelings from our consciousness without our awareness of the process. Painful and traumatic material is simply gone from memory. We have no recollection. Remembering becomes selective. The repressed material, however, continues to influence feelings and behavior. The woman who was the subject of childhood incest but who has no memory of it may, nonetheless, find extraordinary fault with the behavior of men at work who are felt to sexualize work (see reaction formation).

SUBLIMATION

Sublimation takes the energy associated with negative feelings and internal conflicts and permits acting on it in socially approved substitute activities. An individual who hates his or her supervisor may work hard to show up the supervisor. Sublimation is usually an adaptive response to anxieties and frustrations at work; however, if work frustrations are sublimated in the form of recreational activities outside of work, problems at work may not be dealt with, and valuable creative and productive energies may be lost to the organization.

UNDOING

Undoing involves negating a thought, feeling, or past action. Apologizing for a mistake or being punished permits us to start over with a clean slate. We have paid our debt. An employee may feel he or she must work many extra hours to make up for a past mistake. Undoing maintains socialization and self-esteem except in extreme cases where atonement is not seen as possible. Undoing can be used to mediate undesirable behavior, as in the case of an embezzler who gives large sums to charity.

Notes

INTRODUCTION

1. The most popular work on organizational excellence is Tom Peters and Robert Waterman's book, *In Search of Excellence* (1982). This book was followed by a second by Tom Peters and Nancy Austin, *A Passion for Excellence: The Leadership Difference* (1985).

2. Argyris and Schon (1978).

3. The initial concept for this book was an article by the author titled, ''How to Keep Your Superstars Shining'' (1988).

4. Much of the discussion of organizational culture is informed by Edgar H. Schein's book, *Organizational Culture and Leadership* (1985).

CHAPTER 1

1. Argyris and Schon (1978). See also Argyris and Schon (1982).

2. An insightful analysis of Chris Argyris and Donald Schon's work is found in Michael Diamond (1986).

3. Many books inform the student of the irrational side of organizational life. Those that form the basis for this book include Baum (1987); Bion (1961); Hirschorn (1988); Kets de Vries and Miller (1984); Levinson (1976, 1981); and Zaleznik and Kets de Vries (1975).

4. Peters and Waterman (1982).

5. Ibid. Richard Scott's development of four major eras of both management theory building and practice form the theoretical focus for this book. Scott postulates that the first era began with the scientific management principles espoused by Frederick Taylor and with Max Weber's theory of bureaucracy (1900–1930). The second era is described as the human relations movement typified by Elton Mayo and Douglas McGregor (1930–1960). The third era returned to a more rational approach that involved the development of many quantitative methods associated with the MBA degree and the works of Alfred Chandler and Paul Lawrence and Jay Lorsch (1960–1970). The fourth and current era marks the return to a humanist orientation that is more complex and is typified by the works of James March and Karl Weick (1970–   ). In this fourth era, "The rational actor is superseded by the complex social actor; a human being with inbuilt strengths, weaknesses, limitations, contradictions and irrationalities" (Peters and Waterman, p. 100). The limits of rationality are questioned. Four elements of a new theory are put forward: "(1) people's need for meaning; (2) people's need for a modicum of control; (3) people's need for positive reinforcement, to think of themselves as winners in some sense; and (4) the degree to which actions and behaviors shape attitudes and beliefs rather than vice versa" (p. 100). This rather simplistic and limited view of human nature does not permit Peters and Waterman to gain more insight into the aforementioned limitations, contradictions, and irrationalities which are the subject of this book.

6. Argyris and Schon (1982).

7. Peters and Austin (1985).

8. Ibid., p. xviii.

9. Vaill (1989).

10. Hermeneutic science is the study of the subjective without the use of researcher-centered constructs such as researcher-constructed hypotheses, term definitions, and other concepts which are then used to observe, record, and analyze behavior. This researcher-centered methodology does not not preserve the individual's natural state and, far from being objective and empirical, it represents the subjective imposition of the researcher's worldview upon his or her research subjects. Psychoanalytic principles, in contrast, draw all content to be studied from the subjects. The material is analyzed for meaning relative to the individual. In effect, each person has his or her own story and does not become a statistic.

CHAPTER 2

1. A computer-assisted literature search using the key word "superstar" revealed a number of references to articles that are related to sales but are not particularly informative about performance. Sales is an example of a field where results are purely quantitative, a field which facilitates comparability and determination of who is the best. Examples are Levy (1985); Maher (1973); and Murray (1985).

2. A number of books on gifted children were particularly informative, for example, Leyden (1985); Takacs (1986); and Ziv (1977). A noteworthy article on entrepreneurship is by Ross and Unwalla (1986). An interesting book which explores the relationships among intelligence, knowledge, and artistry is by Schon (1987).

3. "The Plight of the Super-Competent" (1981).

4. "Humanizing the Superstars" (1978).

5. Ginsburg (1981).

6. Many scholarly and self-help books for women deal with gender-related issues at

work. Several that are particularly informative are Sanford and Donovan (1984); Lerner (1985); and Westkott (1986).

CHAPTER 3

1. A thought-provoking idea of Wayne Wright (1987), "Escape from Mediocrity," is that an organization may not be ready for the introduction of the pursuit of excellence. A poorly managed organization with marginal strategies, poor information systems, and entrenched performance problems may not be able to deal with the needed changes to develop a new organizational culture that achieves higher level goals through improved teamwork. Wright raises the specter that many organizations may first have to achieve mediocrity before striving for excellence. Brown (1988) also notes that accepting mediocrity, especially at the higher level of management, can weaken organizational performance.

CHAPTER 4

1. Many have written about the psychodynamics of groups. Two books are of particular interest: Bion (1961); and Coleman and Geller, eds. (1985).
2. A popular book that looks at the meaning of anger is Lerner (1985).
3. A thoughtful book on love and attachment is Person (1988).
4. An author who deals with the meaning of shame and guilt in the workplace is Baum (1987).
5. A paper that examines the impact of unconscious neurotic processes at work is Diamond and Allcorn (1984). This paper is based upon the work of Karen Horney (1950).

CHAPTER 5

1. Allcorn (1988b).
2. Two books that shed light on object relations are Greenberg and Mitchell (1983) and Segal (1988).
3. De Board (1978).
4. Many good papers and books deal with the issues of examining the group as a whole. Several papers are Allcorn (1989); Diamond and Allcorn (1987); and Menzies (1960). A book on the subject is Bion (1961).
5. An article dealing with the psychodynamics of role formation is Diamond and Allcorn (1986). A related book is Zaleznik and Moment (1964).
6. Diamond and Allcorn (1987). Another important discussion of regression at work is Kernberg (1979).
7. Coleman and Bexton (1975); Coleman and Geller, eds. (1985).
8. Bion (1961).
9. Mentzberg (1979).
10. Levinson (1981); Maccoby (1976); and Zaleznik (1966).
11. Schein (1985).

PART II

1. Some good books on cosmology are Asimov (1985); Gibilisco (1984); Golden (1976); and Jastrow (1979).

CHAPTER 6

1. Allcorn (1988b); Diamond and Allcorn (1984, 1986, 1990); and Kets de Vries (1980).
2. Horney (1950); and the American Psychiatric Association (1987).

CHAPTER 8

1. Kets de Vries (1979).

CHAPTER 12

1. Diamond and Allcorn (1984).
2. Greenberg and Mitchell (1983), chapter 11; and Masterson (1988).
3. Bar-Levav (1988).
4. Allcorn (1988a); Diamond (1986); and Diamond and Allcorn (1985, 1990).
5. Diamond and Allcorn (1986).

CHAPTER 13

1. I wish to acknowledge a debt of gratitude to Edgar Schein and his very fine book, *Organizational Culture and Leadership* (1985), which informs much of this chapter.
2. Schein (1985), p. 9.
3. McGregor (1960).
4. Bion (1961).
5. Simon (1965).
6. Argyris and Schon (1978).

CHAPTER 14

1. Schein (1985), p. 86.
2. Ibid.
3. Ibid.
4. Ibid.
5. Ibid.
6. Ibid., p. 66.
7. Ibid.
8. Ibid.
9. Ibid.

10. Ibid.
11. Ibid.

APPENDIX

1. Appendix material is modeled after a table prepared by Coleman (1964).

Bibliography

Allcorn, Seth. (1988a). "How to Keep Your Superstars Shining." *Management Solutions*, July.

———. (1988b). "Leadership Styles: The Psychological Perspective." *Personnel*, April.

———. (1989). "Understanding Groups at Work." *Personnel*, August.

American Psychiatric Association. (1987). *Diagnostic and Statistical Manual of Mental Disorders*. 3d ed. Washington, D.C.: American Psychiatric Association.

Argyris, Chris, and Donald Schon. (1978). *Organizational Learning: A Theory of Action Perspective*. Reading, Mass.: Addison-Wesley.

———. (1982). *Theory in Practice: Increasing Professional Effectiveness*. San Francisco: Jossey-Bass.

Asimov, Isaac. (1985). *The Exploding Suns*. New York: Truman Tally Books.

Bar-Levav, Reuven. (1988). *Thinking in the Shadow of Feelings*. New York: Touchstone.

Baum, Howell. (1987). *The Invisible Bureaucracy: The Unconscious in Organizational Problem Solving*. New York: Oxford University Press.

Bion, Wilfred. (1961). *Experiences in Groups*. London: Tavistock.

Brown, Edward. (1988). "Maladies Which Will Weaken Organizations." *NRECA Management Quarterly*, Fall, pp. 7–11.

Coleman, Arthur, and Harold Bexton. (1975). *Group Relations Reader*. Washington, D.C.: A.K. Rice Institute.

Coleman, Arthur, and Marvin Geller, eds. (1985). *Group Relations Reader 2*. Washington, D.C.: A.K. Rice Institute.

Coleman, James. (1964). *Abnormal Psychology and Modern Life*. 3d ed. Chicago: Scott Foresman.

De Board, Robert. (1978). *The Psychoanalysis of Organizations: A Psychoanalytic Approach to Behavior in Groups and Organizations*. London: Tavistock.

Diamond, Michael. (1986). "Resistance to Change: A Psychoanalytic Critique of Argyris and Schon's Contributions to Organization Theory and Intervention." *Journal of Management Studies*, September.

Diamond, Michael, and Allcorn, Seth. (1984). "Psychological Barriers to Personal Responsibility." *Organizational Dynamics*, Spring.

———. (1985). "Psychological Dimensions of Role Use in Bureaucratic Organizations." *Organizational Dynamics*, Summer.

———. (1986). "Role Formation as Defensive Activity in Bureaucratic Organizations." *Political Psychology*, December.

———. (1987). "The Psychodynamics of Regression in Work Groups." *Human Relations*, August.

———. (1990). "The Freudian Factor." *Personnel Journal*, March.

Gibilisco, Stan. (1984). *Black Holes, Quasars and Other Mysteries of the Universe*. Blue Ridge Summit, Pa.: Tab Books.

Ginsburg, Sigmund. (1981). "The High Achievers Job Satisfaction." *Personnel Administrator*, January, pp. 78–81.

Golden, Frederick. (1976). *Quasars, Pulsars, and Black Holes*. New York: Charles Scribner's Sons.

Greenberg, Jay, and Stephen Mitchell. (1983). *Object Relations in Psychoanalytic Theory*. Cambridge, Mass.: Harvard University Press.

Hirschorn, Larry. (1988). *The Workplace Within*. Cambridge, Mass.: MIT Press.

Horney, Karen. (1950). *Neurosis and Human Growth*. New York: W.W. Norton.

"Humanizing the Superstars." (1978). *Managers Magazine*, March, p. 23.

Jastrow, Robert. (1979). *Red Giants and White Dwarfs*. New York: W.W. Norton.

Kernberg, Otto. (1979). "Regression in Organizational Leadership." *Psychiatry*, vol. 42, pp. 24–39.

Kets de Vries, Manfred. 1979. "Managers Can Drive Their Subordinates Mad." *Harvard Business Review*, July-August.

———. 1980. *Organizational Paradoxes*. London: Tavistock.

Kets de Vries, Manfred, ed. (1984). *The Irrational Executive*. New York: International Universities.

Kets de Vries, Manfred, and Danny Miller. (1984). *The Neurotic Organization*. San Francisco: Jossey-Bass.

Lerner, Harriet. (1985). *The Dance of Anger*. New York: Harper & Row, Chapter 5.

Levinson, Harry. (1976). *Psychological Man*. Cambridge, Mass.: The Levinson Institute.

———. (1981). *Executive*. Cambridge, Mass.: Harvard University Press.

Levy, Robert. (1985). "Superstars of Sales Meetings." *Marketing*, August, p. 82.

Leyden, Susan. (1985). *Helping the Child of Exceptional Ability*. Kent, England: Croom Helm Ltd. Provident House.

Maccoby, Michael. (1976). *The Gamesman*. New York: Simon & Schuster.

McGregor, Douglas. (1960). *The Human Side of Enterprise*. New York: McGraw-Hill.

Maher, D. (1973). "Salesman to Superstar: Challenge Is the Key." *Sales Management*, April 30, p. 26.

Masterson, James. (1988). *The Search for the Real Self*. New York: The Free Press.

Mentzberg, Henry. (1979). *The Structuring of Organizations*. Englewood Cliffs, N.J.: Prentice-Hall.

Menzies, Isabel. (1960). "A Case-Study in the Functioning of Social Systems as a Defense against Anxiety: A Report on a Study of the Nursing Service of a General Hospital." *Human Relations*, vol. 13, pp. 95–121.

Murray, Thomas. (1985). "Superstars of Electronics Superstores." *Dun's Business Month*, July, p. 60.

Person, Ethel. (1988). *Dreams of Love and Fateful Encounters*. New York: W.W. Norton.

Peters, Tom, and Robert Waterman. (1982). *In Search of Excellence*. New York: Harper & Row.

Peters, Tom, and Nancy Austin. (1985). *A Passion for Excellence: The Leadership Difference*. New York: Random House.

"The Plight of the Super-Competent." (1981). *Personal Report*, Research Institute of America, October 20, pp. 5–6.

Ross, Joel, and Unwalla, Darab. (1986). "Who Is an Intrapreneur?" *Personnel*, December, pp. 45–49.

Sanford, Linda, and Mary Donovan. (1984). *Women & Self-Esteem*. New York: Penguin Books, pp. 207–26.

Schein, Edgar H. (1985). *Organizational Culture and Leadership*. San Francisco: Jossey-Bass.

Schoeck, Helmut. (1966). *Envy: A Theory of Social Behavior*. Indianapolis: Liberty Press.

Schon, Donald. (1987). *Educating the Reflective Practitioner*. San Francisco: Jossey-Bass.

Segal, Hana. (1988). *Introduction to the Work of Melanie Klein*. London: Karnac Books and the Institute of Psycho-Analysis.

Simon, Herbert. (1965). *Administrative Behavior*. New York: Free Press.

Takacs, Carol. (1986). *Enjoy Your Gifted Child*. New York: Syracuse University Press.

Vaill, Peter. (1989). *Managing as a Performing Art*. San Francisco: Jossey-Bass.

Westkott, Marcia. (1986). *The Feminist Legacy of Karen Horney*. New Haven, Conn.: Yale University Press, pp. 31–41.

Wright, Wayne. (1987). "Escape from Mediocrity." *Personnel Administrator*, September, pp. 109–17.

Zaleznik, Abraham. (1966). *Human Dilemmas of Leadership*. New York: Harper & Row.

Zaleznik, Abraham, and Manfred Kets de Vries (1975). *Power and the Corporate Mind*. Boston: Houghton Mifflin.

Zaleznik, Abraham, and David Moment. (1964). *The Dynamics of Interpersonal Behavior*. New York: John Wiley & Sons.

Ziv, Avner. (1977). *Counselling the Intellectually Gifted Child*. Toronto, Canada: The Governing Council of the University of Toronto.

Index

About the Author

SETH ALLCORN is Associate Dean for Fiscal Affairs at the Stritch School of Medicine of Loyola University in Chicago. He has also served as the Administrator of the Department of Medicine of the School of Medicine and Dentistry at the University of Rochester and was Administrator of the Department of Medicine at the University of Missouri—Columbia. He has published more than forty-five articles, a book, and several chapters on hospital management, medical group and medical school management, and the psychodynamics of organizations, among other topics.